MORE THAN JUST A GAME

MORE THAN JUST A GAME

Coach Bobby Bowden
with Bill Smith

Thomas Nelson Publishers
Nashville • Atlanta • London • Vancouver

Published in Nashville, Tennessee, by Thomas Nelson, Inc., Publishers, and distributed in Canada by Word Communications, Ltd., Richmond, British Columbia, and in the United Kingdom by Word (UK), Ltd., Milton Keynes, England.

Scripture quotations are from the NEW KING JAMES VERSION of the Bible. Copyright 1979, 1980, 1982, Thomas Nelson, Inc., Publishers.

Library of Congress Cataloging-in-Publication Data

Bowden, Bobby.
    More than just a game / by Bobby Bowden with Bill Smith.
      p.   cm.
    ISBN 0-8407-6313-1
    1. Bowden, Bobby.   2. Football coaches—United States—Biography.   3. Christian life.   4. Florida State University—Football.   I. Smith, Bill, 1929–
    GV939.B66A34   1994
    796.332′092—dc20
    [B]   94-6136
                                                CIP

Printed in the United States of America

1 2 3 4 5 6 7 — 00 99 98 97 96 95 94

Acknowledgments

I wish I could find the words to thank all the folks who have been instrumental in molding me into the person I am today. Lord knows I'm not perfect, and I would hate to think where I'd be today if a few of them hadn't grabbed the steering wheel.

Although I dedicate this book to my wife, Ann, I have to thank her again. There is no way I can ever thank her enough. Without her as my guiding light I don't know what would have happened to me. I certainly didn't have a bunch of goals as a youngster. She was the one who kept me headed in the right direction, and made me strive and not yield.

And there are our six children—Robyn, Steve, Tommy, Terry, Jeffrey, and Ginger. I can't begin to thank them for letting their old man spend most of his time being someone else's daddy. I know I was gone a lot of the time when they were growing up, but I always tried to set an example for them.

My mother and daddy are gone now, but they are the ones who put the solid rock cornerstone in the foundation of my life. I owe all my beliefs in Jesus Christ to them. They lived their beliefs as well as any couple I have ever known. I have always been eternally grateful for their direction, wisdom, and influence.

I want to thank Ken Smith, our former team chaplain; Billy Smith, head of our security; assistant coaches Chuck Amato, Mickey Andrews, Brad Scott, Ronnie Cottrell, and Dave Van Halanger; Bill McGrotha, the late sports columnist for the *Tallahassee Democrat* and one who knew more about Florida State's football history than any man alive; and my friend Vince Gibson for their kind comments about me. I'm not sure I'm worthy of all that.

And of course I need to thank my long-time friend, Bill Smith, for the mountains of time and effort and good ol' TLC that he poured into this book. Without him, and my editor, Duncan Jaenicke, and the entire team at Thomas Nelson, this book wouldn't exist.

I'm not going to try to thank everybody because I know I'd leave more than a few out. They know who they are because when I love someone and value their help, support and friendship, I'm not bashful: I tell them what they mean to me. So, before I begin this book, I'll just tell them all again, "I love y'all."

Now, let's get at it.

—Bobby Bowden
Tallahassee, Florida

Contents

Preface

BY BILL SMITH

What is Florida State football coach Bobby Bowden, the man who is fast becoming a legend in the South, really like? Well, the best way to describe the man from Birmingham is to tell stories about him. Bowden would like that because he's a storyteller himself.

One came to mind when trying to figure out a way to begin this book. It was October 2, 1973, and Bowden, then the 43-year-old head coach of the West Virginia University Mountaineers, had his team on the road. He and his Mountaineers were in the heart of Pennsylvania, in the blustery Nittany Valley, a place where West Virginia teams had stumbled time after time, year after year.

No Mountaineer team had won at Penn State since 1954.

Bowden had different ideas this time around. A year earlier his Mountaineers had finished 8-3 in the regular season and earned a spot in the Peach Bowl (where they suffered a 49-13 loss to North Carolina State). But one of those three regular season defeats came on West Virginia's home turf at the hands of Penn State 28-19. And the play that propelled the Nittany Lions to victory came when West Virginia blocked a field goal attempt and the Lions turned it into a fluke touchdown.

And the last time Bowden's team had visited State College, Pa., it had suffered a 42-8 defeat. The coach was determined that would not happen again.

Bowden's team wasn't all that talented. It went into the game with only a 3–3 record. But those wins had been over Maryland (20–13), Virginia Tech (24–10), and Illinois (17–10). Bowden figured, "We can't be all that dad-gum bad. If we play like we did in our victories, we just might be able to stay with Penn State. Those boys put their pants on the same way we do."

Penn State had an outstanding running back named John Cappelletti, who would go on to win the Heisman Trophy. Bowden knew Cappelletti was a threat, but he figured to counter with a threat of his own, in speedy wide receiver Danny Buggs, who was averaging 23 yards per catch and 14.2 yards on punt returns.

Unfortunately for Bowden, his team suffered an embarrassing 62–14 defeat that afternoon. It remains the worst defeat in his illustrious coaching career, one that now spans five decades and has seen him become the fifth winningest coach in the history of the game.

Bowden's name is now mentioned in the same breath with such greats as Bear Bryant, Glenn "Pop" Warner, Amos Alonzo Stagg, and Joe Paterno. Only these men top Bowden in all-time wins.

In that '73 walloping, Buggs caught a school record 96-yard touchdown pass. But Cappelletti scored and scored—four times in all.

Long after the game, and long after all the West Virginia players had left the visitors' locker room, a local sportswriter—me—found Bowden sitting on a bench in a corner of the room with his head down. He had showered, but hadn't dressed. He had a towel draped over his lap. He was obviously depressed.

I said, "Don't worry, Coach, it's not the end of the world. Your team will bounce back." Being his long-time friend, I tried to be cute next by adding, "They only beat you by 48 points. It's just a loss. You'll beat the Hurricanes (University of Miami) next week in the Orange Bowl."

Bowden looked up, shook his head, and said, "Naw, I'm just not getting the job done. I feel like hanging it up."

I said, "What are you saying? Give up coaching? That's the dumbest thing I ever heard you say. Your coaching can't just be measured in terms of wins and losses. You're a great influence on a lot of young men's lives. That has to stand for something."

"I'm not even sure I'm doing a good job of that," he muttered. "I'm so sick I want to die."

"Now don't do that, Coach," I rejoined, not really knowing what else to say.

And Bowden made an effort at a smile and drawled, "Well, I ain't gonna die, but I'm so sick I could throw up." His team did bounce back the next week, with a 20-14 win at Miami.

But while that conversation was taking place in the Beaver Stadium visitors' dressing room, there was another scene taking place. It was in the home team's locker room. This was one of jubilation. Cappelletti was hugging a young boy, his little brother, Joey. Joey, his face wan and body frail, was dying of leukemia. Everyone in the room knew it.

Prior to the game Cappelletti wanted to do something to make Joey happy, to ease his suffering for one brief afternoon. So he asked him, "Hey, Joey, how many do you want me to get today?"

Joey answered, "Four. Score four touchdowns."

"That's a tall order, but OK, you got 'em," said his big brother.

Youngsters sometimes ask seemingly impossible things like that of their heroes. But big brother went out that day and got Joey those four touchdowns, and there was happiness in the Penn State locker room—for Joey.

Years later, Bowden heard about what had happened in the Penn State locker room when a movie, *Something For Joey,* was made of what Cappelletti did for his dying brother. Bowden smiled that smile of his and said, "Lawh, if I had known that . . . well, I just might have wished Cappelletti had scored a couple more. That game meant a lot to me at the time, but I know it meant a whole lot more to John Cappelletti and his little brother. It was more than just a dad-gum game to them."

This book is a compilation of lengthy conversations with Bowden, the man they refer to in the Deep South as "Bobby B." It is full of his stories, because he likes to tell stories. Also, it includes conversations with his wife, his children, his coaches, and others who know him, perhaps know him better than he knows himself.

To know this man is to love him. When others who know him describe him, they always say the same thing. Oh, they may use different words, but the meaning is the same. They will say, "There is just something different, something special about him."

Bowden has genuine love for people. They sense it. When he walks on the Florida State campus, he speaks to everybody. Columnist Edwin Pope of the *Miami Herald* wrote that Bowden once saw a young man, whom he didn't know, walking on an ankle cast and said, "Hey! Ankle's looking pretty good. You gonna play tailback for us tomorrow?"

Talking about the encounter, Bowden told me, "I just plain like people. I don't know of anybody I dislike. Now, I do know some I'd just

as soon not be around. But just because I don't want to be around them
don't mean I don't love 'em. God commands us to love not only Him, but
to love everyone. I gotta do what He says.

"Maybe I'm naive, but I treat people the way I expect them to treat
me. My first reaction when I meet someone is to like 'em. God loves us all
no matter how bad we mess up. If you look at nearly all of Jesus' apostles
you'll find out those guys were pretty sorry at times. There ain't nobody
perfect, nobody that I know."

A former dean at Florida State, Coyle E. Moore, once described
Bowden this way: "He's what we call a 'southern cracker' and perfectly
adapted to us rednecks of northern Florida. He speaks our language, ad-
heres to our religious faith, and fits our needs like a glove."

Bowden speaks in that "cracker" drawl and uses words like "y'all"
and "dad-gum." He admits to not speaking proper American English. "I
use the word 'ain't' a lot too," he says. "I'm bad about that. I know 'ain't'
ain't in the dictionary [it really is], but how else would I express myself?
Sometimes there ain't no better way to say it."

Does he do it for effect, or is it for real?

"It's for real. I'm from Birmingham. My momma and daddy were
born and raised in Alabama. I'm from the Deep South. I will admit I
might just lay it on a little heavy sometimes. When I do, though, it's for a
purpose. For some reason, that drawl seems to get people's attention.
They'll look up and chuckle because I'm talking that way and murdering
the king's English. But at that moment I got all their eyes on me. Maybe
they're waiting to see whether I'm gonna say something else funny. Usually I do, because I like to tell funny stories. But those stories are usually to
make a point too. You know, Jesus was a storyteller. All those parables He
told were just to get His points across.

"I ain't no 'cracker' though. I've never lived in the country in my life.
My family lived in a middle-class section of Birmingham."

Bowden appears to be easy-going and laid back. But because of that
appearance and his down-home humor, he is often viewed as a not-real-
smart, country hick.

Pope once described him in a newspaper column as a "good old
boy." It was a compliment. He wrote, "If Olympic gold medals were
awarded for charm, Bobby Bowden would have a basement full of bullion.
He is irrepressibly up and impossibly down to earth."

"I've always played the hick role," laughed Bowden. Then he added,
"But folks who perceive me as being a good ol' boy who is kinda dumb

are making a little bit of a mistake. It's like the old guy who was challenged to a fight and refused to. He was challenged again. He refused again. Finally, he was backed into a corner and had to fight. And he turned that challenger every way but loose, and then said, 'I said I didn't *want* to fight. I didn't say I *couldn't*.' Well, folks who think I'm dense and somewhat of a pushover better not back me into a corner."

Opponents who face him on the field know better. Bowden is a fierce competitor with a reputation for getting the most out of his talent. He also has the reputation of pulling a trick or two out of his football bag.

"A lot of folks call those trick plays 'high school plays,' " Bowden said with a chuckle. "Well, we just use them dad-gum things against coaches with high school mentalities."

Jake Gaither, the late legendary Florida A & M coach, once was quoted as saying of the late Paul "Bear" Bryant that "he could take his'n and beat your'n, or he could take your'n and beat his'n." Bowden may not have that reputation yet, but he does have the reputation of being the greatest in the game when he has several weeks to prepare for a single game.

His record of being the winningest bowl coach percentage-wise in NCAA history (13-3-1 record) attests to that. Through the 1994 Orange Bowl, Bowden's Florida State Seminoles had won an NCAA-record nine straight bowls and had not lost a bowl game in 12 straight years (11-0-1). No coach, not even "Bear" Bryant, has ever accomplished that. And Bowden needs only three more wins to surpass Bryant's NCAA-leading bowl victory total of 15.

And to use a Bowden term, he "ain't been bad" when it comes to other big games, either. He is 6-2 against Nebraska, 4-2 against Louisiana State, 3-2 against Clemson, 2-0 against Ohio State, 2-0 against Syracuse, 1-1 against Notre Dame, 1-1 against Michigan, 1-0 against Michigan State, 1-0 against Brigham Young, and 1-0 against Oklahoma State.

When Bowden's Seminoles won their 10th game during the 1993 season (their final record was 12 wins, 1 loss), it marked the seventh consecutive season his teams had won 10 or more games. No other coach in the history of major college football has accomplished that. Also, at the end of the 1993 season Bowden was second in most victories by an active coach with 239. Only Joe Paterno, with 257, is ahead of him.

Bowden believes in many things. He said, "I believe in God, Jesus Christ, salvation, family, country, and football—in that order." He believes in prayer and reading the Bible. Also, he recognizes his weaknesses. He said, "Christians are people too."

He is called many things—coach, father, disciplinarian, counselor, teacher, preacher, and even "bigger than life." But above all, he is a Christian.

Bowden speaks at churches and charitable events all the time, and does not charge a speaking fee. He is in a pulpit somewhere on about forty Sundays of each year. He said, "Folks ask, and I gotta go. I can't say no. Jesus tells us that we have not chosen Him, but He has chosen us." His religious convictions are so strong that he once turned down Playboy's "Coach of the Year" award. He simply said, "It wouldn't have been right."

Although it's difficult to believe, Bowden really doesn't care much for the public life. He is famous. He knows that. How could he not know it? Everywhere he goes, adoring fans crowd around just to get a glimpse of him. Fans, who feel the goodness in him, will yell, "Hey, Bobby, how ya doin'?"

Bobby will answer, "Hi, buddy, how y'all been?" He calls everybody he doesn't know "buddy," with good reason.

The truth is that although Bowden loves people, he doesn't like crowds. He would much prefer to be out on the practice field alone with his thoughts, or on a golf course somewhere with a "chaw" of tobacco in his cheek, or at home on the couch in front of the television set, or on a beach somewhere soaking up the sun.

But he spends every waking hour doing just the opposite. He's a man on the go with a calling burning in his heart.

Why does he do it?

He simply says, "I firmly believe God has a plan for my life. I just try to respond whenever He calls. I'm a Christian. What else can I do?"

Brad Scott, former Florida State offensive coordinator and now head coach at South Carolina, summed it up best when he said, "There are many coaches across the country who are Christians. Bobby Bowden is a Christian who is a coach. And therein lies the difference."

What I Believe

I reckon there will be some who will say, "Here comes another of them dad-gum coaches who's gonna preach to us."

Well, those folks are right in a way. I am going to talk about God and keep talking about Him whenever and wherever I have the opportunity. I'm not going to preach and certainly not going to judge anyone who wants to believe differently. But as long as the words will come out of my mouth, I'm going to say what I believe to be true. And if you want to call that preaching, then so be it.

This book is simply about what Bobby Bowden believes. It isn't a message y'all haven't heard before. But I know just as sure as the sun rises and sets that it is a message that can't be repeated often enough.

I know the message is the way to life and is the truth about life. And if you believe it, I believe you will have the life of lives, just as God has promised. It will be a life of peace, contentment, happiness, and fulfillment. The Bible tells us, "And the peace of God, which surpasses all understanding, will guard your hearts and minds through Christ Jesus" (Phil. 4:7). When you have the God of love in your heart and mind, you certainly can't have a lousy life.

I'm almost obsessed with getting the message to young people. That's why I'm a big supporter and spokesman for the Fellowship of Christian Athletes. No matter how busy my schedule is, I rarely turn down an invitation to speak to young kids. Hey, buddy, don't you get it? These youngsters are our future.

During the 1991 season we were ranked number one in the nation and had our sights set on winning a first national championship. It was a dream that wasn't going to become a reality that year. It took two more years before we finally got that elusive, mythical national championship, but that's another story.

Anyhow, we were 3-0 and had an open date. (For folks who don't know what an open date is, it's a week off during the season.) Our next game was a big one—at Michigan. During that open date, I excused myself from game preparation and flew to Williamson, West Virginia, to speak to a youth group at a tiny school in a coal town called Delbarton.

Why did I go? Why didn't I stay in Tallahassee and prepare for that important game at Michigan?

I went because they asked me and I couldn't refuse. I just felt I had to do it. You never know when you will say something, or do something, that might make a difference in a kid's life. (The only thing I didn't like was landing in those dad-gum mountains in that wee little airplane. It seems they make airports in West Virginia by flattening the tops of two mountains and then filling in the hollow in-between. I've never been much on flying anyway, and I've had my share of close calls, but more on that later.)

This book is about what I believe. I'm certainly not going to judge anyone who believes differently. But as long as the words will come out of my mouth, I'm going to say what I believe to be true.

I go out and talk to kids because they can still be influenced. So many of them are at a crossroad in their lives. The right word at the right time might turn them in the right direction, might change them, and might steer them on to productive, happy, Christian lives. I feel as a believer I must try as hard as I can to give them God's Word, because if they don't get that, they might get the wrong word. Too many kids have already gotten the wrong word, and that saddens me.

It really saddens me when I read about some young person getting shot and killed, or dying in a car crash, or coming down with a terminal illness, or throwing his or her life away messing with drugs and alcohol. I think, "Lawh, I pray somebody told them all he or she could about the meaning of salvation before they died."

You know, I'm not getting any younger. I turned sixty-four on November 8, 1993. The years have gone by so fast, and ol' Bobby's time on earth is drawing to a close. Not a single person on this earth can be positive he or she is going to be around five years from now, one year from now, one month from now, one day from now, or one minute from now. I know that. So I want to leave something behind, something that might influence someone's life.

That's the essence of why I've done this book.

I thought about not doing the book until after I retired. Then, I decided maybe it would be better to do it now and not wait. (Now keep in mind, I'm not planning on retiring no time soon. That is, unless we start losing a whole bunch of games. Ol' Bobby just may lose his welcome if that should happen!) I figured, *Bobby, if you wait until after you're gone from football, you may be long gone. It may be now or never.*

I just want to let y'all know right off the bat where I'm coming from in writing this book and sharing my life's philosophy. That's the focus of Chapter 2. If you read that and don't want to read Chapters 3, 4, or any more, that's fine. But I think you will find them interesting. There are some good stories with a good message. I believe with all my heart that the message, God's message of salvation, will never grow old.

We will, but it won't. It's my belief that what we do in the meantime is what's important.

Where I'm Coming From

A s the deer pants for the water brooks, So pants my soul for You, O God."

That's the first scripture I ever learned. I can remember sitting beside my mother on the couch in our living room and listening to her read the Bible. Mother always read the Bible, and she always read that scripture, Psalm 42:1. It's one of my favorites and one I use in a lot of my talks.

Mother must have taught that to me when I was about eight years of age. It's the first one I ever memorized. I think most parents teach their children scriptures like John 3:16: "For God so loved the world that He gave His only begotten Son . . ." I learned that one, too, but that psalm was the first. And at the time I didn't know why Mother picked that one out.

It was years before I discovered the meaning of that psalm. It means that just like a deer running in the woods has a thirst for water, our souls have a hunger for God. It means that whether we know it or not, something is missing. Every person is born with a void, and only God can fill that void. I was born with that emptiness in my soul, and so were you. Everyone is searching for Him. The problem is a lot of folks don't know how to find Him. They ain't got no idea what they're looking for.

I'm a football coach. I love the dad-gum game. And when we have our players on the practice field in August in two-a-day drills, it's always ninety degrees or hotter on the field. Sometimes it is well over 100. It gets pretty warm in northern Florida that time of year. And when our kids come off the field after being out there for a couple of hours, man, they're hot. Many of them have lost eight to ten pounds of fluids in that hot sun. And some of those extra big kids might sweat off more than that.

And what do you think is the first thing they want?

Well, it's not food. No, they want something to quench their thirst.

In our facilities building right down the hall from our locker room is the cafeteria. And the first thing the players pass when they enter is the liquids. And right in front is a big container of orange juice. I'm sure many of our players say to themselves, *Lawdy, I wish that juice was in a great big vat so I could pick it up in my hands and drink the whole thing.*

But they can't. And even if they could, they couldn't drink the whole thing; they'd probably get sick. So, they take a little glass, fill it up, and drink it down. Naturally, it doesn't satisfy them. So they fill up the glass again and drink that one down. And they keep filling it up and drinking it down until they get satisfied. The only way they can satisfy their thirst is by filling up that little glass. There ain't no other way.

To me, it's the same with our understanding of God and Jesus Christ. We can't handle it all at once. To me, the vat of juice is God and the glass of juice is Jesus Christ, and if we know Christ, we know God. They are the same.

Our understanding comes in stages. God doesn't reveal Himself to us all at once. If He did, I'm not sure we could handle it.

I can't figure out all of who God is. I don't know where heaven is. I can't figure out how this thing we call the world—and life—all started. All I know is that I believe and have faith. And my thirst gets satisfied as long as I stay in touch with Him.

I come in contact with so many players who weren't raised in a Christian environment, who don't know God. Lord, that troubles my soul. I was fortunate to have been raised in a Christian home by Christian parents. I don't ever remember a time in my life when the Bible and church weren't part of it.

And that's why I'm going to say at the outset that I'm a Christian. That's the first thing I always say to an audience. "Folks, I'm a Christian. I just want to make sure y'all know where I stand."

And I always tell the audience that I am not ashamed of it. I'm like that deer in the psalm. I'm always thirsty for God and His Word. And you'll hear me say this more than once, "The Bible tells us that 'In the beginning was the Word, and the Word was with God, and the Word was

God. . . . And the Word became flesh and dwelt among us, and we beheld His glory . . .' "(John 1:1,14).

A lot of times when I speak to church groups I start out by telling them what I look for in football players. When I get young men and try to teach them how to play the game, I tell them there are two things they have to do if they are going to have what it takes to win: faith and commitment.

The first thing they must have is faith. I tell them, "Men, y'all must have faith in me. Y'all gotta trust me." Of course, I have coached some boys who didn't trust me. I have pitied them because that's the one thing I won't stand for and don't want—mistrust.

I tell them, "I'm going to trust you. I will assume you are abiding by the rules and behaving yourselves. I'll assume that until I see otherwise. And if I see otherwise, then I will take steps to correct it. But I will always give y'all the benefit of the doubt."

And the second thing I tell my players is that they must commit themselves to me. Sometimes kids just can't do that. That's a tall order. But to have a winning program the players must believe. They can't tell me they believe and have faith in me, and then turn around and not do what I tell them to do.

And I say to my players, "When I tell you not to do a certain thing, y'all must not do it. And if I tell you to run a certain amount of laps around the field, y'all gotta run them laps. And if I tell you to go to class, y'all gotta go to class." That's the way I see it. They have to do what I say.

I'm a football coach. I love the dad-gum game.

And then I tell them, "If I have your faith, trust, and commitment, then we're gonna win a heckuva lot of games."

I think God is looking for the same ingredients in each of us. He wants us to believe in Him and have faith in Him. And believe me, there is a difference in believing and having faith.

A lot of folks claim to believe in God. They stand up and say, "Yes, Lord, I believe. Look at how good I am." That doesn't mean a thing. Even pagans believe in a supreme being. Now, those pagans might not have a set religion, but they believe there is something somewhere that is more powerful than they are.

So folks might believe in God. Lord knows, I believe in Him. The problem is we want to accept Him on our terms, not His. It's following Him and obeying Him that causes us to balk. You might say a lot of us try to live our way in God's world. That's where we get in some mighty tall cotton.

There are a couple of stories about faith I use in my talks. One is funny and just an attention-getter. The other may make you smile, but it's not funny. It makes the point and illustrates the difference between belief and faith.

The first story goes like this: My wife, Ann, and I were sitting in the front row of a Baptist church during a revival one Sunday night. Ann was sitting on one end of the row and I was sitting on the other. Our six children were in the middle. I think their ages then were from about four to fourteen. We kind of had the entire row nailed down.

Anyhow, this evangelist is preaching this revival. Suddenly, he pointed his finger at me. I thought, *Oh, Lord, he wants me to do something.*

But he said, "Sir, I see you have six children."

I nodded and thought, *Yeah, they're all mine. And I got the bills to prove it.*

The preacher went on, "Well, let me ask you a question. If I put a 40-foot I-beam here in the front of the church and fixed it so it was only about one foot off the floor, would you get up on it and walk across it for $20?"

I figured that wouldn't be any harder than walking a curb, or walking on a rail on a railroad track, so I said, "Yeah, that'll be an easy $20."

The preacher smiled and said, "All right, let me ask you another question. If I took that I-beam to New York City and put it between two skyscrapers fifty stories in the air, then would you walk across it for $20?"

"Ain't no way," I replied with no hesitation.

"Well, sir, let me ask you a final question," the preacher continued. "If I put that I-beam up there fifty stories high, and on one side I was holding one of your children over the edge and said if you walked across the I-beam then I wouldn't drop the child, would you do it?"

I pondered on it a moment, then said, "Which child?"

Now that really didn't happen. It's just a joke I tell to perk up the audience. Works every time too. I get those folks kind of leaning forward in their seats to see if I'm going to tell another joke. Then I slip in my point with the other story.

It goes like this: Once upon a time there was a man who traveled from one small town to another performing a tightrope act. One day, he came to a little farming community. He stood in the center of the town square and announced that he was going to go to the outskirts of town and stretch a rope across the wide river canyon out there and walk across the rope while pushing a wheelbarrow.

Naturally, the farmers were skeptical. They didn't believe he could do it.

So, the man went out on the edge of town and put his rope between two trees about five feet off the ground and began to practice. He got up on that rope with his wheelbarrow and walked back and forth, back and forth.

I tell my players, "If I have your faith, trust, and commitment, then we're gonna win a heckuva lot of games." I think God is looking for the same ingredients in each of us: faith, trust, and commitment.

One farmer came out and began to watch. And the longer the farmer watched, the more he became convinced that the man could do what he said he was going to do. So, the farmer went back to the town square where the skeptics were and said, "Do y'all remember that man who said he was going to walk a tightrope across that wide canyon?"

The farmers nodded.

"Well, I believe he can do it," said the one farmer.

"Ha!" laughed the skeptics. "No, he can't."

The believing farmer said, "Well, come on out to the edge of town. I want y'all to watch him."

And they all went out to where the man was practicing on the rope. The one farmer said, "See, he's doing it. I told you he could do it."

The disbelievers laughed again and said, "Yeah, but that rope is only five feet off the ground. It ain't hundreds of feet in the air across that big canyon."

And the believer said, "Well, I'll tell you how much I believe. I'll betcha $10 he can do it."

And when he said that, the man on the rope stopped, turned in his direction and said, "Do you believe I can walk across that wide canyon on this rope while pushing a wheelbarrow?"

The farmer replied, "I sure do. I bet $10 on you, didn't I?"

And the man on the rope said, "OK, get in the wheelbarrow."

You see, it's one thing to stand on the sideline and say, "I believe." It's quite another to get in the wheelbarrow. God wants us to get into the wheelbarrow. That's real faith, folks; the kind of faith God requires of each of us. We have to have that kind of faith to follow Christ. I may not always get in the wheelbarrow, but I'm always trying to.

God is our only chance to live real life, both here and in the hereafter. And the key is believing in Him and then trusting in Him; getting into His wheelbarrow.

That's one ride I ain't passing up.

There Had to Be a Plan

You will hear me say more than once in the ensuing chapters that "I'm not perfect, and I have certainly never done nothin' of any significance." But the important thing is, I have turned my life over to Christ, and He has done it for me. I've probably slowed God down. I'm sure He would have had a whole lot more success if I hadn't gotten in His way.

Thank the Lord, though, Jesus came to save all us sinners. He tells us that in Luke 5:32, when He says, "I have not come to call the righteous, but sinners, to repentance." I'm pretty darned sure I qualify in there somewhere.

I do believe God has a plan for my life. I believe that with all my heart. I feel I am right where He wants me to be at this time in my life. And it has nothing to do with coaching and winning football games and championships and making a lot of money. I am sure God has gotten my jobs for me. He handpicked them. He must have because I certainly didn't apply for them.

Every job I ever applied for, I didn't get. Not a single one. All through my career people have contacted *me*, not vice versa. They would call and say, "Bobby, we'd like to have you. Will you come?" Somebody was picking those jobs; it sure wasn't me.

Honestly, when I was young I didn't have all that many goals. All I knew was that I wanted to play football. I didn't even think about playing college football. My goals weren't very deep. I had no goals of being a football coach or of being a teacher. I thought more about a career in the military. Back then all my heroes were military men or football players.

I almost joined the Marine Corps Reserves once. I think I was interested in doing it because some of my buddies had joined up. But my daddy talked me out of it. He just said, "If I were you I wouldn't do it. I wouldn't sign anything until I had to." So, I didn't. And you know what? About three or four months after that, the war broke out in Korea and all those buddies who signed up were in Korea. I reckon God didn't want me there.

There have been many incidents in my life that have convinced me I'm where I'm supposed to be. Two stand out.

The first was way back in 1968 when I was an assistant coach at West Virginia University. I was offensive coordinator there, under head coach Jim Carlen. I had been there two years when I was offered the head coaching position at Marshall University in Huntington, West Virginia. The job came open when Perry Moss, who had coached there for two years, was fired because of alleged NCAA violations.

I believe God has a plan for my life. And it has nothing to do with coaching and winning football games and championships and making a lot of money.

Just prior to that, I had applied for the head coaching job at Wake Forest. I didn't get it, naturally; it seems that my efforts never panned out; it was only when the Lord set things up that they came to pass.

Anyhow, Eddie Barrett, then the Marshall athletic director and a former sports information director at West Virginia, called and wanted to know if I would be interested in the job. I said I'd have to know more about it. So, the next day he drove up to my home in Morgantown. I opened my garage door, and he put his car in the garage so nobody would know he was in town—it might leak to the press before we wanted them to know. We talked most of the day. At the end of it, he offered me the job. I said I would think about it and let him know.

I thought about it, and one day later called him back and said, "Naw, I don't think so, Eddie. I don't mean to belittle Marshall at all, but I want something a little better. And I think if I'm patient I can get on at a bigger school. Thanks for the offer." He thanked me for considering the job.

Oh, yeah, I also turned down an offer to coach at Louisville. I don't know why I didn't take those jobs, because I really wanted a head coaching job again. Something in my heart just told me, "Those jobs ain't for you, Bobby."

So, I didn't take the Marshall job. And Marshall hired Rick Tolley. And an eerie occurrence happened just after that. In case you don't remember, on November 14, 1970, Tolley, his coaches, his entire team, and some Marshall boosters all died in a horrible plane crash at the Huntington airport. They were returning from a game at East Carolina. Lordy, it's been more than twenty years since that happened, and it still makes me sad.

When that plane crashed, I was in my first season as head coach at West Virginia and we had just beaten Syracuse that afternoon. I was feeling pretty good because we were 7-3 with one game left on the schedule, at Maryland. We would win that one, too, to finish 8-3. But when I got home that evening I heard about the plane crash on the radio. Can you imagine, seventy-five people, many of them people I knew, had their lives snuffed out in an instant in that tragedy?

Why had I turned down that job?

I don't know.

Why wasn't I on that plane?

I don't have an answer to that one either.

I don't dwell on it because I believe it just wasn't in God's plan for my life. He wasn't ready to call me home yet. I think God must have said, "Bobby, I've still got some things for you to do." That's the only explanation I can come up with.

Let me tell you the second thing that happened to get my attention. This was in 1979, my fourth year as head coach at Florida State. That was the year we went 11-0 in the regular season. It was the first time any FSU team had ever gone undefeated playing a major college schedule. (Our final record was 11-1 after we lost to Oklahoma in the Orange Bowl.)

Anyhow, about the third game that season, I got a call from Paul Dietzel, who was then athletic director at Louisiana State. The reason he called was because it had become evident that the '79 season was going to be Charlie McClendon's last there as head coach. Dietzel wanted to know if I would be interested in the job.

And at that time I was interested. We had gone 5-6, 10-2, and 8-3 my first three seasons in Tallahassee. I felt we were making good progress. But this was early in my fourth season there. I had no idea we would go 11-0.

Yeah, I know you think that coaches think they're going to win them all, all the time. Well, that's not exactly true. We'd just *like* to win them all; we don't really 100 percent expect to.

Check it out. There haven't been many 11-0 seasons by any team anytime, anywhere. I've been in the business forty-one years and have gone 11-0 only once. And like I said, we lost the bowl game that year. It ain't that easy to go totally undefeated from wire to wire.

I was interested in LSU because at that time I honestly felt the program there was probably a cut above ours.

Dietzel kept calling. He called me a week later. A week after that he called again. He continued to call right up until we went over to Baton Rouge to play LSU. This was about the third week in October. By that time we were 6-0 and rolling along pretty well. We had beaten Miami, Southern Mississippi, and Mississippi State at home, and had won at Arizona State, Louisville, and Virginia Tech. But despite that, I still thought LSU would be a pretty good place for ol' Bobby to coach.

The last time Dietzel called he said, "Bobby, you're going to have to turn down the job, because we're going to offer it to you. But we're going to have to know something pretty soon."

From the way he said it, I knew it would all probably come to a head in Baton Rouge. I knew all those Louisiana writers would nail me as soon as that game was over. They would ask questions like, "Has Dietzel talked to you? Has he offered you the job? Are you leaving Florida State and coming to LSU?" I kind of figured our Florida writers would hit me with the same questions too. Maybe I could dodge them during the postgame press conference, but I knew I couldn't dodge them for long. Anyway, question-dodging is one game I don't like to play.

So, I said to myself, *If we lose to LSU I'm gonna take the job.*

I don't know what God's voice sounds like, but I think He's talked to me a couple of times. I may not be very smart, but I'm smart enough to know that His power intervened in my life.

My reasoning was that this was the best Florida State team I'd had in four years there. LSU was having a pretty good year, something like 4-2-1. But I reckoned if we couldn't beat them with our best club, then maybe I'd be better off to get into that Southeastern Conference (SEC) where I might have a chance to go all the way (at FSU we're now in the Atlantic Coast Conference, generally considered not quite as strong as the SEC, but we weren't in the ACC then).

Well, we didn't lose. We won, 24-19. Now we were 7-0. Only one other Florida State team had ever won its first seven games. That was in 1950 when the Seminoles played teams like Troy State, Randolph-Macon, Newberry, Sewanee, Howard, Stetson, Mississippi College, and Tampa.

After the game I told Dietzel I would not be a candidate for the job. And the following Monday I signed a new five-year contract at Florida State. I got a big pay raise and all that. I'm sure some folks thought I used that LSU offer to get a better contract and more money, but that's not true.

Shortly after I turned down the job in Baton Rouge, LSU hired Bo Rein from North Carolina State. And not long after that, Rein was on a private plane returning from a recruiting trip, or banquet, or some other function. Something went wrong with either the pilot or the plane, or both. Anyhow, the plane went way off course and vanished out in the Atlantic Ocean. As far as I know they never found a trace of it, or of the people on board.

So, now I have turned down two jobs, and the coaches the schools hired instead of me have died in tragic airplane accidents. It could easily have been me in those airplanes. My prayers go out to all their families, but at the same time I have to honestly say that I heave a sigh of relief.

I don't honestly know why I didn't take those jobs. Something just told me, "Bobby, don't take 'em." Now, I have no idea what God's voice sounds like, but I think He's talked to me a couple of times. I may not be very smart, but I'm smart enough to know that some power had intervened, and that power sure wasn't mine. The only thing I can figure out is that God had something else planned for me.

Those incidents are just two of the reasons why I'm convinced that God has had a hand in my career. There are plenty more.

When I was at West Virginia I used to fly to visit recruits in a private plane owned by a coal company in nearby Fairmont. It was a wee little two-engine plane. It was so small I had to crawl over the pilot's seat to get into the backseat. I will not fly in them little old planes now. I feel safer in a bigger plane. But back then that was the only way we had to get around.

The pilot, who worked for the coal company, was an excellent pilot. I used to fly with him in all kinds of weather. Believe me, when you fly in some thick soup, you find out real quick how good the guy in the cockpit is.

I remember once we went up to Bethlehem, Pennsylvania, to try and recruit Mike Hartenstine, who went on to Penn State and then on to a great career with the Chicago Bears. After visiting the kid, we had to spend the night because of a bad snowstorm. The next morning we started back, and as soon as we took off we were in the clouds. We couldn't see a dad-gum thing, nothing but white. And the wind was terrible. That little plane really bounced around. We had to make an emergency landing in Williamsburg, Pennsylvania. How that pilot ever got that plane on the ground I'll never know. We couldn't see the ground at all. We finally made it back safely, but that was one time when I was really scared.

About a year or so later, that same pilot was flying that same plane on a business trip to Pineville, West Virginia, and was killed in a crash. He flew into the side of one of those mountains. He was a good man.

I had another pilot who used to fly me around; he worked for the state of Florida and flew one of the state's planes. His name was Bill Martin. He was an excellent pilot, too, one of the best pilots I've ever flown with. The thing I liked about his flying was that he was cautious. He didn't take chances. He was a great guy and a good Christian.

In the spring of 1992, Bill was killed in a crash. The way I heard it was he was flying from Tallahassee to St. Augustine and the visibility was bad. He had about 500 feet clearance and was at 2,000 feet elevation. He was going to dive down under the clouds and then try to find the airport. He never pulled the plane out of the dive and went straight into the ground.

I've had other scares in planes too. Often it's bad weather that causes those scares. Nowadays, I will back out in a minute when the weather is bad. I used not to do that. I used to jump on anything and go, no matter what the weather. I think the incident that started me worrying about the weather was when that coal company pilot got killed up in West Virginia. I knew what kind of a pilot he was, and after that I figured if it can happen to a sharp pilot like him, it can happen to anybody, at any time.

Another scare I had was my first year at Florida State. I hadn't moved Ann and the kids to Tallahassee yet from West Virginia, so whenever I'd get an invitation, I'd go. I mean, going to a speaking engagement beat sitting around in a room by myself. I got a call from Mississippi State, and they asked me if I would come over to speak at a coaching clinic. I said, "Sure. But I don't have any way to get there."

They said, "Don't worry. We'll come and get you."

So, they sent a plane over. I found out later that the pilot wasn't a regular pilot. Oh, he could fly, but that wasn't how he made his living. Flying was his hobby. He made his living as a professor at Mississippi State. I found out after I got on that plane that it had a new radar unit on it. And I found out soon after that—much to my horror—that the dad-gum pilot loved to experiment with new equipment.

And wouldn't you know, soon after we took off we ran into stormy weather, and this pilot started dodging them storm clouds. He'd fly around one, up over another and down under another. That plane was bouncing around like a pogo stick. All the time he was watching his new radar. He wasn't even looking out the window. He was flying strictly by that instrument and having fun. Me? It wasn't fun to me, and I wasn't feeling too well. I thought, *This ain't no movie, and he ain't no stunt pilot. This is real life.* Finally, the weather got so bad he had to set the plane down in Birmingham.

When I got off that plane I said to myself, *I am never going to let anybody send a plane for me again. I don't want no pilot who has a new gadget to play with to fly me anywhere.* I mean, this guy was like a kid with a new toy. I don't think flying, particularly flying in bad weather, is something to play around with.

I did fly once with the Blue Angels. It was around 1986. The Blue Angels had come to Tallahassee, and one of them was a Florida State graduate. He asked me if I would like to fly with them, and I said, "Yeah." Now, I knew it would be scary, but I knew it would be exciting too. The excitement part of it won over the scary part. (Don't ask me why. Like I said, I never was very smart.)

I went out to the airport the next day and got all decked out in a flying suit and a flying helmet. And when I climbed up the ladder of that double-seater jet, I felt like I was wearing one of those old diving suits. I guess that's about how those astronauts feel.

Anyway, when we took off, I was sitting in the seat behind the pilot and enjoying the view. Right in front, between my legs, was a stick to fly the plane with. I was sitting there watching the pine trees fly past, and then all of a sudden that pilot pulled back on the stick and . . . Whoosh! . . . that plane went right straight up, and I mean straight up. We must have climbed 5,000 feet in about twelve seconds. At least, it seemed that quick. Man, did it ever snap my head back.

Then, after we had been up there for a few minutes, the pilot said to me, "Coach, you want to take the stick and try a few things?"

I said, "Yeah."

He gave me a few instructions over the intercom, and then I took the stick. I moved that stick about one or two inches to the side, and that dadgum jet just rolled clean over. One second we were right side up, the next we were upside-down, and then, we were right side up again. Wow! I couldn't believe it. Then, I did a complete loop. I started doing dives and everything.

When we landed, some folks asked the pilot how I did, and he said, "Well, I think he had a good time, but he did get a little aggressive up there."

I really did have some fun. I was up there making believe I was some hotshot pilot. I'd push that stick forward and go screaming down, and then I'd pull it back and that plane would go screaming straight up toward the heavens. It was so easy. Unbelievable. I know the pilot was doing all the other stuff to keep that jet in the air.

After about twenty minutes, the pilot said, "We have about ten more minutes up here, Coach. What do you want to do?"

I said, "You better get me down. I think I'm gettin' sick." My stomach really was feeling queasy.

As we were coming in for the landing, the pilot said, "I'll show you how we land on aircraft carriers." And he came swinging around almost parallel to the end of the runway. Then, he put the stick over and just slung that jet around and dropped her on the runway. Bam! I wasn't ready for that quick turn, and it snapped my head over against the cockpit canopy. Now I know why they wear those helmets. I thought I never was going to get my head back to where it was supposed to be.

I had been up in the jet for only a little over twenty minutes, but when I got out of it I could hardly walk. And I was so tired that I went right back to my office, stretched out on the couch, and slept for two hours. I guess it was all the tension and the pressure that kind of flying puts on your body. All I know is I was dead tired.

There are other incidents that have helped convince me that God has a plan for my life. One year after turning down that LSU job, I was sitting in my office one morning and Sue Hall, my secretary, told me I had a call from Auburn. I picked up the phone and it was one of Auburn's administrators. He asked if I would be interested in meeting with their president, their five-man committee, and some of their big hitters (their more influential boosters). They were looking for a coach and I reckon they wanted to see if I would be interested in them, and if they might be interested in me.

I said, "Sure, I'll meet with you." We met in Childersburg, Alabama, at my uncle's house.

Basically, they wanted to know what it would take for me to come to Auburn. This was after my fifth team at Florida State had finished 10-1 and was going to play Oklahoma again in a second straight Orange Bowl. In two regular seasons we had lost just one game, and that was by a single point (10-9) at Miami.

If you had said to me, "Bobby, someday you are going to be offered the head coaching job at Auburn and you're going to turn it down," I would have told you, "There's no way I'd turn that one down. You'd better get your head examined."

I listened to what they had to say, and they listened to what I had to say. But something just wasn't right. We had worked so hard that year at FSU, and our kids had accomplished so much. So, I thought about the discomforting thoughts rolling around in my head and said, "Men, I cannot talk to y'all any more about this job. I have a bowl game to get ready for. If my players find out I'm talking to y'all I'll lose their trust and respect. Those are things I don't want to lose. Also, I'd certainly lose their attention when we start to prepare for Oklahoma. I just can't get involved in this thing right now."

A few weeks after that meeting—I think just before the bowl game— Auburn's president called and said, "We want you." (I later found out that Auburn had first offered the job to Georgia's Vince Dooley, and he turned it down. I was their second choice.)

Now you have to remember, I was born and raised in Alabama. All my roots are in Alabama. And you know where I always dreamed of someday coaching, don't you? Sure, it was either Auburn or Alabama. Man, when I was young the thought of being coach at either of those schools seemed about the same as going to heaven.

But when Auburn called and made the offer, I found myself looking for excuses to tell them no. I mean, here I was with an offer to be the top man at Auburn, and I was looking for reasons not to take the job. I started talking to their president and it didn't even sound like me talking. I said, "First of all, I have a big ball game coming up. My team doesn't need any distractions. Also, I have a five-year contract. You would have to buy out my contract. That would cost you about $700,000. I certainly ain't got that kind of money."

Auburn's president said, "Well, why don't you go ahead and resign and we'll find some way to handle the rest of it?" I guess he was talking about going to court or something. I don't know.

I said, "Naw. Why don't you just take my name out of it and look for somebody else?" And I added, "The guy you ought to hire is Pat Dye." Dye was coaching out in Wyoming at the time, and I knew he was interested in the job. Auburn ended up hiring Dye, who served until December 1992, when he resigned in the face of NCAA recruiting violations. Ironically enough, they then hired my son, Terry, for the head coaching job. He went on in his first season as head coach to an undefeated regular season.

So now I've turned down the Auburn job. Unbelievable. If you had said to me years earlier, "Bobby, someday you are going to be offered the head coaching job at Auburn and you are going to turn it down," I would have told you, "There's no way I'd turn that one down. You'd better get your head examined." As I look back today, I probably came closer to taking that job than I thought at the time, because it was a tough decision.

Then shortly after that, Coach Bryant retired at Alabama and they hired Ray Perkins. Perkins coached there until 1986 and then resigned under more than a little pressure. I suspect it was tough being the man who succeeded Coach Bryant; he left huge shoes to fill. Unfortunately, the only way Perkins could go was downhill.

About the time Perkins resigned, we happened to be in Birmingham to play Indiana in the All-American Bowl. I had been at Florida State for eleven years, and we were playing in our fifth straight bowl and the eighth in ten years. We had it going pretty well. At least, I thought so.

A couple of Alabama representatives, I think one was the university president's right-hand man, contacted me and said, "Bobby, our president wants to meet with you. He wants to talk about the coaching job. Would you be interested in talking to him?"

I said earlier that when I was young I dreamed of someday coaching at either Auburn or Alabama. Well, if you think I wanted to coach at Auburn, then you'll figure out that I really wanted to coach at Alabama.

But I played it cool. I said, "I'll talk to your president on one condition. I'll talk if he offers me the job. That's the only way."

A few years earlier I wouldn't have wanted to have been in Perkins's shoes. Being the man who succeeds a legend is an impossible no-win situation. However, being the man who succeeds the man who succeeded the legend is a whole new ball game; I figured that out real quick.

Anyhow, those Alabama representatives said something to the effect that "you're the president's choice." I took that at face value and felt pretty good about it.

We set up a meeting to take place after we had played our bowl game. I thought the meeting was to be a secret one with just me, the university president, and maybe two or three of his big shots. Well, when I got to the hotel where the meeting was to take place and opened the door to go in, I saw that the dad-gum room was full. It was a committee. Well, it was actually more than that. There was the Alabama president. There was the head of this department, the head of that department, and Lord knows who else.

I walked in and my first thought was, *Uh, oh, Bowden, this ain't gonna be what you thought it was.*

When we drove up in front of our house there must have been at least three television crews camped in our front yard. I thought, *What are all these media people doing here? Did somebody in our family die?*

Also, I was smart enough to realize that with all those people in that room, any chance of this being a secret meeting had long since gone out the window. But I figured since I had gone this far, I might as well take it all the way. So, I said to myself, *OK, Bobby, you might as well go on in and listen to their offer.*

I went in and sat down and the questions began. They asked me questions about everything. And I answered them. I kept thinking, *This is an interrogation. What the heck is going on?*

When the meeting was breaking up, the Alabama president came over and said, "Coach Bowden, we want to thank you for coming. We enjoyed talking to you." I shook his hand and left. As I walked out I thought, *I didn't hear that man say anything about no dad-gum job offer.*

And when I got to the car that had delivered me to the meeting, I asked the driver, who was an Alabama man, "What went on? Did your president offer me the job?"

He said, "Naw."

I figured right then and there things hadn't gone my way. It had been a dad-gum interview. That wasn't what I wanted. I had told them prior to the meeting that the only way I'd meet them was if I were offered the job.

I had been in college coaching at that time for twenty-five years. I had been a head coach at the major college level for seventeen years and we had won 132 games and lost 62. Overall our teams had won 163 games. I had coached teams in ten bowl games. We had just beaten Indiana in that All-American Bowl 27-13. That meant we hadn't lost a bowl game since 1980. We'd had consecutive seasons of 10-2, 8-3, 11-1, 10-2, 6-5, 9-3, 8-4, 7-3-2, 9-3, and 7-4-1.

I didn't want to be interviewed. Shoot, no. Why would I have to be interviewed for a head coaching job? If I had been a young coach that would have been one thing. But I wasn't a rookie. I'm not bragging, but the plain truth was my record wasn't too shabby. It should have stood on its own merit. I didn't feel like I needed to prove myself. And I certainly didn't feel I needed to answer questions of some committee.

I know that maybe doesn't sound right, but that's how I felt. My pride was bruised, and I was kind of bent out of shape over the whole thing. Pride can be an awful thing. But as I said earlier, I never did claim to be perfect.

Anyhow, I got the feeling that it wasn't me Alabama was interested in. If it had been, I kind of figured they would have offered me the job. (By way of update, my name popped up again at Alabama in 1990, just before the school hired Gene Stallings to replace Bill Curry. That time I let 'em know I wasn't interested.)

The next day Ann and I drove back to Tallahassee. It took us six hours. And all that time we talked about what went on. We never did turn on the radio. If we had, we would have learned that the big news was, "Unconfirmed reports are that Bobby Bowden is going to become the new head coach at Alabama."

When we drove up in front of our house there must have been crews from at least three television stations camped in our front yard. I thought, *What are all these media people doing here? Did somebody in our family die?*

When I found out what they were there for, I excused myself and went into the house and called Wayne Hogan, our sports information director. I told Wayne to get out a news release stating that I had withdrawn my name from the Alabama job. And I told him to make sure in that release that he said that "Bobby Bowden says he is not interested." Alabama went ahead and hired Curry, and that was fine with me.

Let me say this, though, if they had offered me the job it would have been hard to turn it down because being head coach at Alabama was always something I dreamt of. When I took the Florida State job back in 1976, I said to myself, *Bobby, you're not there yet, but you're gettin' close. And there's only one other move you gotta make: from Tallahassee to Tuscaloosa.*

I feel like God handled that one too. He might have thought, "Ol' Bobby is fixin' to take that dad-gum job. Well, he ain't gonna get it, because I've got something better planned for him than coaching at Alabama. That job ain't gonna be his no matter how bad he might want it."

So, now God has kept me off various airplanes that crashed; He protected me all those years driving those winding two-lane highways in the mountains of West Virginia. He made me turn down the Auburn job, and then He fixed it so I didn't get the Alabama job, the one I had wanted all my life.

I've kind of gotten the message that there's a plan in there somewhere.

The
Road to
Florida State!

In my mind, God's plan for my life goes even farther back. Sometimes when I'm alone with my thoughts, which isn't often, I think about the way the path to coaching was laid out for me.

If it had been left up to me, I honestly don't know where I would have ended up. I might have become a schoolteacher and let it go at that. I really did think of doing that. This happened after I had graduated from Howard College (now Samford University) in Birmingham and had gotten my master's degree in education from Peabody College in Nashville. I came back to Howard and was hired as an assistant football coach. That was in the fall of 1953. I thought, *Well, Bobby, here you are barely wet behind the ears and you're already an assistant coach at your alma mater. You're on your way.*

Then two years after that, head coach Earl Gartman, who had coached me when I played at Howard, resigned to take another job. Suddenly, I was the only coach left on the staff. And I was only twenty-five years old.

I figured I was in a perfect position to move up to the top spot. And I felt even better about it when Gartman said, "Bobby, I'm going to recommend to our president that he hire you." Man, I was up in the clouds.

The problem was the president, a man named Major Davis, didn't pay any attention to Gartman's recommendation. He turned me down. He said, "You're too young. You've played ball with some of the players on the team. I don't think you can coach them."

That just about killed me. When you're young, ambitious, and anxious to get on with your career, you don't have much patience. I have to admit I didn't have much. People are always asking God for patience, but they always add, "But Lord, be quick about it." It doesn't work that way.

Anyhow, I had been so full of dreams of being a coach, and now it was 1955 and it seemed like my coaching career had ended before it got started. I didn't see much in my future, so I began to make other plans. I sent my money in to Columbia University in New York City and planned to go there and work toward a doctorate degree in education. I was accepted and all set to depart for New York on June 1.

As I look back, I can see now that this little old southern boy would have been like a fish out of water in that big city. But as I was getting ready to head for the Big Apple, I got a letter from a Dr. William Smith, the president of South Georgia Junior College. In the letter he said, "If you are interested in being the head football coach at South Georgia College, phone me." And I think the letter said to call collect. That kind of impressed me. And believe me, the letter sure surprised me.

I'll never forget what Dr. Smith said to me. "Son, do you want to coach, or do you want to be a dad-gum schoolteacher?" I said, "I want to coach, sir." That decision changed my life forever.

I read the letter twice, and then I had to start asking some questions like, "Where is South Georgia College?" I had never heard of it. I found out it was located in Douglas, Georgia. Where in the heck was that? Somebody told me it was over near Waycross. That didn't mean anything. I got a map and found out where it was.

I phoned Dr. Smith. We set up an interview, and I drove over to Douglas. Oh, yes, during the phone conversation Dr. Smith said, "We give athletic scholarships too." Howard College wasn't giving scholarships at that time. The idea of being able to offer recruits scholarships really perked up my interest.

During the interview the president let me know right off that he wanted me to be his coach. That pleased me, but it also put me in a dilemma. I said, "Sir, I don't know what to do. I'm supposed to leave for Columbia University in a few days. I won't get back until right when practice is supposed to start. I won't know the players. Maybe I should forget it. Maybe I should go on up to New York City and get my doctorate and just teach."

And then I'll never forget what Dr. Smith said to me. He said, "Son, do you want to coach, or do you want to be a dad-gum schoolteacher?"

I said, "I want to coach, sir."

He said, "Then I recommend you don't go to Columbia. I recommend that you get yourself over here and start to work."

And that's what I did. I canceled my reservations to Columbia University and moved to Douglas. All of a sudden I've gone from thinking I was out of coaching for good to being a head coach and athletic director at a two-year junior college, one that even gave scholarships. This was sure something I hadn't planned on.

I coached there four years and we won three state junior college championships and tied for a fourth one. We compiled a 22-11 record. Then in 1959, Dr. Smith called me into his office and said, "Bobby, we're gonna have to drop football. Even though you've been winning championships, we've been losing money. We just can't take the financial losses anymore."

I said, "How about if we could get more money from the merchants and businessmen?"

He said, "No, we're already getting all the money we can from those folks. We gotta drop football and get our finances back in order. But we want you to stay. You can serve as athletic director and baseball coach. And you can teach. We'd love for you to stay with us."

I didn't give him an answer because I didn't have one. I didn't know what to do. I'd worked my tail off for four years. We'd won championships. I had loved it. Now it was gone. I didn't know what was going to happen, but this time I was sure of one thing: I wanted to coach football. The problem was I had a wife and four young children and needed a job. So, once again I didn't know what was in my future. And this time I was really down in the dumps.

I went back to my office and sat down at my desk. And as I was sitting there feeling sorry for myself, I looked down, and there on the desk was a letter addressed to me. It was from Howard College. I opened it, and it was from Dr. Leslie Wright, the new college president. I don't remember the exact words, but basically it read: "If you're interested in becoming our new head football coach, please let me know."

I couldn't believe it. It happened so quick I didn't even have time to really worry about South Georgia dropping football. I wrote a letter to

Howard College athletic director James Sharman (back in those days we didn't make as many long-distance phone calls as we do now). I said in the letter that I would be interested.

I went back to Birmingham for the interview and got the job. Now I was back at my alma mater as the top man. In my thinking I had gone from the pits to the top of the mountain. I was back home.

Later, I found out how they had decided to offer me the job. One day, after I'd been on the job a while, Sharman said, "Bobby, did I ever tell you how I selected you to come back and be our head coach?"

I had no idea.

He said, "Well, when we decided to make a change, we thought about a lot of candidates and couldn't come to a decision. So I prayed about it. I didn't get an answer, or didn't think I did. Anyway, the day after I prayed about it, I was sitting in my office and an old school yearbook was on my desk. For some reason the book was open. And when I looked at it, the first thing I saw was your picture. And I thought, *By golly, maybe God wants me to hire this young man.*"

Four years earlier, they wouldn't hire me when I really wanted the job, saying I was too young, and I left in a huff. I was really angry, and hurt too. Now I didn't even apply for the job and they hired me back. I was beginning to figure out that when things happened, it certainly wasn't because of anything I did.

My first year (1959) as head coach at Howard, we won nine games— six of them by holding our opponents scoreless—and lost one. It was the best record in school history.

Then in the winter of 1963, I got a call from an old boyhood friend, Vince Gibson. Vince was then an assistant coach at Florida State under Bill Peterson. He said, "Bobby, Peterson is looking to hire an assistant. It might be worth looking into. I've told him about you."

Well, I didn't know Peterson. I wouldn't have known him if he had walked in my front door. And to be honest, I wasn't sure I wanted to move. Oh, there were some things about being coach at a small school that I didn't like, but I kind of liked being a head coach, and so the prospect of an assistantship wasn't exactly super-attractive.

Shortly after that, I went to Atlanta for the Atlanta Touchdown Club banquet. When I got to the banquet I discovered I was one of the few head coaches there from a small school. I mean, I was from little Howard College. Most of the coaches were from big schools—Georgia Tech, Georgia, Clemson, and so forth. But when I looked to see where they had me seated, I'll be darned if they didn't have me seated at the head table right next to Bill Peterson. Now figure that one out.

During the dinner he said to me, "Coach, you know I have an opening on my staff. Would you be interested?" We talked briefly, but that was about it. I didn't indicate my interest one way or the other.

I went back to Birmingham, and about four or five days later Peterson called and said, "I'd like for you to come on down and interview for this job. Also, it would give you a chance to look us over and see if you'd like it down here."

I figured it couldn't hurt to listen and look, so I agreed.

Ann and I drove to Tallahassee. I was interviewed and was offered the job. But like I said, I kind of liked being a head coach. Yet I also knew that someday I wanted to get into major college coaching. Ann and I talked it over and decided if I wanted to move up a step in my career, this might be the best way and the right time to do it. So, I took the job.

Now I was an assistant coach at Florida State University. And again it was a job I didn't apply for. When I think back, I wonder if maybe God had a hand in making sure I was seated next to Peterson at that banquet.

I was at Florida State for three years; and to be honest, they weren't happy ones for me. Things just didn't work out in Tallahassee. I felt I wasn't going anywhere under Peterson. Maybe it was because I had been a head coach and had kind of gotten used to running the show. I don't know. I reckon what I was doing was pouting. I didn't really have a title on the coaching staff. Oh, I coached receivers some and the quarterbacks some. But what I wanted was a title. At the end of my third year at Florida State, the offensive coordinator's job opened up. I thought I would get it. But instead of promoting me, Peterson brought in somebody else. That didn't hit me too good either.

Coaches steal ideas from one another all the time. There ain't any secrets in coaching.

So I was applying for jobs. I had heard that West Virginia's coach, Gene Corum, had resigned. I wrote to Red Brown, the athletic director there, and said I would like to be considered for the job. Brown thanked me for my interest but gave the job to Jim Carlen. That was another job I applied for and didn't get.

I had met Carlen when he was an assistant at Georgia Tech. He used to come with other coaches to Florida State in the spring to study what we were doing. In 1964 we had gone 9-1-1 and whipped Oklahoma 36-19 in the Gator Bowl. That year our offense scored 263 points and our defense gave up only eighty-five. Man, we put points on the board. When you have a good year, coaches come from all over to try to find out how you did it. That's when I first met Carlen. And the next spring I went up to Georgia Tech and studied what they were doing.

Coaches steal ideas from one another all the time. There ain't any secrets in coaching.

Anyhow, when Carlen got the West Virginia job, he called and wanted me to come to West Virginia and join his staff. I flew up to West Virginia and interviewed for the job and got it. What sold me was when Carlen said, "Bobby, you will run the offense and call all the plays." I liked that.

Meanwhile, "Shug" Jordan at Auburn had called and offered me the same position—offensive coordinator. After visiting West Virginia, I came back to Tallahassee and drove up to Auburn and visited with Shug. Then I went back home and talked everything over with Ann. We decided the best thing to do was to take the West Virginia job. I called Carlen and told him of my decision. Then I called Shug and told him I was turning down his offer.

Don't ask me why I took the West Virginia job and turned my back on Auburn. It was another of those decisions people make that don't make any sense at the time. Like I said before, I had always wanted to coach at one of the big universities in my home state. But when Ann and I talked, we tried to look at it in a rational way. I figured Shug wasn't going to retire and leave anytime soon. So, if I took the Auburn offer, there wouldn't be much chance for advancement there.

I just felt at that time that West Virginia was a better opportunity. I liked Carlen's positive style. And he was a heck of a salesman. I felt since West Virginia's program was down, folks up there would be hungry for success, any kind of success.

But you'll never know what a tough move that was. Here I was a guy raised in the Deep South and a guy who had never been out of the Deep South, and I was going to a part of the country I had never been to before. I was going to a state I knew nothing about, a state they called the "Mountain State." I figured I knew about mountains. After all, we have some mountains in Alabama. I learned I didn't know anything about mountains, because I sure hadn't ever seen any like the ones they had up there.

It turned out to be the right move, because four years later Carlen suddenly left to take the head coaching job at Texas Tech. This was in 1969, when we had gone 10-1 and had beaten South Carolina 14-3 in the Peach Bowl. That was the game where we surprised South Carolina by installing the wishbone offense just for that bowl game. We had never run it before, and never ran it after that. But that night the wishbone was perfect. It rained and rained; the field was muddy and perfect for a running attack like the wishbone. We looked like geniuses. (Besides, we couldn't have thrown the ball if we had wanted to, it was so slippery.)

Anyhow, while we were in Atlanta for the bowl game, the rumor was flying around that Carlen was going to leave for Texas Tech. And to show you how naive I was, I thought, *Jim ain't going anywhere. Where would anybody get a dad-gum idea like that?*

But it wasn't a rumor. It was all true. And the funny thing was Jim had already told all of his assistants—all of them except me—that he was leaving. I guess he wanted to find out how many of those guys would go with him. And after the game, he called all of us into a room. This time I was included. He said, "Men, I want to talk to y'all. I have been offered the job at Texas Tech, and I'm gonna take it. And I'd like for all of y'all who want to to come with me. I will give all of you jobs."

I always sort of figured Carlen, who was younger than me and equally ambitious, would use West Virginia to make a name for himself and then move on. I just didn't figure it would be that soon. So, you can say I was slightly dumbfounded.

When we left the room, he called me over and said, "Bobby, I would love for you to come with me, but I'm going to recommend you for the head coaching job here." I figured out later that Carlen knew I was going to get the job all along, and he had lined up his assistants to go with him before I could ask them if they wanted to stay.

At the same time this was going on, my daddy was in a Birmingham hospital having a brain operation. He came out of it brain dead and lived only about four months after that. So, still dumbfounded over Carlen's announcement, I had to shower, change clothes, get Ann, and then drive to Birmingham as quickly as I could. I didn't even have time to stay around and campaign for the West Virginia job.

We arrived in Birmingham around 3 A.M., and early the next morning I went to the hospital to see my daddy. It was one of the toughest things I ever had to do. I loved him so much, and it wasn't easy seeing him in the condition he was in.

When I got back to my parents' house after seeing Daddy, I got a call from West Virginia University athletic director Red Brown. He said, "Bobby, I met with our athletic council, and we want to offer you the head coaching job. Will you take it?" Man, that was quick, because we had just played the bowl game the night before. And Carlen hadn't dropped his bombshell until after the game.

How long did it take me to accept the job? Well, I had to wait until Brown got through offering it to me. Then, I answered so quick that his question and my answer probably sounded like one sentence: "Will I take it yeah I sure will."

So, I was finally a head coach at a major university.

I stayed at West Virginia as head coach for six years. Then after our 1975 regular season was over and we had won eight and lost three and accepted a berth to play North Carolina State in the Peach Bowl, I started getting calls from some big boosters at Florida State. This was early in December. The Florida State program was in a sorry state. Darrell Mudra, who had won only four games in two years, was going to be let go, and those Florida State people wanted to know if I would be interested in the job. I was but didn't want to get involved until after our bowl game.

After we beat North Carolina State 13-10, I was picked to coach in the All-American Bowl in Tampa. That's when it got serious. I met with John Bridgers, then Florida State's athletic director, and we talked about the sad state of the FSU program. I was kind of interested, but not all that much. I wasn't about to move anywhere until I got the assurance that the school was ready to make the commitment in terms of money and improved facilities needed to rebuild the program.

Folks say I left West Virginia because of the cold weather up there and because I had slipped one too many times on the ice. That's not true. I took the Florida State job because I thought it was worth taking. And I took it because it would get me back near my Alabama roots.

God has a purpose for everyone. Things that happen in a person's life are just brief stops along the highway as he or she travels to get where God wants him or her to be.

But anyhow, I was back near home, a place I am still at today. Lord willing, this will be my last job. And again, it was one I didn't go after. They came after me.

All that has happened in my life has reaffirmed what I had always believed, and believe more than ever today, that God has a purpose for everyone. I believe the things that happen in a person's life are just brief stops along the highway as he or she travels to get where God wants him or her to be.

Like I said, if it had been left up to me, I don't know what I would have done, or where I would have ended up. I have no idea.

I feel like I've been led by a power greater than myself all my life. It just seems like everything in my career has fallen into place. I applied for a lot of jobs and never got one of them, not a dad-gum one. Things just worked out. I can look back and see that all the things that have happened to me have shaped my career. Now, if things hadn't worked out the way they have, I would have said, "Well, Bowden, you just weren't listening to Him, were you?"

It's like the old joke about the Christian who was stranded on top of a house with flood waters rising all around him. As the water continued to rise, rescuers sent a boat out for him. They said, "Get in! Hurry! We're here to save you."

The Christian said, "No, I'm all right. You go and save others. The Lord will take care of me."

The water continued to rise. The rescuers sent out another boat. They begged the man, "Get in. The water is getting so high that we might not be able to come back for you."

But the Christian said, "The Lord will take care of me. Save the others."

Finally, the water got up around the man's chest. This time the rescuers sent out a helicopter. They dropped a rope ladder and yelled down to him, "Grab it. We'll save you."

The man said, "No, save the others. I have faith in the Lord. He will take care of me."

The water got higher, up to his neck, up to his mouth, up to his nose. No rescuers came this time. The man drowned.

When he got to heaven he said, "Lord, I was faithful to You all my life. I trusted You. I kept Your commandments. Why did You let me drown?"

And the Lord replied, "You fool, I sent two boats and a helicopter. What more did you want?"

I'd like to think I'm smarter than the guy in that story. I followed wherever He led me. I hopped in every rescue boat He sent out. I figured if God had wanted me out of coaching, He had plenty of opportunities to get me out. If that's what He had wanted for me, He would have led me down a different path. I know this; I couldn't have planned it to work out as well as it has. If I had tried to plan it, I would have messed it up somehow.

Sometimes I tell an audience, "I'll bet there's not a soul here who knows where I went to college. I'll bet y'all think I went to Alabama, or Auburn, or Notre Dame, or Georgia, or Southern Cal, or some other big famous school. You probably think ol' Bobby had to have gone to some-place like that to have the big, important head coaching job at a school like Florida State."

Then I'll tell them, "Naw, I didn't go to any of those schools. I went to little ol' Howard College, a Southern Baptist school in Birmingham. And it's not even called Howard College anymore. It's Samford University. But I am living proof that it doesn't matter where you come from, or how big or little you are, if you turn your life over to God, He will do unbelievable things.

"And if y'all don't believe that, well, here I stand."

CHAPTER 5

Always Church and Football

I cannot remember a single day when church and football were not central parts of my life.

I'm sure my mother and daddy took me to church right after I was born. It was just something the Bowden family did. On Sunday mornings nobody in our house got up and went out to play golf. And nobody sat around and read the Sunday newspaper. We got up and got ready for church. And there was never a vote taken. We were in that church every time the doors opened. It was almost like it was the house of a close relative, one we visited all the time.

As for football, well, my uncle George Hendricks, who married Momma's sister, Jessie Mae, gave me my first football for Christmas. I don't remember how old I was, but I couldn't have been more than five or six years of age.

My daddy's name was Bob Pearce Bowden. Most folks think I was named after him, but I wasn't. His name wasn't Robert. It was just Bob. I was named after my grandaddy on Momma's side. He was Robert Cleckler. And that is where they got Robert Cleckler Bowden, my full name.

My grandaddy (my mother's daddy) lived with us for the first fifteen years of my life. At one time he was pretty well off. He had money. But when the big depression hit in 1929—the year I was born—he lost everything. The way he told it to me was that he had heard things were going to go bad, but before he could get to the bank to get his money out, things went from "going to gone."

He said, "Bobby, when I marched into that bank and told them I wanted my money, they told me, 'Sorry, Mr. Cleckler, we ain't got no money, yours included.' " So, my grandaddy went from having plenty to having nothing.

Grandaddy lived with me in my room. Oh, once in a while he would go and stay a month or so with one of his other daughters, but the rest of the time we were roommates. I was very close to my grandaddy.

I didn't have any brothers, so my grandaddy was almost like an older brother to me—a much older brother. He was German. He wasn't first generation, but pretty close to it. That's one reason I've always been so interested in World War II history, especially the German part of it. I read every book about that war I can get my hands on.

Daddy, whose ancestors were French, was raised on a farm near Clayton, which is about 100 miles south of Birmingham. I don't remember that, because when I came along he had already left the farm and had a job as a teller in the First National Bank of Birmingham. Daddy had a high school education, but he never did go to college. Oh, he might have gone to night school some. At least, I think he did.

Daddy worked at that bank for seventeen years. After that he went into the real estate business with a man named Bishop. Those two formed the Bowden-Bishop Realty Company. Daddy and Bishop would purchase land. Then Bishop would build houses, and Daddy would finance and sell them. Daddy knew how to borrow money, and he knew how to get other folks to spend theirs.

My daddy was what folks today would call conservative. I mean, he wasn't one for taking a lot of chances. If Bishop set about to build a house, Daddy had it sold before it was built. He didn't like doing it the other way. He was very excitable, too, in that he got worked up about sports. And he loved football. I've got a lot of my daddy in me.

Mother's name was Sunset. That's right, S-u-n-s-e-t. I have never heard of anyone else having a first name like that. I don't know where in the world her mother and daddy got that name. Maybe she was born at sunset.

Her family was from Anniston, Alabama. She was a short woman and a little heavy. In that respect, I've got a lot of my momma in me too.

My first memories of football were of sitting up on the garage roof with my daddy watching the high schoolers. I was so young I didn't have any idea what was going on, but it sure looked like fun. Someday I wanted to do that too.

Mother was a housewife and stayed home and raised the family, which included my sister, Marion Sunset, and me. I was the baby. When my sister and I got out of high school, Momma went to work with Daddy in his real estate office. Oh, how I loved her. She was a great woman.

When I was born, we lived in the Woodlawn section of Birmingham, right behind the Woodlawn High School football field. Woodlawn was always a high school football power in the state. Back when I was young, it seemed like Woodlawn was always winning the state championship.

Now, when I say we lived right behind the high school football field, I mean we lived right behind it. Our garage in the backyard faced an alley, and just on the other side of the alley was the fence, which was covered with some kind of hedge or vines, that bordered the field.

I still haven't figured out why we had a garage; we didn't have a car. Back then, more folks didn't have cars than did. I was seventeen years old before Daddy bought his first car. It was a 1947 Plymouth. I remember that day. Before Daddy bought that car we did all of our traveling by streetcar. Daddy rode it to work; Momma rode it to shopping. My sister and I rode it to school. And if we went to a picture show, we either rode the streetcar or walked.

That garage came in handy, though. I can remember Daddy getting out the ladder. It wasn't one of them fancy painter's ladders, either. It was homemade. He would prop it up against the garage, and we would climb up on the roof and watch the high school football team practice. We used to do that a lot.

We also sat up there and watched the band practice. I guess that's where I got my love of music.

I can remember chasing the chickens out of the way to get to the ladder. It seems like those dad-gum birds were always in the way. They were never in the chicken coop. But since I couldn't have been more than three or four years old at the time, maybe the chickens chased me, instead of me chasing them. Some of those old roosters were pretty daggone mean.

Anyhow, my first memories of football were of sitting up there on the roof with my daddy and watching those young high school guys, guys I thought were big men, in those helmets and pads running around on that field. I was so young I didn't have any idea what was going on, but it sure looked like fun. I knew right then that someday I wanted to do that too.

We were so close to the field that when an extra point sailed off to the right, it landed in our yard. And when that football would land in the yard and bounce around, it would scare those chickens to death.

Oh, the hours we used to sit up there and watch football practice. Even today I can still hear the sound of the head coach barking out orders. I can still hear the sound of the pads crashing together during a scrimmage. I can still hear that distinctive "thud" of a foot striking the ball when a player would boot a punt. I can still hear the sound of the band as it practiced its marching formations and played the school fight song. And I think I can still smell those vines that covered the fence.

When I was five, maybe six, we moved from Woodlawn across town to East Lake. And our new home was only one block from the Howard College football field. I could stand in my new front yard and see the field up on the hill. So, we moved from the shadows of a high school football field to the shadows of a college football field. And when I started grammar school, I had to walk up the hill, across the field, and across the campus to get to school.

I couldn't wait for each fall to roll around because that meant football. It meant that when Daddy came home from work, he'd get out the old ball my uncle got me that one Christmas, and we'd toss it back and forth out in the yard. And on Friday nights he'd take me to Legion Field to see Woodlawn High School play. And on top of that, here I was living right down the hill from where the local college team practiced and played.

When it was time for practice, I'd grab an apple, get a pocketful of raw peanuts, and head up the hill to watch. I'd chomp on that apple and shell those peanuts and watch those players go at it. Boy, I thought they were giants.

I remember one time I shinnied up the goalpost and sat on the crossbar so I could see better. And about that time the team was fixin' to practice extra points. They kicked one and the ball sailed right past my ear. If that thing had hit me it would have tumbled me off that crossbar like a clay pigeon.

The coach saw me and let out a yell, "Boy, get off that dad-gum goalpost! You know you ain't supposed to be up there."

I didn't know I wasn't supposed to be up there. All I knew was that my love for the game was growing and growing. It was becoming part of my life. All my early memories were of growing up with a football field practically in my backyard. I thought all kids had the same thing.

Church was becoming part of my life too. My parents were very devout. Church was always the center of their lives. We attended Ruhama Baptist Church, which I think might be the oldest church in Jefferson County.

On Sunday mornings nobody in our house got up and went out to play golf; nobody read the Sunday newspaper. We got ready for church. And there was never a vote taken.

Daddy and my sister sang in the choir. I was in the Sunbeams Sunday School class when I was about five. Later I was in the R.A.'s (Royal Ambassadors), which was an organization for young boys ages eight through twelve. There has never been a time when I haven't gone to church. And there is no doubt that the impact of religion on my life comes from my parents' influence—an influence I am so thankful for.

My daddy was a lot of fun away from church. Man, he played with me and took an interest in everything I did. But when it came to church, there was no monkey business. Daddy taught me the meaning of the word *holy* early in life. He would say, "This is God's house. It is a holy place. And when we're in here, we listen to God. So shut up."

Daddy laid out the rules real plain.

There wasn't any laughing, joking, cuttin' up, or playing around while we were in God's house. If we did any of that stuff and Daddy found out, when we got home he might just give us a good whipping. I think if he hadn't been up in the choir loft, he might have done it while we were still in church. He just figured when you went through the door of the church you should be silent and reverent and get everything out of your mind that might interfere with hearing the Word.

I ain't going to lie. When I was young I resented it to a point. Whenever I could, I would duck out. If I could find an excuse to miss church I sure would try it. It didn't work very often with Daddy though.

He was stern when it came to taking the Lord's name in vain or being sacrilegious in any other way too. Now, we didn't read the Bible much as a family, but we sure read it a lot in church. And we always had prayer before every meal. And when I say we bowed our heads and prayed, that's exactly what I mean. There was no peeking out of the corners of your eyes, or giggling, or any kind of fooling around.

I know for sure if we did some of the things kids do today he would have backhanded us so fast it would have made our heads spin.

In today's society there is a breakdown in the family. I think that's a major part of the problem with what is wrong in our culture. Back when I was growing up, it was a different time. We were a family. I obeyed my parents. I obeyed my grandparents. I obeyed my aunts and uncles. They were the grownups; they were family. I was taught to have respect for them all. I loved them, and I know they loved me.

We lived in a neighborhood where we knew all our neighbors. We shopped in neighborhood stores; we went to a neighborhood church. Just about everything our family did, it did in the neighborhood.

The difference today is, church might be ten miles away. You have to get in your car and drive to church. Back then we never did that. First of all, like I said, we didn't have a car. We walked, and on the way, met our neighbors. And after church we all walked home together.

Nowadays, the people you go to church with don't even live in your neighborhood. The kids you go to church with don't even go to the same school. You never see those folks except in church. There's not the closeness there was years ago when everybody went to a community church. Back then the church was our second home. It was kind of like an extended family. Shoot, when I was growing up everybody knew me; they knew my mother and daddy. If I got into any kind of trouble, it didn't take long for the news to get back to my house.

I definitely had my heart set on football. I had those sounds from the practice field ringing in my ears. And it was sweet music to me. It still is.

But times have changed. I go to a church in Tallahassee where the members of our congregation live miles apart. I don't think I know half the people in my church, and it's partly my fault.

I know that forcing kids to go to church and preaching to them all the time will drive some away. That just proves that acceptance of Christ is a personal thing. It's like a vaccination. Sometimes it takes, and sometimes it doesn't. Church isn't some club you can go join. I've seen kids raised in a church environment turn out as ornery as any kids you've ever seen because they resented it.

Like I said, I had a little resentment when I was young. But I was taught by my parents the same as you were taught by yours. And sooner or later, I had to make a decision to accept Christ personally. My parents couldn't make it for me. I had good parents, a good pastor, and good Sunday school teachers. I was very lucky because all the teaching I received "took."

But for some kids, the teaching doesn't take. They don't get the message. Maybe they don't have any outside interests. I don't know. All I know is I had the church, school, and football. Now, I will admit I wasn't too keen on studying. I had to, though, if I wanted to play football and other sports.

And I definitely had my heart set on football. I had those sounds from the practice field still ringing in my ears. And it sounded like sweet music to me. It still does.

CHAPTER 6

Heart Problems

There was a time when it appeared that any kind of physical activity wasn't going to be in my future. It all happened in January 1943. I was thirteen, and what happened then probably made Mother and Daddy wonder if I was going to make it to fourteen.

One afternoon I came home from playing YMCA basketball, and my knees were sore. Man, they were killing me. They had been hurting for days. I hadn't been sleeping much at night because of the pain. I wasn't very old, but I was old enough to know that something wasn't right. My knees had never bothered me before. When you're young and full of vinegar and your joints have always worked, you just take for granted they always will. Well, mine weren't working, and I was scared.

And this particular day they were worse. I could barely make it up the porch steps. My feet and ankles were swollen too. Momma really got worried. So, she took me to see Dr. Mahaffey. Doc Mahaffey was a general practitioner. Back then that was all we had. In the early 1940s they didn't have specialists all over the place. Most families just depended on their family doctor. And if you couldn't get to his office, then he came to your house.

Anyway, Momma took me to his office. Since we didn't have a car, we had to walk, and with my knees hurting and my feet and ankles swollen, it wasn't the most pleasant walk I ever took. Doc Mahaffey checked me over. It seemed like it lasted forever. And when it was all over he told Mother, "Mrs. Bowden, your son has rheumatic fever. That's why his joints are so sore. I can hear a heart murmur and I'm afraid the fever will do permanent damage to his heart. This disease is very serious."

Momma started crying. I didn't feel so hot either.

The doctor ordered me to bed, and I mean in bed flat on my back, for six months. I wasn't allowed to get up for nothing—not to eat, not to go to the bathroom, not to stretch my aching back. Nothing. I still remember having to use a dad-gum bedpan. Ugh! That was humiliating.

Even though I was ordered to stay in bed, I still kept up with sports. I listened to every football radio broadcast I could. And I compiled quite a scrapbook on Alabama and Auburn football. Also, Daddy bought me a football board game and I spent countless hours plotting ways for Alabama and Auburn to win. That might be where I learned to love the strategy of the game.

When you're young and full of vinegar and your joints have always worked, you just take for granted they always will. Well, mine weren't working, and I was scared.

I did a lot of praying during those months. It was Momma who suggested I ask God to heal me. And I know she did a lot more praying than I did. Momma always believed if you wanted something from God, you had to ask. She taught me that too.

Doc Mahaffey would come to the house almost daily to examine me. And as the weeks went by I got to feeling pretty good. One day when he was there and I was laying in that bed, somebody, either Mother or Daddy, asked a question, and I made as if I was going to get out of bed. The doctor almost threw a fit. He shoved me back down and yelled, "Don't get up! Don't even try! If you do, I won't be responsible." I guess he thought if I got up I would die or something. He sure got worked up.

After six months flat on my back, he finally let me get up and move around. But he still wouldn't let me go out of the house. Oh, I think I did sneak out on the porch once in a while. He wouldn't even let me go up and down the stairs. I couldn't lift any kind of weight at all. I couldn't do a thing. And most of all, that rheumatic fever kept me out of school for a whole year. That put me back. All my buddies were now one grade ahead of me.

When you're a teenager that sort of thing really hurts. You always want to do what your buddies do. And if they move up to the next year in school, you sure don't want to be left behind. I was left behind.

The doctor would come by the house. I would be in there listening to the radio or playing some game, and I would hear him pull up in front of the house in that old black Model A Ford he drove. I'd say, "Momma, he's here again. Do I have to see him? He scares me."

Mother would just kind of stare at me. She knew that I knew what the answer was.

He'd come in and check me over. And he'd always reach into his black doctor's bag and pull out that big ol' needle. I never knew why he always had to do that. But he'd say, "Young man, stick out your arm." I guess I was a good patient, as good a patient as a youngster can be, but I sure hated to have him stick that needle in my arm and draw out that blood. It hurt, and I hated it. Also, I didn't know then how your body manufactures blood. I figured he was taking blood out of me and I wasn't ever gonna get it back.

I'm not too crazy about needles to this day.

When I finally did get to go back to school, I enrolled at Woodlawn High School. It was a four-year school. The problem was I wasn't allowed to go out for football. I wasn't allowed to go out for any sports. Doc Mahaffey told Mother, "No football for him. No physical activity of any kind. Remember, he has to take care of that weak heart."

I did some begging, but Momma was sure the doctor knew what he was talking about. So, I figured, "Well, if I can't play football on the field, I'll get on that field somehow. I'll just go out for the band." And I did.

Even though I was ordered to stay in bed, I still kept up with sports. Daddy bought me a football board game and I spent countless hours plotting ways for Alabama and Auburn to win.

I played in that band my first two years in high school. I played trombone. I played the piano and a little bit of trumpet. I started taking piano lessons when I was about eight. I had played the trumpet in grammar school. But there wasn't any way I could play a piano in a marching band, and they had too many trumpet players. The band director said, "Bobby, here's a trombone. You're now a trombone player."

That was all right with me. You blew into a trumpet, so I figured I could blow into that trombone. I got pretty good with that old slide instrument too. In fact, a bunch of us formed a jazz band and went out and played on weekends and special nights. We played at a club called the Rose Club in east Birmingham and played at weekly high school dances at Colonel's Corner in Woodlawn. We made a lot of extra money. I played in that jazz group until I went to college.

Two years of the high school band was enough though. I wanted to go out for football. Sitting in the Legion Field stands and watching my buddies run up and down that field just didn't quite get it. And marching on the field at halftime didn't get it either. I kept after Mother and Daddy. I said, "How come that doctor will allow me to march up and down the field with the band, but he won't allow me to run up and down the field? Ain't marching physical activity?"

But Doc Mahaffey kept saying, "No, Mrs. Bowden, your son can't do any of that strenuous physical activity. He's not supposed to run. He can't play football. I don't want him to do anything that might damage his weak heart. If he does, his heart might give out before he's forty."

And when he'd say that, Momma would cry some more. Me? I thought when you were that old, your life was about over anyway.

Finally, my pleading must have gotten to my mother, because she weakened. She took me to another doctor. I reckon now they call it getting a second opinion. This doctor was a heart specialist. And, like I said, there weren't too many heart specialists back in those days.

Anyhow, after this doctor examined me, he said, "Mrs. Bowden, I don't see any problems with your son. Oh, he does have a slight heart murmur, but a lot of folks have heart murmurs. It doesn't sound serious. I don't see any reason why he can't go out for football."

Looking back, I kind of think Doc Mahaffey and my parents over-reacted a little bit. But I finally got to go out for football.

This time *I* cried.

Finally
Football

remember the first time I put on that Woodlawn High School uniform. Lawh, I must have been a sight. I didn't weigh but 130 pounds. And I might have been about 5'6" at the most. To be honest, I probably looked like a runt. But I was a quick and eager runt. I had played some football in grammar school, so I wasn't totally lost out there. The problem was I was now a junior. If I wanted to do something in football at Woodlawn, I didn't have much time.

The coach, a man named Kenny Morgan, made me a halfback. The team ran the single-wing, and in that system the halfback did about everything. Today a 130-pound back wouldn't even get a glance from a coach. He sure wouldn't get a glance from me. About the only thing he'd get today would be a "get out of here before you get hurt, son."

But back then, I was big enough to get by in high school. However, I was beginning to think about playing college ball. And I knew if I wanted to go on and play college ball like I hoped to, then I would have to somehow get bigger.

About two weeks before the first game of the season—my first game —I was going out for a pass in practice. I slipped making a cut and went down, and as I went down, I put my right hand out to try to regain my balance. When I did that, something went "snap!" It sounded almost like a small twig breaking. I looked down at my hand and my thumb was laid clean back against my wrist. It was a terrible-looking thing. For a second it didn't sink in, but when it did I said to myself, "Oh, Lawdy, it's broke. I broke my dad-gum thumb."

I got up, held my hand against my stomach, and went over to Coach Morgan. I showed it to him and he said, "It'll be all right, son. I'll take care of it."

Back in those days we didn't have trainers. The coach was the trainer. And Coach Morgan simply reached down and grabbed my thumb and yanked it back in place, and then he slapped some tape on it. Whooeee! Did that thing ever hurt! It cleared up my sinuses, and then some.

I said through gritted teeth, "Thanks, Coach."

What I thought was, *I think he's ruined it.*

Anyhow, I went back to practice and worked out the rest of the afternoon. But that dad-gum thumb was hurting. I just didn't want to show it. I didn't want to miss out on a chance to play in my first game.

But that night the thumb had swollen to about twice its normal size. At least, it looked that big. I didn't think much about the thumb, except that it hurt. I figured it would get better. What do kids know?

The next day Coach slapped some tape on it and I went through another full practice. By that time, though, it was really getting sore. And now it was extremely swollen.

I probably looked like a runt. But I was a quick and eager runt.

You have to understand, back in those days you just weren't supposed to get injured. And if you did get injured, you were supposed to suck it up and play anyway.

The coach would say, "We ain't having no injuries. And y'all better do what I say."

Those coaches didn't know any better. They just taught the way they were taught. And as a young player, I thought that was just the way it was supposed to be. It was a Spartan mentality. No matter how hot it got, we were never allowed to drink water or take off our helmets, either. Only sissies did that. Coach didn't want no dad-gum sissies on the team. And I sure wasn't gonna be a sissy.

Nowadays, we let players have all the water they want during practice. And when they're not actually involved in a drill or a scrimmage, we tell them to take off their helmets. We've learned through sports medicine that you have to replace the fluids you lose and that the body cools itself through the head. It's a wonder that years ago players didn't faint right and left. It's a miracle somebody didn't get killed.

I must have practiced about three days with that swollen thumb. And all that time it throbbed like the worst toothache you can imagine. No, it was worse than that. I don't think I've ever had a toothache hurt that bad. But I didn't really know for sure it was broken. Back then they didn't x-ray every little hurt like we do today. I suppose they should have, but they didn't.

The next day I was sitting in class. The teacher was fixin' to give us an English test. I hadn't studied for it at all. I hadn't even cracked a book. Besides, my thumb was hurting. So I came up with a bright idea. I said to myself, *Bobby, I know how you can get out of this English test.* So, I went up to the teacher and put the most pitiful expression on my face I could and said, "Ma'am, look at this thumb. The dad-gum thing is killing me."

When that teacher saw that thumb, which by now was really swollen and turning black and blue, I think she came close to fainting. She said, "I'm going to write you an excuse to see the principal. He had better look at your thumb."

So, I went to the principal's office and showed him the thumb. He said, "Son, that thing looks awful." I couldn't disagree with him. And he added, "You'd better see the school doctor."

And he sent me to Dr. Hurley Knight. Dr. Knight x-rayed my thumb and when he looked at the X-ray he said, "Son, that thumb is broke clean in two."

I sort of had a hunch the coach had finished the fracture that day on the practice field when he yanked it back into place.

The doctor set my thumb. It must have taken him forty-five minutes. And if you think those needles hurt when Doc Mahaffey used to draw blood from me back when I had rheumatic fever, you have no idea how this hurt. I'm talking about *bad* pain. It had been about three days since I hurt that thumb. Now, it was broken, swollen, and probably getting infected. And in those days they didn't give you a shot to numb it. That dad-gum doctor just grabbed hold of it and started yanking. I thought he was going to yank it clear out of the socket.

I must have spent the whole forty-five minutes yelling, "Aghhh! Ughhh! Ohhh!" I couldn't believe what that doctor was doing to me. Finally, he got it where he thought it was right, and then he put a lot of tape on it and sent me back to class.

I did get out of that English test though.

Unfortunately, Dr. Knight didn't help me much more than Coach Morgan did. My thumb was still hurting something awful. And it was getting worse. I finally had to go to a specialist and have the thing reset—again—and put in a cast.

So, after waiting all this time to play football at Woodlawn High School, I ended up with a broken thumb just days before my first game. I still wasn't able to play the game I loved more than anything. I was beginning to wonder if I would ever get to play.

Then, although I didn't realize it at the time, a strange and wonderful thing happened. Coach Morgan called me into his office and said, "Bobby, I don't think you'll be much use to us this year. I have an idea though. Why don't you drop out of school this semester? That way I think I can get you another year of eligibility. And instead of this being your junior year, next year will be your junior year. You'll be a year older and you just might get bigger. You might get good enough to win a college scholarship. What do you think?"

What did I think? Well, first of all, I had never thought about being good enough to get a college scholarship. What I thought was that I was going to miss an entire season of football and miss an entire semester of school. That seemed like a daggone eternity. I did kind of like what he said about maybe having a chance to win a scholarship, but that wasn't enough to raise my spirits. I was really down. First, rheumatic fever; now this.

I tell my athletes, "Men, believe me, when things seem the darkest, have faith in Jesus. No matter how impossible things look, don't ever give up."

I went home and told my parents what the coach said, and they went to see him. He told them the same thing he told me.

Until Coach Morgan brought up the word scholarship, I hadn't even thought about such a thing. Mother and Daddy hadn't either. But I think they figured it would be an inexpensive way to go to college. So, they let me drop out of school for that semester. So, now I was behind in school a year-and-a-half.

That semester I worked for Daddy, who was building houses. The truth was, I didn't do very much. I couldn't very well handle a pick or shovel, or push a wheelbarrow with one hand.

The semester passed and my thumb healed. And before I knew it, it was time for spring practice. My weight had gone up to 150. I wasn't any muscular body builder-type, but 150 pounds was a lot better than 130. In those days, a 150-pound back wasn't too bad. I ran as third-team tailback in the spring, but when the season rolled around in the fall I had worked my way up to the first team. We ran the Notre Dame box, and the tailback in that system was the same as a quarterback today. That meant I got to run and pass. I was pretty quick and kind of liked the idea of running the ball. I could throw it pretty well too.

It had taken a long, long time, but I was finally a football player. And my senior year my weight was up to 155, which was about the same weight as the backs on all the teams we played. Oh, occasionally you would see a team with a 180-pound back, but not very often. When you saw one that big, you thought the guy was a giant. Remember, this was back in the late 1940s.

I made All-City, and the University of Alabama came calling. Well, that wasn't exactly right. What they did was send me a letter. Basically, the letter said, "We're interested in you. Why don't you come on down to Tuscaloosa?"

So, I guess they kind of semi-recruited me on some sort of scholarship. I never did sign a paper though. Back then there wasn't a letter of intent or stuff like that. But Alabama did pay my tuition and fees, and I got free meals at the training table. I thought that was pretty good. I was really thrilled when they paid my tuition. It wasn't but thirty-eight dollars, but I'll never forget it.

So I went to Alabama. This was in the winter of 1949. Remember, I had dropped out of high school that one semester and had graduated at mid-year. I was all set to go out for Alabama's spring football. And I did. I had a couple of problems though. One had to do with football. The other didn't.

When I went out for football that first spring at Alabama—well, man, you talk about a team having a lot of players. They must have had about ten or eleven players at my position alone, and I was at the bottom of the list. I didn't see any chance of me ever getting much playing time there. And believe me, I wanted to play, and thought I could play. The problem was numbers. Also, Alabama at that time had a couple of great backs in Bobby Marlow and Eddie Salem. I think Salem made some All-American teams, and I know Marlow held some sort of Southeastern Conference rushing record for a while.

The problem of playing, or rather not playing, was bothering me. And on top of that, I began to get homesick. I had never really been away from Birmingham. I missed my folks. And more than that, I missed my high school sweetheart, Julia Ann Estock. Ann was still in high school that semester. I was three years older than she was, but since I had missed that year-and-a-half of school, I was only one semester ahead of her. I just couldn't stand being away from her.

So, I stopped going to practice and started hiding from the coaches. I didn't know how to face them, and didn't want to. I admit I wasn't very mature about it. I'm still kind of ashamed about the way I did that.

I think I was a good small college player at Howard. I was fast and could scramble. And I was feisty.

I finally left Alabama and went back home and enrolled at Howard College, and eventually was a Little All-American quarterback there. I think I was a good small college player. I was fast and could scramble. And I was feisty. To be honest, Howard was the perfect place for me. Looking back now, I really don't think I could have been a good major college player. I'll never know for sure because that's water over the dam.

When I give talks to young athletes today, I tell them, "Men, believe me, when things seem the darkest, if you have faith in Jesus, He promises each of us that whatever the difficulty, He will take us through it. And no matter how impossible things look, don't ever give up. He will take us from darkness to light.

"When I got that broken thumb, I was about the sorriest guy you ever saw. My head was down, and I figured my whole career had ended before it started. In truth, though, that injury shaped my whole career. If I hadn't gotten hurt and gotten that extra year, I would have come out of high school so small that nobody would have been interested in me. So, something I thought was bad turned out to be something good."

Until I got that so-called scholarship, I had serious thoughts about a military career. I had dreams of being a general. Well, that's the way kids dream. But because of that injury, I was able to go on to a college football career.

I'll be honest, though, if I hadn't been able to play football I probably never would have gone to college. Man, I hated to study. I don't know why, but I couldn't stand it. The only reason I studied was so I could play football. At Howard College there was no way they'd let you play if you didn't make the grades. They didn't fool around with you. I kept studying just to play.

And four years later, I said to myself, *Well, I'll be dad-gum. Bobby, you just need a few hours to graduate.* And I graduated. And then I went on and got my master's degree. And a few years ago I was given an honorary doctorate from my alma mater.

"Dr. Bobby." How about that?

I'll bet some of my old buddies really had a good laugh about that.

Marriage

When Ann and I met, she was about fourteen; I was about seventeen. I thought she was a dream the first time I ever saw her. Boy, she was something! Still is.

Ann was born in Gadsden, but her family had just moved to Birmingham from Oak Ridge, Tennessee, where her daddy had worked at the atomic plant during World War II. I had seen her at a church social function. It was a wiener roast at East Lake Park. That was back when churches used to have wiener roasts, hayrides, and stuff like that.

Oh, she was a cute little thing. I can even remember what she was wearing. It was a brown seersucker suit. When I saw her, I said to myself, *Bobby, there ain't but one way to meet that pretty girl, and that's to charge right on in.*

She was standing around the fire with a boy named Benny Clayton. He was her so-called date. Well, maybe not; I don't think her momma and daddy allowed her to date then. Anyhow, she was roasting a wiener on a stick. In that firelight she sure did look pretty.

So, being the tactful guy I was, I just went up to her and said, "Boy, you sure are cute. I like the way you model that dress."

She just kind of flashed that pretty smile of hers to let me know she knew I had paid her a compliment. I'm not sure I impressed her all that much though. After seeing her at that wiener roast, I knew I had to find out more about her.

I found out she lived just a few streets over from my house. So, I

51

made every excuse I could to go visit a high school teammate, a guy named Mort Vaserberg, who lived about three doors from where Ann lived. And I spent a lot of time walking back and forth in front of her house too. Oh, I must have been a sight.

Did you ever have a dog come up to you and want your attention? And then, when he's got your attention, he kind of turns his head away, like he really isn't all that interested in your attention? Well, that's the way I walked in front of her house. When I was out there, I'd kind of act like I didn't know she was watching. But I knew she was. And I was pretty sure she knew that I knew.

Ann lived on the corner and there was a streetlight there. Mort and I used to spend a lot of evenings sitting under that light shooting the bull, as they say. Now, I liked Mort, but he wasn't the main reason I was there. All I was doing was waiting to get a glimpse of Ann, or to let her get a glimpse of old cool Bobby.

Sometimes to get her attention, I would pitch rocks up on her porch. And when she'd be out in the yard, or out sweeping the sidewalk, I'd kind of pitch a rock her way. When a youngster is strutting around like a peacock, he can act mighty weird. I was struttin'. And believe me, I was weird. Boys will sure do dumb things, won't they?

Ann was a brain in school. She graduated when she was sixteen. And she was really popular. Before she got out of high school, she was a cheerleader and a beauty queen.

On Sunday mornings Ann sang in the Ruhama church choir. I sat on the back row with my buddies and spent a lot of time acting like a smarty. A lot of Sundays she'd wear a red sweater. I always liked her in red. Boy, I sure remember her in that sweater.

When anyone asks Ann how we met, she will say, "Well, I was singing in the church choir when we met. I'd like to think I got Bobby off that back row and up in the front of the church with me. But the truth is, he got me out of the front of the church and on the back row with him, where he was misbehaving."

I thought Ann was a dream that first time I ever saw her. Boy, she was something! Still is.

Anyhow, when I was at the University of Alabama that spring of 1949, I sure did miss her. Also, I had heard a rumor from my roommate, a guy named Paul Crumbley, who was from Birmingham, too, that she was going out with a running back from a rival high school named Shorty White.

Paul had just come back from a weekend at home and he said, "Bobby, ain't Ann Estock your steady girl?"

I said, "She sure is. Why?"

And he proceeded to tell me what he had seen when he was in Birmingham that weekend. Well, that did it. The next weekend I was heading up the highway to Birmingham to find out what was going on. There wasn't nothing going on. She was still my sweetheart.

The problem was, we both knew we were fixing to get into trouble if things kept progressing the way they were. We were getting real intimate. And neither one of us believed in sex before marriage. I wasn't taught that, and she wasn't either. So, we took care of that by running off and getting married. She was sixteen and I was nineteen. Yep, we were young.

We had heard that other couples from Woodlawn High School had done the same thing. They had gone just over the Georgia state line to a little town called Rising Fawn. It was up Route 11, near the triangle where Alabama, Georgia, and Tennessee meet. Now, I don't really think Ann and I planned to run off and do that. It just sort of happened.

You know, if a young boy and a young girl are determined to be together, there's not much you can do about it. They are going to find a way to be together. And we definitely wanted to be together. That's a fact.

I didn't have a car. And I didn't have any money either. So, I wasn't sure how we were going to get to Georgia and get married. But you know young folks, they don't worry about little details like that.

It turned out that on this one weekend my mother and daddy were going to Atlanta for some kind of convention. This was the end of March. They took the train to Atlanta. Back then most folks, at least most folks we knew, traveled by train when they went somewhere. Daddy left the family car at home. More important, he left the car keys at home too.

And on Sunday morning, April 1, 1949, I got Daddy's car, borrowed twenty dollars from a buddy named Dennis Hudson, and went to pick up Ann. We skipped church that morning and took off for Georgia. I was in such a hurry to get to Rising Fawn that I got caught for speeding through Gadsden. The policeman said, "Son, y'all didn't see that speed limit sign back there, did you? That's gonna cost you ten dollars."

So, I had to donate half of the twenty dollars that Dennis had loaned me to the Gadsden economy. Now we had only ten dollars to finance our trip and pay the justice of the peace for marrying us. That wasn't exactly doing it up in style.

When we got to Rising Fawn, we had to find the justice of the peace. His house, which was also his office, was located down at the end of an old dirt road off the main highway. Man, this was really in the country. We knocked on the front door.

The justice of the peace's wife answered and promptly announced, "State your business, son. We're just sittin' down to Sunday dinner."

I tried to stand up as tall as I could and said in what I thought was a deep grown-up voice, "Me and my sweetheart want to get married."

The woman just turned and hollered over her shoulder, "Hey, Pa, there are two youngsters here who want to get hitched."

Pa hollered back, "Bring 'em on in, Ma."

So, she invited us in and told us to sit down, and said that they'd be with us in a few minutes. I think they went ahead and finished eating. Anyway, we sat there and tried to relax while they got things ready for the wedding. That justice of the peace didn't ask us our age or anything like that. They didn't require proof of age in Georgia back then. That's why some of the kids from school were running up there to get married.

The justice of the peace asked me, "Boy, you got a ring?"

Ring? I hadn't thought that far ahead. Shoot, all I had on me was the ten dollars left from the twenty dollars I got from Dennis. I said, "Naw, I ain't got no ring."

He said, "Well, we'll use your high school ring." It was a long time before I was able to get Ann a proper ring.

And we got married. I gave the justice of the peace five dollars. That left me five dollars to buy gas to get us back to Birmingham. Talk about faith.

We decided to keep our marriage secret. After all, I was in college and Ann was still in high school. We didn't have any money, not a dime. I didn't have a job, and at that moment didn't have any prospects either. So, the plan was for her to continue to live with her parents and I would continue to live with mine. We tried to act like everything was the same as always. We kept on dating just like we always had. We figured we would announce it when we thought the time was right.

Ha! Within a month, everybody at our schools knew our secret. I reckon Ann told some of her cheerleader friends. At least I accuse her of being the one who let it out of the bag. But I probably told a buddy or two too. Anyhow, that was that. It was out. And it wasn't long before our parents found out what we had done. Facing them wasn't exactly the easiest thing I've ever done.

After everybody found out Ann and I were married, the next move was to find somewhere to live. It's tough finding a place to live when you don't have any money and don't have a steady job.

When a youngster is strutting around like a peacock, he can act mighty weird. I was struttin'. And believe me, I was weird.

My parents were living with Daddy's sister, who was badly crippled with arthritis. I'm not sure why Daddy moved in with her, except maybe to help her out. It wasn't that he didn't have his own house. He did. And it wasn't that he was in financial trouble. He was making good money. So it must have been for that reason.

Daddy's sister lived in a big house. There was plenty of room. So, Ann and I moved in with them. We lived downstairs in a little apartment with a bedroom and bath. We lived that way for about a year until we got our own apartment near the college campus. By that time, both of us were enrolled at Howard College.

I had a work scholarship at Howard. There wasn't any such thing as a full free-ride scholarship in those days. My job was to fire up the furnace in the gymnasium. The furnace heated the boiler so folks taking showers could have hot water. So, early every morning I would get up and go chop wood to get the fire started. Once I got it going, I would shovel in coal. And if that fire ever went out, or I overslept and didn't get it started, I'd get in trouble.

There were more than a few mornings when I turned off that alarm and rolled back over for a few extra winks. When that happened, I'd come flying out of that bed, jump into my clothes, and go racing across campus toward the gym. I might be a block away when I'd hear somebody yell, "Bowden! Bowden! There ain't no dad-gum hot water." I'll bet the athletic director and coaches said more than a few things about me that I can't print here!

I also worked as a basketball and baseball coach at the YMCA. That's how I got through college.

And guess what happened in 1951? Yep, Ann got pregnant. She finished the first semester that year and then dropped out of school to have the first of our six children. First child was a girl, Robyn. After Ann gave birth to Robyn, she started back to school again. That didn't last long. Before we knew it, she was pregnant again and had to drop out of school again. This baby was a boy, Steve. Then after Steve was born, Ann enrolled in school a third time, and the first thing we knew we were expecting a third child. Along came Tommy. And that was the end of Ann's attempts to go to college. Ann never did finish school, because after Tommy came Terry, Jeffrey, and Ginger.

I told that story one time to St. Petersburg (Florida) sports columnist Hubert Mizell and he laughed and said, "Oh, three tykes and she was out, huh?"

When I give talks today, I sometimes tell the story of having those babies. I say, "When Robyn was born, I told Ann, 'She is our cheerleader.' When Steve came along, I told her, 'He's the quarterback.' When Tommy came along, I said, 'He's the wide receiver.' And when the sixth child came along, Ann said to me, 'This is the end.' "

I have to tell a funny story that illustrates some of the things that can happen to you when you have a large family. Well, it wasn't funny at the time. It was one Christmas when I was an assistant coach at Florida State. It must have been about 1964 or 1965 when Ann and I got all the children up early and set out for Birmingham to spend Christmas day with the grandmommas.

We left Tallahassee about 4 A.M. and got to Prattville, Alabama, about 7:30. We were still about eighty miles from Birmingham, so we decided to stop at a nice little restaurant there for breakfast. When we were through eating, I paid the bill and we loaded the kids up in our station wagon and headed up the highway.

After we had gone about forty miles, a highway patrolman came up behind us. He flashed his lights and motioned for me to pull over. I looked down at the speedometer and thought, *I'm not speeding. I wonder what I've done wrong?* (Usually I was speeding, but I wasn't that time.)

The state trooper got out of his car and walked up alongside ours. I rolled down the window and said, "Was I speeding?"

He said, "Naw. But aren't you missing somebody?"

Ann and I looked in the backseat and started counting heads. Sure enough, we were shocked to find that we were missing somebody. Ginger, the baby, who was about three years old then, wasn't in the car. She had gone into the bathroom or something when we had finished breakfast and we had forgotten her! Now, you have to understand when you have a big family, you don't count heads each time you load them up in the car. You just figure all the kids have hopped in.

The trooper said, "The folks at the restaurant called us and told us they thought the little girl belonged to those folks who were heading up to Birmingham." So, we turned around and drove back to get Ginger.

Ann cried all the way back. I didn't feel so hot either.

Jeffrey, the next-to-youngest, probably knew Ginger wasn't in the car. We always accuse him of knowing we had left her behind and not telling us. He was that ornery.

When we got back to the restaurant, Ginger was perched up on the counter and those folks were feeding her candy. She was having a high old time.

But I've gotten way ahead of myself. After we had our third child and Ann dropped out of school for good, I was still going to college and playing football. We didn't have any money to start with, and now we had three more mouths to feed. By that time, Daddy had built a new home, a real spacious house. We gave up our apartment and moved back in with my folks. I'll admit living with my parents wasn't an ideal situation, but I've always been grateful for their love and support. It was the way we had to do it. We didn't have nothing, nothing but three kids.

When I graduated from Howard in January 1953, Coach Gartman said to me, "Bobby, I'd like to hire you as an assistant coach, but I can't unless you get a master's degree. You go off and get one and I'll put you on my staff."

We got married. I gave the justice of the peace five dollars. That left five dollars for gas to get back to Birmingham. Talk about faith.

That sounded all right with me. I knew I wanted to be a coach and figured this was my chance. I enrolled at Peabody College, which was about 190 miles away in Nashville. I would get up at 4 A.M. every Monday morning, kiss Ann and the babies good-bye, and head up Route 31. I fixed my class schedule so I had classes through Thursday afternoon. And late every Thursday I'd head back to Birmingham. One of those trips back home was interesting.

If I had a car to drive, which most of the time I didn't, I would drive back. There were about four or five of us from Birmingham going to Peabody and we would carpool. Sometimes none of us had a car available. When that happened, I would get out on the highway and stick out my thumb. I used to do a lot of thumbing.

Man, I wouldn't do that today. People don't stop and pick you up like they used to. I don't blame them. There are too many crazies out there.

I remember one night I was thumbing out of Nashville. I had caught a ride to Decatur. Actually, the guy let me out of his car on the highway between Decatur and Hartselle. It was about midnight and I was still about ninety miles from home.

When that guy drove off, there I stood in pitch-black darkness in the middle of nowhere on Highway 31. Have you ever been out on a highway late at night when there's no traffic? Man, that's a lonely feeling. I couldn't see a sign of car lights anywhere.

I said to myself, *Well, if you're gonna have to walk home, you might as well get started.* So, I started walking. I walked and walked. I must have walked about eight miles.

Finally, I saw some headlights come over the rise off in the distance. I thought, *Here comes one, Bobby. This may be your only chance. If you don't get this car to stop and give you a ride, you might be stuck out on this highway until morning.* The thought of that didn't exactly excite me.

I got as close to the highway as I could, but made sure if the driver didn't see me until I got in his lights he wouldn't run over me. I stuck out my thumb and that car went by me so fast the breeze practically dang near blew me over. I figured, *Well, start walking.* But about 300 yards or so down the road the car came to a screeching stop and began to back up. I ran up to it, and the driver said, "Where you goin', boy?"

I said, "Birmingham."

He said, "Hop in."

Then before I could hop in, he added, "You got a driver's license?"

"Yeah."

"You don't mind driving, do you? I been driving all night and I need to get some sleep."

I didn't mind driving. So, I got in behind the wheel and the guy moved over on the passenger's side. The guy looked like he had money, because he had this brand new car and was dressed up in fancy duds. He said, "I'm from Detroit. I'm going to Bessemer to visit my family." That was fine with me. That meant I had a ride all the way home because Bessemer was on the other side of Birmingham.

I pulled out onto the highway and we were off. When we had gone about three or four miles, this guy reached into the glove compartment and pulled out what looked to be a .38-caliber pistol.

I took one look at that big ol' gun and my Adam's apple did a flip-flop. I said to myself, *Uh, oh, Bowden, you done had it this time. Lordy, this man is fixin' to rob you and shoot you and dump your body out here in the middle of nowhere.* That was what I thought. What I said was, "Look, if you need money, I got money. I got enough to get you to Birmingham. I'll buy you some gas. If I can, I'll buy you anything you want."

This guy didn't say a word. He just looked at me. And then he rolled down the window and started firing that pistol out the window. Bang! Bang! Bang! I didn't know what he was shooting at. It was dark. He couldn't see anything. I think he was just letting me know that I'd better not try anything while he was napping.

I wasn't about to. I was too scared.

I did stop and fill up his gas tank. I don't think I did that out of the goodness of my heart; that big gun might have had something to do with my generosity. Maybe that was what he wanted, I don't know. I know this, that's the second and last time anyone ever pulled a gun and got my attention. (I'll tell you about the first time later.) Anyhow, that guy sure got my attention in a hurry.

The guy let me out of the car about a mile or so from my house. By then it was after 4 A.M. I was tired and didn't want to walk the rest of the way. Along came another car, so I figured I might get one more ride, maybe all the way to the house (in thumbin' again so soon, I guess my judgment was impaired, or I figured my luck was bound to improve after that episode). So I stuck out my thumb.

The car stopped and the guy inside made a motion for me to hop in. He opened the door, patted the seat on the passenger's side, and said in a real high-pitched feminine-like voice, "Well, come on, honey. Get in."

I'd had about enough for one night. I gave him a long look, and then I slammed the door and said, "No, thanks, honey. I'll walk."

I ain't tried to hitch a ride since.

Tough Times

After I got that graduate degree, I did get hired on as an assistant coach at Howard. But money became a major problem in my rapidly growing family. Ann and I had moved out of my parents' house and into a small apartment less than two blocks from the college campus. It was time to get our brood out of Mother and Daddy's hair.

Besides, by this time Ann was pregnant again.

The money problem had to do with my salary as an assistant. I was told that my salary would be $3,600 a year. But when I got my first paycheck I did some quick mental arithmetic and figured out that they were paying me only $3,300. I marched right into the athletic director's office and said, "Look here, you got me making only $3,300. You promised me $3,600. What's going on? I want that money. I need it."

He said, "I applied for $3,600, but the administration wouldn't approve it. What you got is all they would authorize."

"Well, that's not fair," I complained.

He simply said, "I don't know about 'fair.' All I know is what they authorized."

"Who do I go talk to?" I asked, not wanting to back down.

"The president," he replied.

So, I went and got an appointment with the college president. And I complained again. I know by today's standards an extra $300 a year might not seem like much, but believe me, it was a lot back then. It figured out to twenty-five dollars a month, and that extra twenty-five dollars would make a lot of difference. Anyhow, since I was only twenty-three years old and had a wife, two kids, and one on the way, I think the president felt sorry for me. I got that extra $300.

I was on Coach Gartman's staff for two years. I was his assistant in football and head coach in track. And after my second year he came in and said, "Bobby, I'm leaving. I'm taking the head job at Austin Peay, and I'm recommending you to take my place as head coach." And like I said earlier, I had hoped to get the job, but President Davis turned me down because he thought I was too dad-gum young. I remember going to see him and saying, "I want that job and think I ought to get it." I still wasn't very mature. I've since learned that's not the way to get a job.

President Davies said, "Have you talked to the athletic director?"

I said, "Yeah. And he said he didn't think you were gonna give it to me."

Then he said something like, "Well, that's the way it is." And he turned his back on me and went back to doing whatever it was he had been doing before I walked in. The meeting was over. He was through with me.

Well, I was through with him too. In fact, I was so daggoned mad I felt like telling him what he could do with my great $3,600 salary. And that's when South Georgia College contacted me.

The year before, the athletic director at West Georgia College had called and wanted me to come up for an interview for the head coaching job there. The athletic director was Leven Hazelgrove, a graduate of Howard College. I drove up there, had an interview, and turned the job down. It didn't look very good to me. West Georgia didn't give scholarships. I didn't want to coach at any school that didn't offer scholarships.

The next year, apparently Dr. Hazelgrove had run into President Smith of South Georgia College somewhere and learned that he was looking for a head football coach. I found out later that Dr. Hazelgrove had recommended me. So, that's how South Georgia came to be interested in me and to offer me the job there.

My new salary at South Georgia was $4,200. Man, that was a big jump from what I had been making as an assistant at Howard. And I was to be the athletic director and head coach. I couldn't believe it. I was only twenty-five years old, and here I was in charge of a whole program. I thought that was about the best thing that ever happened to me. At that point, it was.

But Dr. Smith put one little obstacle in the way. He said, "Bobby, you'll have to take the basketball coaching job too."

Basketball? The only things I had ever done in basketball were to play second-string ball in high school and college and to coach a little YMCA ball. I didn't want to coach basketball. But I had to coach that sport if I wanted the job. And I sure wanted the job. So, now I was a basketball coach too. This was going to be interesting.

South Georgia College and the surrounding community was a beautiful place. I guess Douglas, Georgia, had a population of about 10,000 souls. It was only about fifty miles from the Florida state line. It had palm trees and tall pines and didn't look much like I thought Georgia would look. It looked more like Florida, which I liked. And the weather was about the same too.

About the end of July 1955, Ann and I moved our growing family to Douglas. And it wasn't like we moved there and football practice was to start the next week. Back in those days, football season didn't start until late September. Some schools didn't even begin classes until October. I had time to go to some high school all-star games and look for players.

I had eighteen work scholarships to offer. They were only partial scholarships and didn't cover the full cost of tuition. So, to raise extra money for our program, I started going around to local merchants. I managed to raise pretty close to $3,000. I was pretty proud of that.

The team had some veterans returning, but they hadn't won a game the year before. I think they might have tied one. Now, some of those veterans were good players and good boys, but we needed more. I had to get more players.

Ann and I moved into what used to be an officers' barracks at an old World War II U.S. Army Air Corps base just outside of town. It was sort of a strange arrangement. The barracks consisted of small rooms and to get from one to another, you had to go outside. There weren't any connecting doors inside. The floors were concrete and they would sweat in the winter. Man, I can't tell you how many newspapers we spread on those floors to soak up the moisture.

Also, the bathrooms were too large: we must have had six toilets in ours! So, here we were—Ann and I and the children—living in a military barracks. By this time we had three babies. You couldn't beat the rent though. It was only twenty-five dollars per month.

I'll have to tell you a couple of stories about those years at South Georgia. To earn extra money to pay bills, I had to go out and scratch every summer. Believe me, was I scratching. It seemed like we always owed somebody some money. And we kept having babies. I don't think we were ever able to put any money in the bank until I became the head coach at West Virginia in 1970.

When I look back now, it scares me. If I had died, Ann wouldn't have had a penny. I didn't have any insurance. Until I went to West Virginia, I never had any kind of full hospitalization coverage. Oh, I had some from the college, but it wasn't much. If we'd had a child with a serious illness or birth defect, or if Ann or I had gotten sick, I don't know how we would have paid those medical bills. We sure prayed a lot to cover the lack of insurance.

Anyhow, I got a summer job in a tobacco warehouse. My job was to weigh in the tobacco that the trucks brought in. I worked from 8 P.M. to 8 A.M.

When you think you know everything, that's when you'll find out real quick that you don't.

During the day I was a lifeguard at a swimming pool too.

So, I worked at that pool from about nine in the morning to about five in the afternoon. Then I'd go home, sleep a couple of hours, and then head for the warehouse.

I'd sit up on a big scale and truckers would drive in and load the bales of tobacco on big wooden trays. Then I'd weigh them. When I'd go to work the trucks would be lined up waiting for me. And I'd work steady until about two in the morning. After that things slowed down some, and I'd push a couple of bales together and stretch out on them and go to sleep.

The thing I remember about that job was that the warehouse was full of big ol' rats. And I mean big ones. When I stretched out to sleep, I made sure my arms and legs weren't hanging down near the floor. I didn't want any rodent trying to make a late night snack out of me.

For that I made fifty dollars a week. I did that every summer while I was at South Georgia College.

During the Christmas holidays I would work for the post office delivering mail. The post office in Douglas was about the size of a small house. Anyway, one day the postmaster gave me a wagon full of Christmas packages to deliver. Now, you'll have to get the picture. This little wagon was one like a horse would pull. It was about twice the size of a golf cart and it had big old steel wheels. The only way I could move it was either to push it, or pull it. If I pulled it, I looked like a two-legged horse. If I pushed it, I looked like some guy out collecting old clothes and junk.

I figured the best way to move it was to make like a horse. I figured I might be less conspicuous that way. So, there I was going right down the middle of the main street in Douglas pulling that wagon full of packages. Every time those steel wheels would hit a crack or bump in the pavement, they would make a "kuh-whack, kuh-whack, kuh-whack" sound. Lordy, that wagon and I sure made a racket. It was like me beating a drum and announcing, "Here I come." Everybody in town would stare at me. I was sure scratching to make money to pay some bills. There I was, a junior college athletic director, the head football coach, and the head basketball coach, who still had to work at all those extra jobs to make ends meet. I'm glad those days are over.

Anyhow, this one day Ann was downtown with the kids doing some shopping and she heard this horrible racket coming down the street. She turned around to see what fool was making all that noise. And there I was coming down the street making like a horse pulling that wagon. Kuh-whack! Kuh-whack! Kuh-whack! Oh, she was embarrassed. I had a notion to whinny for her, but I didn't. I didn't think she would have liked it. I can still hear that "kuh-whack."

Our first season at South Georgia we went 5-3-1 but won our league championship. We began by winning our first two games and I thought we just might be pretty good. And I kind of thought I had this coaching stuff down pat. But in our third game we had to go to Mississippi and play Jones Junior College. We got killed 61-14. That brought old smarty Bobby down to earth in a hurry.

But remember, this was my first season as a head coach and only my third year of coaching. You know, when you think you know everything, that's when you'll find out real quick that you don't. For instance, I didn't know anything about scouting. We didn't have movies on opponents and stuff like that. We didn't have much of anything except enthusiasm.

The coach from Jones College called me and said, "Coach, we can't scout y'all and you can't scout us. We're too far apart. And I don't reckon you have any more money than we do. So, let's just tell each other over the phone what we're gonna do." So, I told him what we were doing— what defenses and offenses we used. I told that dad-gum coach everything!

Boy, was I gullible. And he told me what he was doing. He didn't lie to me either. But I think I would have been better off not swapping information.

I mean, I knew what the Jones coach was going to do. The only problem was his team did it better than I thought. Jones was the number one team in junior college football at that time and went on to win the Junior College Rose Bowl that year. They were the elite of junior college ball.

Anyhow, we went over to Mississippi to play them. It was a night game and I was so dumb that I got my players up for breakfast and then made them go back to bed. I got them up for lunch and then made them go back to bed in the afternoon. I wanted to make sure they were well-rested. I had them rested all right. I had them so dad-gum rested they couldn't move.

Golly, I can't believe how dumb I was. I was learning the right way and the wrong way—the hard way.

On the way to the game I dropped off my only assistant, Sam Mrvos, a guy from Connellsville, Pennsylvania, who had attended Georgia, at Troy, Alabama, to scout Troy State. So, when we played Jones College the next night I coached the team by myself. I was the coaching staff. And after the game we drove back and picked Sam up alongside the highway. He just estimated about what time we would come by and stood there like a hitchhiker. Oh, that was big-time football!

Also, after that shellacking was the first time when I wondered whether I ought to be a coach. I really wondered if I had picked the right profession. I've wondered about it a few times since too. But I did learn from that licking. In four seasons at South Georgia we won twenty, lost eleven, and won three state championships outright.

I said earlier that I had to coach basketball too. That was just plain awful. No, it was worse than awful, but awful will have to do because I can't think of a worse word to describe it. I wasn't much into basketball, so, when I say our team was bad, I mean our team was real bad.

First off, I wasn't about to waste any of my eighteen scholarships on basketball. What I did was get a few of my football players to come out for the roundball team. I figured, "Heck, these guys are athletes. They ought to be able to play some dad-gum basketball."

The junior college league we played in had twelve schools, but only six played football. They all played basketball and some were pretty dag-gone good.

My first basketball team at South Georgia won only one game all season. We beat a U.S. Navy team. They managed to out-awful us, which took some doing. I always say, "Our claim to fame that year was that we didn't get shut out." (There were a couple of times, though, when I was afraid we might. Man, we were sad.) I still think the only reason they let me get by with such a pitiful job in basketball was because we had been successful in football. At that time I wasn't really concerned. All I cared about was coaching football.

I remember once we played a team in our league called Brewton-Parker Junior College. Brewton-Parker was coached by a man named Glen Wilkes and was the top team in our conference. They almost always went to the nationals. I think they even won a few national titles.

Golly, I can't believe how dumb I was. I was learning the right way and the wrong way—the hard way.

We played them at our place, and we were so bad that the Brewton-Parker coach didn't even dress his starters. He figured he could beat us with his second team and might as well give his starters the night off. He added insult to injury by letting his starters sit up in the stands. Well, our claim to fame in that game was we managed to hold a slim lead at the half. And we made that dad-gum coach get his starters out of the stands, suit them up, and put them in the game. They tore us up in the second half and won by something like 80-40. We scared 'em for a half though.

I was such a sorry coach I didn't even know how to instruct our players to get the ball to mid-court against a zone press. That was back when teams were just beginning to use that zone press. And I had so little interest in basketball that I didn't even know what the zone press was. There were lots of games when we couldn't even get the ball across halfcourt. That press ate us alive.

We had a little football player named Ronnie Kelly who played guard for us. And I figured since lowering your head and plowing straight ahead worked in football, it would work in basketball. So, I told him, "Son, you get that dad-gum ball, and when they get all over you with that press, you just duck your head and head down the court. If they get in your way, run over em. Knock em out of the way." Oh, my roundball coaching was awful.

Mvros left to go back to Georgia after that first season. So I needed to find another assistant. I hired Vince Gibson, who grew up with me in Birmingham. We played together a couple of seasons at Howard College and then he transferred to Florida State. Vince grew up about three blocks from where Ann lived and we all went to Woodlawn High School. I was three years older than Vince. I think Vince kind of looked up to me when I was young, the way I looked up to the guys who were older than me.

Anyhow, Vince was an assistant coach at a high school in St. Augustine. And when Mrvos left I called him and said, "Would you be interested in coming up here and coaching college ball with me?" I kind of stressed the college part of it. I figured that would sound a lot better to him than being an assistant at a high school.

Vince said, "Yeah, Bobby, I think I just might."

I said, "Well, Ann and I will drive down and visit with you and we'll talk about it."

So, we put the four kids in the car and headed for St. Augustine. The route we traveled meant we had to cross a big bridge south of Jacksonville. The problem was, the bridge was a toll bridge. I didn't know there was a dad-gum toll bridge on that route. When we got there the guy at the toll booth said, "That'll be fifty cents."

I didn't have fifty cents. I didn't have any money on me at all. There were a lot of times in those early years when I didn't have money. The only thing I had was a Gulf gasoline credit card.

Now, if we had crossed that bridge we would have had only about twenty more miles to go to Vince's house. But we had to turn around and drive about eighty-five miles out of the way. Those were the days. Can you imagine starting out on a long trip today with your family and having no money in your pocket—not even fifty cents? I reckon we're a lot braver—or maybe dumber—when we're young, huh?

Vince took the job and I think he took a cut in pay. He used to laugh and say, "I take a cut in pay to come with a man who is trying to hire me and he doesn't even have fifty cents to get himself across a toll bridge? I think he's crazy. And I gotta be crazier." I reckon he was right on both counts.

Anyhow, I had Vince as my assistant in football. And since I figured he had to know more about basketball than I did, I stuck him with the head basketball job. I had humiliated the school enough with my sorry efforts to coach that sport. He didn't.

Vince and his wife moved into those air base barracks and since their apartment was smaller than ours, their rent was only fifteen dollars a month. We all lived out there for two years. Those years were tough, but as I look back we sure had a lot of fun.

Then, after the second year the school decided to let us move into Powell Hall, one of the campus dormitories. And believe me, we thought we had a real deal. We had free utilities. We had free use of the telephone. I could walk to my office and save on car expenses. Plus, I even got a pay raise. I was now making $4,500 per year.

We thought we were really living in high cotton.

Learning the Passing Game

I know a lot of folks will find this hard to believe, but up until about 1959 I had been a defensive-minded coach. Defense always came first with me. I wasn't into the passing game all that much, and I certainly didn't have any trick plays in my offense. I pretty much played it straight with what I thought was good ol' rock 'em, sock 'em football.

General Bob Neyland, the legendary coach at Tennessee, was one of the men instrumental in the formation of my coaching philosophy. The other one was Coach Frank Thomas of Alabama. In my book, Neyland was—and still is—one of the top men who ever coached the game. And if you know anything about his philosophy, you know it was all defense and kicking. He figured if the other team couldn't score, it sure couldn't beat him.

I remember two stories they always told about Coach Neyland. Both had to do with defense. In a book written about him years ago, when asked if he prayed before games, he replied something like this: "No, I don't. . . . I would never ask God for victory, because the other team wants to win as bad as we do. I always figured if we prayed and the other team prayed too, God would answer the prayer of the team with the best pair of defensive tackles."

Also, Coach Neyland is credited with saying something to the effect that "when the other team is driving and gets inside our 10-yard line, we got 'em because they can't throw it. They gotta run it."

So, when I came back to Howard College as head coach in June of '59, defense was really my thing. If you remember, I got the Howard job when South Georgia College decided to drop football. I went back to my alma mater with the full intention of staying there the rest of my life. At that point in my career, I couldn't picture anything any better than that.

What more could a man want? I was the head coach at my alma mater, which was in my hometown. It was certainly a place where I felt mighty comfortable.

I brought Ann and the kids back to Birmingham that summer, and to make ends meet I worked for my daddy, who had bought into an automobile repair shop. They fixed cars and sold tires. Daddy put me to work and my job was to go around town and try to drum up business. I'm not sure how much business I drummed up; probably not much.

Then around the end of August I was ready to begin my first preseason camp at Howard. I didn't know what to expect, because the team had gone 1-8 the previous year.

I will have to tell you one thing I did to my players at that first preseason camp at Howard. Oh, I wasn't exactly honest with the players, and I'm not proud of it.

I went out and rented a camp and planned to do it like Coach Bryant had done when he was at Texas A&M. I had been told what Coach Bryant had done by his assistant, Gene Stallings, who later became head coach at Alabama. I was going to get my players off away somewhere where we could close the gates and let them go at it, and I mean really go at it. I wanted a "survival of the fittest" camp.

The camp, a Baptist camp called Cooke Springs, was located about thirty-five miles from Birmingham, where we could work the players without any interruptions. So, I wrote all my players a nice letter, and, oh, I painted them a pretty picture of that camp. I made it sound like I was going to take them on a nice seven-day retreat.

I wrote:

"Do you know football season is nearly upon us? It is hard to believe that in approximately three weeks we will be wearing the togs again. I hope you are as excited about the coming season as I am. I don't ever remember being as optimistic over prospects at Howard College as I have been this summer.

"I have a pleasant surprise for you about our first week of practice. We will spend the first seven days at a camp, where you will be able to swim, fish, and recreate yourselves between practice sessions."

Ha! Boy, was I stretching the truth in that letter. We turned that training camp into a dad-gum boot camp. My idea was to separate the men from the boys.

Man, we practically worked those kids to death. You couldn't do that nowadays. Kids today would die. Kids today are used to air-conditioned rooms, air-conditioned cars, air-conditioned classrooms, air-conditioned everything. They wouldn't be able to stand the heat. Even I am accustomed to air-conditioning today. There's no way I could stand all those hours in the hot sun like I used to. Of course, I'm not as young as I used to be either.

Back then, though, we didn't know what air-conditioning was. My idea of air-conditioning was to sit under a shade tree, or go to a room and turn the fan on full blast and then sit in front of it.

Also, we never worried about players dying in football. Then the kids were used to the heat. And we didn't know anything about heat exhaustion. I thought it was good to work out the kids in the hot sun and make them sweat. The more they sweated, the better shape they would be in.

I remember at that camp we almost did lose one kid. His name was Bill Kinghorn. He was from Jacksonville. One day, when it was really hot, he just collapsed. I thought he was going to die. It took us a long time to revive Bill. No telling how close that boy came to dying. That really was scary.

It was kind of shameful to score that many points against those teams, but winnin' is winnin', and the forward pass helped us out significantly.

Anyhow, we worked those boys like dogs. About the closest they came to swimming was when they walked past the pool on their way back from a tough workout and jumped into the pool with their uniforms on to cool off. They were so hot and tired they didn't have any energy left for swimming.

The pool was a dad-gum dump anyway. It had water in it, but it was covered with some kind of green slime, or algae, or something. No way I would have gone into that pool, but they didn't let that stop them. It's a wonder some of them boys didn't come down with typhoid!

And the boys didn't do any fishing either. When we finished with them, they went back and ate lunch, and laid down and slept like dead men. Then we got them up, and took them back out and worked them hard again. And in the evenings we had long meetings. By the end of all that it was time for lights out. If they had caught any fish, those fish would've had to have jumped out of the river and into their beds! We sure didn't have to worry about those boys getting into any kind of mischief.

It was seven days of rough, tough, hot, exhausting, hard-hitting football. My goal was to find out who was tough enough to play and who wasn't. I'll be honest, we did run off a few good kids.

I'm not proud of that, because now as I look back, I was pretty rough on those boys. I didn't know any better. That's not an excuse; it's just a fact. I was just doing what everyone else was doing. Remember, it was one-platoon (players played offense and defense) football back in those days. To play one-platoon ball you had to be tough. If you weren't tough mentally and physically, you couldn't play, because you wouldn't survive.

Nowadays, it's two-platoon, and you can have sissy kids playing out at wide receiver. You can have a guy who can't do anything but catch the ball play for you. These are guys who are talented at doing one thing, but they won't hit nobody. You can have a kid who don't know a dad-gum thing about football on your team because he's a good kicker. There's a spot now for everybody. I hope I don't hurt anybody's feelings, but some of them are sissies. And some of them have no idea how the game was played back when it was one-platoon.

But those kids who survived that camp—with all that wonderful swimming and fishing—are the ones who went 31-6 the next four years at Howard College. Those kids were tough and I was proud of them.

Now, when I came back to Howard College, thirteen of the players I had at South Georgia came with me. My first season there, we had an incredible start. We began by winning our first five games by shutouts; our opponents didn't score a single point. We finished the year with an 8-1 regular season record, which was the best record in school history. We sure surprised a lot of folks. Our only loss was to Mississippi College. Part of the reason for our early success was those junior college boys I brought with me. They were a little more mature, and knew me and knew how I coached. I did have about fifteen returning lettermen, and I went out and got some freshmen too.

After the regular season we went to a little thing called the Textile Bowl in Lanett, Alabama, which was right on the Alabama-Georgia line.

We played Gordon Military College out of Barnesville, Georgia, and beat them something like 50-14.

I do remember that we scored in that Textile Bowl on our first play from scrimmage. We had a quarterback named Joe Milazzo, and he faked a sweep and rolled out on a naked bootleg and hit receiver Buddy Bozema, who ran it in for a touchdown.

So we finished 9-1 overall that first year. It was a pretty daggone good beginning.

At Howard I had two assistant coaches. I'd had only one at South Georgia, so I was moving up in the world, it seemed. Those two assistants were Virgil Ledbetter, who also coached the baseball team, and Walter Barnes, who coached basketball. Walter hadn't played football and didn't know all that much about it. I let him coach our receivers and tight ends. Virgil, who had football experience, coached the line and linebackers. I coached the backs.

My first spring practice at Howard the next year was when I began to really learn about the passing game. It came about this way. That spring Walter got so tied up with basketball that he couldn't get to practice much, so I told him to go ahead and stay with basketball. And Virgil had to coach his baseball team. I really had the team by myself. Believe me, coaching a college football team by yourself isn't the ideal way to do it.

Anyhow, I was sitting in my office one day thinking about how to improve the team, and a thought struck me: *What about Bart Starr? Maybe I could get some ideas from him.*

I knew that Bart, who had just broken in with the Green Bay Packers, was living in Birmingham during the off-season. He had an automobile dealership and was also doing some kind of radio show. Bart was a Montgomery boy and had gone to the University of Alabama. When I was in high school, our schools had played each other, but I never played against him because he was two or three years behind me. Also, I had known of him when he played at Alabama. I don't think he knew me though.

Bart was just beginning to make a name for himself with the Packers. This was 1960. Vince Lombardi had become coach of Green Bay about 1958 and had made Bart his quarterback. I think Bart had just taken Green Bay to the NFL playoffs. Maybe he had taken them all the way to the championship game. Anyway, I knew Bart was becoming a star.

So, I called him on the phone and said, "Bart, this is Bobby Bowden out at Howard College. If you got time, how about coming out one of these days and talking some football?" Bart not only sounded like he was interested, he sounded excited about it. And an hour later he was sitting in my office.

Now, I figured I just might learn more about the passing game. I always kind of figured that passing was a quick way to move the football upfield. Some of the old-school fans will give you grief for not runnin' it all the time, but modern strategy calls for both styles of play.

Coach Neyland said, "I always figured if we prayed and the other team prayed too, God would answer the prayer of the team with the best pair of defensive tackles."

When Bart came to my office it wasn't no time before he was up at the blackboard with a piece of chalk and was diagraming pass plays. He was more than willing to tell me everything he knew about the passing game. And I was more than willing to listen.

Then I said, "If you got time, and it's not too much of an inconvenience, why don't you come on out and work with my quarterbacks some?"

He didn't even hesitate. He said, "Sure. Let's go do it."

So, I got him some shorts and sweats to wear, and he went out on the field and started working with the quarterbacks and receivers, while I worked with the linemen. He ended up staying the whole spring practice. So that spring it was me and Bart coaching the team.

Now, I didn't pay him for that. He did it for free. I couldn't have paid him anyway. I didn't have any money. My football budget was so tight it squeaked. Nowadays, you wouldn't even think of asking somebody to do something like that without paying them. But back in those days I think Bart was having as much fun as I was. If I hadn't had a wife and family to feed and bills to pay, I'd probably have done it for free too. Since I wasn't able to offer him any money, I did invite him and his wife over to our house for dinner. They came over pretty often and we got to be good friends.

In our spring game that year, we decided to divide the team, with me taking the best running backs and Bart taking the best quarterbacks and receivers. We billed it as a "throwing vs. running game." Bart's throwing team beat my running team 22-18. It was exciting. But more important, I began to see what a real weapon the forward pass could be. I thought we threw the ball a lot the year before, when Milazzo threw for about 1,000 yards in ten games. As I look back, I know now I didn't know what throwing was, but I was learning.

After that, I made several trips to Green Bay to observe Bart and the Packers. I was learning from Bart what Lombardi was teaching him. So, you might say I got my first phase of the passing game from Green Bay from Vince Lombardi by way of Bart Starr.

That year I remember we scored sixty points against Memphis Navy, eighty against Troy State and then we beat Georgetown by about eighty-four points. It was kind of shameful to score that many points against those teams, but winnin' is winnin', and the forward pass helped us out significantly.

Later that year we played Wofford College and trailed by about four points with a minute to play. Wofford had the ball, and all they had to do was hang onto it and they would win. But they didn't. They fumbled and we recovered. On the first play after recovering that fumble we hit a long bomb to win the game. It was exciting. I said it to myself, "Man, we never could have won that one by running the ball. This passing game really puts excitement into it."

And that's the one thing the forward pass can do. If you got a good running game and can mix it up with an exciting passing game, you're going to have your fans on the edges of their seats because they know their team is capable of scoring on any given play, and capable of doing it in a hurry.

In the years that followed we pulled off a few big upsets. We beat Furman. We beat Chattanooga. Those schools may not sound like big names in football today, but back then they were. And they were much bigger than we were, in terms of number of scholarships available. Both schools are now Division 1-AA powers.

The one team that always gave us fits, though, was Mississippi College over in Clinton, Miss. We lost to them my first year. It was our only loss that season. The second year we lost to them again, and again it was our only loss. The third year they beat us again. In my three years at Howard we won twenty-four and lost four, and three of those dad-gum losses were to that bunch from Clinton.

Mississippi College was a Baptist school like we were, and they always had good teams. They were coached by a man named Hartwell McPhail. He had major college experience. I think at one time he was at Ol' Miss.

He was a good coach and really knew what he was doing. To be honest, he was a much better coach then than I was.

We finally beat that dad-gum bunch my last year at Howard. Playing those Mississippi Baptists, it took four tries to get it right.

Help from Coach Bryant

Learning from Starr what Lombardi was teaching him wasn't the only great break I had in the four years I was head coach at Howard College. I also had the opportunity to be around Coach Paul "Bear" Bryant and his great University of Alabama coaching staff.

I've often said that one of the big mistakes I made in my life was when I up and quit my freshman year at Alabama and came back home to Birmingham. That's the only thing I ever quit on. At least, I don't think I ever quit on anything else. I've often wondered what would have happened if I had stayed there.

I was raised so much under the influence of Alabama football. The majority of folks in Birmingham support and pull for Alabama. They always have. Tuscaloosa was only about sixty miles down the road. Oh, there are some Auburn people, too, but Birmingham isn't the real Auburn town. Montgomery is more Auburn country.

Harry Gilmer, who was four years ahead of me at Woodlawn High School, went to Alabama and had a great, great career there. A lot of my high school teammates went to Alabama. My high school coach left and went to Alabama. And when I was a young kid back in the 1930s and 1940s, Frank Thomas, who was head coach at Alabama then, was a hero to me.

Like I said earlier, sometimes I think I was led away from Alabama to Howard College. That was the way my life was supposed to go. It might not have shaped up so good if I had stayed there. However, if I had stayed I might have learned more about the game a little quicker. I don't know. I've always kind of regretted that move though.

Coach Bryant came to Alabama as head coach in 1958. I came back to Howard as coach one year later. One of the first things I did was write him and ask if I could come down to Tuscaloosa and watch his team practice.

He wrote me back and said, "Yeah. Y'all come on down."

I had first written him a year earlier when I was at South Georgia Junior College. I didn't know in less than a year my school was going to drop football. That time Coach Bryant not only wrote me back, he called me on the phone.

Now, I'm not patting myself on the back at getting special attention from him. Coach Bryant didn't know Bobby Bowden from Adam. I knew he was new on the job and was probably writing and calling every coach who wrote and called him. I figured ol' Bear was smart enough to know that it would be a good idea to make friends with all the high school and junior college coaches he could. That way he could get his trump cards arranged. I'm sure he thought we might have some kids he'd be interested in.

Anyway, I started going to Alabama to observe how Bear operated and how he ran his practices. By watching his teams practice, I learned how great he was at teaching the fundamentals. Now, he had his own way of doing things, things that probably wouldn't have worked for anyone else. Man, I didn't know what tough was until I saw him in action.

I think he sort of took a liking to me, because he let me sit in on meetings. And I went to every meeting I could. And when you sat in on one of Coach Bryant's staff meetings it was all X's and O's on the blackboard. He never missed a single detail.

Also, I used to watch how Coach Bryant observed all the little things that went on in his practices. I do that now. I walk around and observe. I used to keep a tape recorder with me to record little things I would want to bring up at the next day's staff meeting. I did that when I was coaching at West Virginia. I would go into the meeting, put the tape recorder in the middle of the table, and tell the staff, "All right, men, I want you to listen to this."

I quit doing that, though, because I figured some of the stuff I'd seen in practice was wee little stuff and wasn't worth me getting all bent out of shape over. Now I put my criticisms on a little index card. That gives me time to sleep on them, and the next day I'm able to see that some of the things I put on the card aren't all that important. And if I decide they aren't, I don't even bring them up.

Coach Bryant let me study his films too. He let me eat at the training table. Also, I got to meet his staff, and, believe me, he surrounded himself with some great young coaches, guys like Gene Stallings, Jerry Claiborne, Howard Schnellenberger, Phil Cutchins, Charlie Bradshaw, and Pat James. All of them, except James, later became head coaches. Pat never did become a head man, but he was a brilliant line coach.

One of the biggest mistakes was when I quit the Alabama football team. That's the only thing I ever quit on. I've often wondered what would have happened if I had stayed there.

Stallings was just a young fellow then, but he had played for Coach Bryant at Texas A&M. I used to spend all day in Stallings's office talking football with him. He would tell me what Coach Bryant used to do at A&M. It was kind of the same thing I did with Starr. I learned from Lombardi through Starr. Well, I was learning the way Coach Bryant did things through Stallings.

As for Bear? Well, I was always awed by him. I was only twenty-nine and just learning the game. I really looked up to that man. Oh, occasionally he would call me back into his office and we'd chat, but most of the time he would just pass by and nod, or say, "How ya' doin', Coach?" That was about it. It wasn't like we were bosom buddies.

Now, you have to understand, I wasn't the only one in awe of him. His assistants were too. Plus, they were scared to death of him. I figured if those guys who knew him were scared of him, there had to be a good reason. And I wasn't about to do anything to find out what that reason was. Most of the time I stayed out of his way.

Coach Bryant had a big tower out on the practice field and that's where he would watch practice from. He'd climb up that ladder. Later, as he got older, the tower had steps.

It was almost like God was sitting up there looking down on you. And whenever something didn't go right in practice, the coaches would all check the tower to see what Coach Bryant was doing. If he was just sitting there, they'd go back to what they were doing. But if he got up and started toward that ladder, they'd say, "Oh, Lawh, look out! He's comin' down the ladder."

I remember one time a big tackle did something wrong. Ol' Bear came down that ladder, came striding up behind that kid, and hauled off and knocked him flat. I think he got that kid's attention. He sure got mine. Coach Bryant had a unique way of getting your attention.

It got to the point where Coach Bryant would send me players, players he didn't want. Back in those days they were cutting scholarships down to forty-five a year. Of course, today it's only twenty-five. But then Alabama always had too many players. Bear wanted it that way. He wanted to make sure he got the best players he could. And those who survived his tough training camp were usually the best.

To get rid of the extra players, Bear would do what he would call "lose a kid." Those were kids he was sure would never play for him. He would just get them to leave.

Now, it wasn't like he really intended to run them off. He just didn't want to waste any scholarships. If a kid wasn't going to play for him, he did make an attempt to get the kid in a school where he could play.

I wasn't the only one in awe of Coach Bryant. His assistants were too. Plus, they were scared to death of him.

A lot of times he'd let me come to what he called a "closed practice." Other than his staff, I might be the only other coach there. Bear would get one of his assistants, usually Hayden Riley, who then was kind of his public relations coach, to give me a list of maybe fifteen or sixteen players. He would say, "Here's the list. I'll walk you around so you can watch them. If you see any you like, let me know."

So, I'd walk around and watch practice, and when I saw a kid on the list I liked, I would point him out to Hayden. Hayden would tell Coach Bryant, and then Coach Bryant would call the kid into his office and recommend that he transfer to Howard College. He'd say, "Son, I don't think you can play here. You're a good boy, but you ain't good enough to play for us here at Alabama. Why don't you go on up to Howard College? Go on up there and play for Bobby Bowden."

You have to remember, I was just a young coach and I jumped at the chance to get some players that Coach Bryant thought were almost good enough to play for him. Hey, back then I was willing to take players any way I could get them.

I used to call Coach Bryant for advice when I was head coach at West Virginia too. I especially called him when things started going bad in 1974. That was the year we lost a lot of players to injuries and had to win two of our last three games to finish with a dad-gum 4-7 record.

Coach Bryant gave me one good piece of advice that year. I called him and told him what was happening. I said, "Coach, what do I do?"

He said, "Bobby, I'll tell you one thing you better do. You better give them boys plenty of lovin', because if you're counting on the ones you have left winning for ya', you better give 'em love—and lots of it."

I'll say this about Coach Bryant, if you called him and asked for help, he would try and help you. I know this, he never turned me down.

I don't think I've told this to too many people, but after my first year at Howard College I wrote him and asked him for a job. In my letter I said, "Coach Bryant, if a position ever opens on your staff, I'd sure love to have the opportunity to work for you."

He wrote me back and said, "Bobby, I can't hire you, 'cause if I did, I'd have every Baptist in Alabama mad at me." I think that was his polite way of saying, "No."

That was another job I tried to get and never got.

My Major College Initiation

I have always felt sorry the West Virginia fans had to suffer while I was learning what to do, and what not to do, as a head coach. Boy, did I make a bunch of dad-gum dumb mistakes in the six years I coached in Morgantown. I try to rationalize and say it was because it was my first experience at being in charge of a major college program. The truth is, I just wasn't as smart as I thought I was. We did have some good times at West Virginia, but we had our share of bad times too.

When Jim Carlen suddenly left after the 1969 season to take the Texas Tech job and I was promoted to head coach, I had ideas about the way I wanted to run things. Remember, though, this was Division 1-A football. It wasn't like it was at South Georgia and Howard College, or like it was being an assistant at Florida State.

West Virginia had gone 10-1 in '69, and we had some lettermen returning, including the late Jim Braxton at fullback and Bob Gresham at tailback. Braxton had made some All-America teams as a junior, but we were strong at fullback, so we moved him to tight end. He made All-America there, too, and went on to a great career as a fullback with the Buffalo Bills. I don't know of many players who ever made All-America at two different positions. Braxton was the guy who paved the way for a lot of the yards O. J. Simpson gained. Gresham went on to a fine career with the New Orleans Saints.

We also had a quarterback named Mike Sherwood returning. Sherwood was a fine passer and had a great touch. I think he held a lot of West

Virginia passing records for a time. A year earlier, he had thrown for 416 yards in a win over Pitt. I think that's still a West Virginia record.

Now, big linemen were pretty scarce on that team. I remember we had a defensive tackle named Charlie Fisher. That boy couldn't have weighed more than 190 pounds soaking wet. He was tough though. He just wasn't very big. But I thought we could get by and maybe outsmart and out-quick some folks.

We won our first four games over the likes of William and Mary, Richmond, Virginia Military, and Indiana. Then we played Duke at home and lost 21-13.

Despite that loss, we were still 4-1. Our next game was at Pitt. I remember the date of that game. In fact, I'll never forget it. It was October 17, 1970.

Now, back in those days Pitt wasn't all that good. They were having a few problems up there. We had beaten them three years in a row. So, we went up to Pitt and wore them out in the first half. It seemed like we scored on every possession. At the half we held a 35-8 lead. I'm sure our fans had visions of us winning by fifty or sixty points. I didn't think we'd win by that much, but I certainly thought we had the game won.

The second half? Well, it was a dad-gum nightmare. Like I said, I made a bunch of mistakes at West Virginia, but the one I made in this game topped them all. My strategy for the final thirty minutes was to sit on the lead. I figured, "We ain't gonna gamble and lose this one." I learned right then and there that when you go conservative, you're in a heap of trouble. It's like they say, there's a big difference in playing to win and playing to keep from losing. When you play to keep from losing, you can almost guarantee you're going to lose. That's what happened to us.

Pitt scored on its first possession of the second half and went for a two-point conversion and made it. Now, our lead was 35-16. If Pitt had gone for just one point after their first two scores, it would have been only 35-14. But because of those two two-point conversions, they had almost cut the deficit in half. They got fired up. And old smart me, I was content to run three plays and punt. Pitt scored again. We ran three plays and punted again. And Pitt scored again.

We ended up losing 36-35. There's no way we should have lost that one. All we had to do was make one or two first downs and they couldn't have pulled it out. Oh, it was horrible, and I felt about as low as I ever felt in my life because I knew what had happened was all my fault.

At Pitt Stadium, the visitors' locker room is a tiny little place just off the tunnel exit at one end of the stadium. Most of the fans go out that way. After that game, many of our fans, and we had a lot of them there, made a beeline for our dressing room.

They stood outside and yelled, screamed, and cursed. All of it was directed at me. Some of them even kicked and beat on the door. I thought they were going to tear the dad-gum thing off its hinges. I think they wanted a piece of my hide. I felt like letting them have it. (Naw, not really. But I had never seen any fans act the way those Mountaineer fans did. To say they were unhappy with my coaching is an understatement.)

Later, I tried to be cute with the media again. That was another dumb decision. I don't think I was thinking too clearly after that loss, because when the writers asked me why we didn't make any adjustments at the half, I said, "What adjustments? We were ahead 35-8. I told 'em to keep doing what they were doing." That not only was dumb, it wasn't the truth, because if we had kept doing what we were doing, we would have won going away.

I've been coaching now for forty years, and that October 17 afternoon in Pitt Stadium is still the blackest day in my career. I've had some tough defeats, but not like that one. It was the worst loss any team I coached ever suffered. Even the 17-16 loss to Miami in 1991, the one that knocked us out of a chance to win the national championship, doesn't compare with that Pitt loss. After that game I questioned whether I should be in coaching.

I did learn from it though. For one thing, I have never sat on a lead since. I don't care how big a lead we have, you'll never catch Bobby Bowden ever letting some team up when he's got them down. And if I had the chance to coach that game again, I would have come out in the second half with our offense wide open and tried to get a bigger lead. You should never lose a game when you have a four-touchdown lead, not unless there's an earthquake, or a flood, or something.

Boy, did I make a bunch of dad-gum dumb mistakes in the six years I coached in Morgantown.

Since then there have been games where our Florida State teams have won by forty, fifty, and sixty points, and we have been accused of running up the score. Folks can say what they want, but I am not going to sit on the lead. If they want to say we ran up the score, that's fine with me. That Pitt game is permanently etched in my memory; I know what can happen when you pull back on the throttle.

I learned something about fans from that Pitt loss too. I began to see the other side of them. Whooee! Boy, did I ever. Now, that didn't make me lose faith in the goodness of people, but it sure showed me how bad folks can be at times. And what I say about fans isn't a reflection on the fans at West Virginia. We had some great fans there. If the same thing happened here at Florida State, some of our Seminole fans would act the same way. Fans are the same everywhere. Some are good, and some are bad. Some are with you through thick and thin. And some are just with you through thick. They don't like that thin stuff.

The next week we bounced back and managed to squeak past Colorado State 24-21. I don't know how we managed to do that after that Pitt loss. Then we had to go to Penn State. I think I was twenty-three years old the last time a West Virginia team won up there. Some things never change. We lost, 42-8. We had some tough kids on our Mountaineer teams, but I reckon deep in their hearts they knew those Nittany Lions were better than they were. We'd always go there hoping to play well and not make mistakes, and then we'd go out and make one dad-gum mistake after another.

We did finish the season a respectable 8-3, but we didn't get any bowl bids. And the next year we went 7-4. Yeah, we lost to Duke and Penn State again. We did get even with Pitt though. We beat them 20-9 at Mountaineer Field, but nothing could make up for that 36-35 loss the year before. Nothing ever would.

In 1972 we had another 8-3 regular season record.

But we did go back to Pitt Stadium—back to the scene of the crime —and beat those Panthers again. This time we got 'em 38-20. I remember in the third quarter of that game, we were up something like 20-6 and had the ball way down on our 4-yard line. We threw a bomb and completed it for a long gain to get us out of the hole. We went on and scored, and that took all the bite out of the Panthers. They'd had it.

After the game, a Morgantown sportswriter named Mickey Furfari, who has covered West Virginia for what seems like forever, said, "Bobby, you were clear down on your 4-yard line and threw a bomb. Don't you think that was kind of risky?"

I said, "Mickey, don't you remember two years ago when we played here and went conservative in the second half and blew that 35-8 lead and got our tails stomped? Have you forgotten so quickly? I ain't never gonna let that happen again. From now on, if we lose, we're gonna go down with both barrels blazing."

Maybe Mickey forgot, but I sure hadn't.

That year we got a bowl bid. We were invited to play North Carolina State in the Peach Bowl. I learned a lesson there too. It had to do with the public relations aspect of coaching.

Lou Holtz, who's now at Notre Dame, was then the North Carolina State coach. And at one of the pregame press conferences, I was given the microphone first. I got up and talked about our team and what I thought our strengths and weaknesses were. Then I talked about what I knew about our opponent. I played it straight all the way. Then Holtz got up and started using those one-liners of his. He had the writers in stitches, and he poked fun at us, most of it at my expense. He really upstaged me. I made up my mind then and there that I would never be upstaged again. And since then I've developed quite a few one-liners myself.

In 1973 we had a bunch of injuries and struggled, and had to beat Virginia and Syracuse in our last two games to have a winning (6-5) record. That was the year when Penn State beat us 62-14, which is still the most points anybody has ever scored against one of my teams. Oh, Lordy, that was a terrible afternoon. That was another time when I really questioned whether I was in the right profession.

And then came the 1974 season, a year that still remains the worst I ever suffered through. I thought I had been through some tough years, but nothing I had ever experienced prepared me for this. To be honest, teams I had coached had always won more than they lost. And up to that point, I'd never had a losing season. I've had only two in my entire career. We finished 4-7, and that's when I really began to learn the facts of life. I had gotten a glimpse of the bad side of fans after that 36-35 loss at Pitt in 1970, but I got the full view in '74.

I don't care how big a lead we have, you'll never catch Bobby Bowden ever letting some team up when he's got them down. I ain't ever sittin' on a lead again.

We started the year by losing to Richmond at home 29-25. It got worse after that. We did have a lot of injuries, especially at quarterback, but nobody wanted to hear that, and I wasn't about to come out with a bunch of excuses.

Some of the fans got pretty nasty: I was hanged in effigy. That's a funny dad-gum feeling to see a dummy with your name printed on it hanging from a post. People put "for sale" signs in our yard. Everywhere I'd go around campus I'd see "Bye, bye, Bobby" bedsheets hanging out the windows of the dormitories. I don't think I could have run for office in Morgantown that year. If I had, I'd have gotten only two votes—mine and Ann's. (At least I think she would have voted for me.)

I began to get a lot of criticism from folks I thought were my friends. I was close to a lot of folks at West Virginia, but some of them really turned on me. They were people I enjoyed being around and playing golf with. That really hurt because I never had any trouble getting along with folks. I couldn't believe they would do that just because we had lost a few dad-gum football games.

All of a sudden, they quit calling. All of a sudden, they stopped inviting me to their homes. I saw how ruthless some people could be. When they'd see me, they'd wave and say, "Hi, Coach. See you later." And I reckon they meant much later.

As I look back, I can see that the folks who acted like that were nobodies. At that time, though, it really hurt. Now, I had the support of the people who counted: the university president, the athletic director, and the athletic council. I'll always remember them for their support. They told me, "Bobby, you are our coach; we're behind you."

Trouble was, at that point in my career, I just couldn't handle the criticism. It just plain killed me. It hurt Ann something awful, and I know it hurt the children.

It bothered me to the point that I almost wanted to find out who was doing and saying that stuff and go look them up. I reckon the devil tried to get a hold of me, because I thought about what I might do to them to get even. Believe me, that was a real test of my faith. I'm not sure I handled it very well, and that bothers me to this day.

My son Tommy, who was a wide receiver on our team, set about to do what his daddy couldn't. He and Dave Van Halanger, an offensive tackle and now our strength coach at Florida State, were driving by a dormitory one day and saw one of those "Bye, bye, Bobby" sheets hanging out a window. They slammed on the brakes, hopped out of the car, and went in to find out who the scoundrel was who did it. They got the guy's room number, went to his room, and pounded on the door. The way they told it to me was that they had every intention of beating up on the guy.

Tommy said, "When this guy opened the door he was the skinniest, scrawniest, most pimply-faced kid you ever did see. He was only about 125 pounds and wore big, thick glasses. Dave and I decided he wasn't worth us wasting our time and energy. We just laughed at him and came on home."

Now, I wouldn't have condoned them beating up on that boy, but I knew it was just Tommy sticking up for his daddy.

Anyhow, all that happened that year helped me realize right then and there that folks who do things like that are small people. The only way people like that feel important is if you take them seriously.

Now, don't misunderstand, there were plenty of folks who were loyal to our program, folks who stuck by us. All teams have those loyal fans. But I'm no longer naive. I know that all teams have the other kind too.

I was also getting criticism for not calling the team's plays. Remember, I had taken the job as an assistant at West Virginia back in 1966 partly because Jim Carlen said, "Bobby, you'll call all the plays." So, when I moved up to head coach I figured since letting an assistant call the plays had worked for Carlen, it would work for me. I had to learn the hard way that something that works for somebody else won't necessarily work for you. Anyhow, I let my offensive coaches run the offense. In my first five years as head coach at West Virginia, I don't think I called a dozen plays.

After that year I said to myself, "Bobby, if you're gonna get criticized and maybe lose your job, then you better make sure it's because of what you did or didn't do, and not because of what someone else did or didn't do." I've called all the plays, except for one year at Florida State, ever since.

Some fans are with you through thick and thin; others are just with you through thick. They don't like that thin stuff.

We ended that season at Virginia Tech. That was a game I still believe they tried to steal from us. We were leading 21-20 in the closing minutes. Tech had the ball. On one play the officials called one of our players for roughing the quarterback, when our kid did everything he could to keep from landing on the boy. He did graze him with one leg, but it certainly wasn't unnecessary roughness, not to me. One official didn't see it that way. He dropped his flag and walked off fifteen yards.

Dad-gum, I was mad. I stormed out on the field and let that official have it, and dad-gum it if that guy didn't walk off fifteen more yards. And later, he walked off fifteen more! On that last drive, forty-five of the yards Virginia Tech got were thanks to the referees.

I probably said more than a few bad words about those officials after that game because I remember asking God for forgiveness.

Before that game I had said to myself, *Bobby, your job might be hinging on this one.* So I reckon I was feeling the pressure. It was a new kind of pressure, because up until then I had never felt any job I ever had hinged on the outcome of a single game.

Anyhow, Tech was down about our 3-yard line with a fourth down, and the clock was winding down. All they had to do was kick a chip-shot field goal. Golly, it wasn't any longer than an extra point. The week before, Tech's kicker had booted a 60-yarder to win a game.

Well, we blocked it. But the officials had a conference. Usually when officials have a conference and you're the visiting team, the decision they come up with isn't going to be in your favor. These officials decided there had been a dead-ball penalty. Tech got to try the field goal again.

I thought, "Lawh, we ain't got a chance. They're going to steal this dad-gum game from us after all." The kicker lined it up and the ball was snapped, and he missed it! We won. I've always figured that miss was poetic justice.

I have to say something here about officials. Up until that time, I always believed all officials were good. Oh, I knew there were some who were incompetent, but I always figured they were trying the best they could. I don't believe that anymore. I still believe most of them are good, but I also believe there are some that are just like some coaches I know. I don't trust them. I have blackballed some officials. I just plain don't want some officials working our games.

There are so many close calls that can go either way. And when you are in a close game, one call can affect the outcome. With some officials, I've felt whenever there's a call that can go either way, they always seem to call it the other way.

I figure in officiating they have bad folks just like we have in coaching. There are bad folks in everything. There are some bankers I don't trust. There are some lawyers I don't trust. There are some writers I don't trust. There are some coaches I don't trust. And I have to be honest, there are some officials I don't trust.

Anyhow, everything that happened that year at West Virginia helped me come to the conclusion that if the chance ever came for me to leave any job, I wasn't going to have to apologize to anybody. I said to myself, *Bobby, if you ever want to leave here, you go ahead and do it. This is a ruthless game and people are fickle, and if you want to take another job, take it.* I saw just how important I was: as important as my last victory. It's the old story, "What have you done for me lately, baby?" I was only important until we lost.

And I don't have any illusions about fans at Florida State either. If we start losing down here with regularity, good ol' popular Bobby will find out just how popular he is with some of them.

What folks at West Virginia didn't understand was that the program was in a transition period. We had been in the Southern Conference where we played teams like William and Mary, Richmond, Virginia Military, and The Citadel. Also, we played Villanova, which later dropped football.

Now, we still played the regular rivalries like Pitt, Penn State, Syracuse, and Maryland, but we were adding teams like Duke, California, Stanford, Illinois, Indiana, Southern Methodist, Kentucky, Tulane, and Miami, Florida. The schedule was getting a lot tougher. It certainly wasn't Southern Conference anymore where we were practically guaranteed a certain number of wins every year.

Most of those teams we added to the schedule had great programs and great facilities. Our facilities stayed the same. We played in old Mountaineer Field, which seated only about 34,000. Now, don't get me wrong: it was a great place to play and those 34,000 sounded like 75,000. But all our facilities, if you could call them that, were at that old stadium. Today the school has a new stadium and all-new facilities. But back then our locker room was a dingy, cramped place under the stands. Our weight room, if you could call it that, was a wee little room partitioned off from the ladies' bathroom. We had to scrounge around town for some old carpets and mirrors. I don't remember how many weights we had in there, but it wasn't very many. I might have been able to lift them all myself. Our offices were in a Quonset hut-type building at the bowl end of the stadium.

In 1975, my last year at West Virginia, we went 8-3 and were invited back to the Peach Bowl to play North Carolina State again. We were pretty dad-gum good. We had a good running back named Artie Owens, who later played for the San Diego Chargers. Two of our three losses were by a total of three points—to Tulane 16-14 and Syracuse 20-19.

I was as important as my last victory. It's the old story, "What have you done for me lately, baby?"

We went to Clemson and used their facilities to prepare for the bowl game. And when we looked at all the facilities Clemson had compared to what we had at West Virginia, it made us wonder how we won at all. Clemson had acres and acres of nothing but practice fields. At West Virginia we had to share an old field with the band, the soccer team, and the intramural teams.

I thought, *Our facilities ain't nothin' compared to this.*

We beat North Carolina State this time 13-10. And I felt that just maybe the program had finally turned the corner. However, I had already been contacted by some big supporters of Florida State about going back to Tallahassee as head coach. I hadn't been happy at Florida State ten years earlier when I was an assistant, but this was different. This was the head job.

I didn't know what to do. Four of my own kids were in school in West Virginia. I kind of felt that maybe the time wasn't right to move. But when the talks got serious with Florida State and Ann and I went back to Tallahassee for an interview, everything changed.

But I have to be truthful, if all that stuff hadn't happened at West Virginia in 1974, I probably would have stayed there because I am a loyal person. I did like it up there. Ann liked it there. Our children liked it there. Some of our children married West Virginians. And we made a lot of great friends there, people who are still our friends.

I made a joke once that the reason I left those mountains to return to Tallahassee was because I was getting out of my car one time on a cold winter day and slipped on some ice. Well, that wasn't quite true. It is true, though, that I slipped on the ice a few times. I even wrecked a state car up there once when I skidded on the ice and lost an argument with a fence.

And a lot of folks think I left because at that time all I had was a one-year contract and wasn't making much money. I was only making something like $28,000 per year then. Now, I wasn't too happy with only a one-year contract, because it didn't give you much security, and it sure didn't give my assistant coaches much either. But those things weren't why I left.

The main reason was that Florida State was in the Deep South and I had been born and raised in the Deep South. I think deep down, every person would like to go back home. I kind of think being home is like being in church. You feel safe and secure there.

Going Home

I've heard a lot of stories about why I left West Virginia and came back to Florida State. Most were fiction, some of it created by me, I guess. I think I ought to set the record straight.

For some reason, there are a few folks around Tallahassee who think Ann and I sat around in Morgantown for ten years and hoped a job would open up down south so we could get back where it's warm. That's not the way it happened. We didn't sit around and constantly say, "Oh, it's awful up here. These mountains are so terrible. We just gotta get out of here."

First of all, folks down in the Deep South don't understand that it does get cold, sometimes darned cold, in West Virginia, but it's not like you were living in Minnesota or North Dakota. Sure, West Virginia has winter, but a lot of nice places have winter. Sometimes the winters in those mountains are fairly mild.

Now, you have to remember, when I took the Florida State job back in 1976, it wasn't exactly a plum. The program wasn't exactly in the top ten charts, not unless they had a chart for a team that in the previous three years had gone 0-11, 1-10, and 3-8, and had won only one home game: a big 17-8 win over mighty Utah State!

In that same time frame the Seminoles had a twenty-game losing streak and gave up 774 points and nearly 13,000 yards total offense. Dadgum, 13,000 yards is about seven-and-a-half miles. Somebody wasn't playing much defense.

No, Florida State sure wasn't a plum.

Also, back then the stadium in Tallahassee had only 40,000 seats. I think they were averaging only about 17,000 to 20,000 for home games. And I'm not sure, but I think the program might have been operating in the red. The facilities weren't great, but they were great compared to what we had at West Virginia. Florida State didn't have all the facilities it has now.

What happened was that after the 1975 season, Florida State was getting ready to fire Darrell Mudra. And, like I said, certain Seminole boosters called and said they were interested in me, and they wanted to know if I would be interested in them. They started calling about late November. I guess they had already made up their minds about Mudra. But it wasn't like I was the only guy they were calling. They were calling other coaches and feeling them out too.

As I understand it, all this was being done without the authority of Florida State's administration. Those boosters were doing it on their own. But the same thing was happening to me at West Virginia. Even though we won that Peach Bowl, there were still some big Mountaineer supporters who were mad at me for what happened in 1974. I have no doubt that they were calling around to see if they could find somebody to replace me.

You know, this coaching profession isn't anything but a popularity contest, and you're popular only as long as you win. In 1974 I wasn't the most popular guy in those mountains.

I didn't put a lot of stock in the calls I was getting from those Florida State fans. However, I knew the folks calling were high-profile alumni. They might have been part of a search committee. Anyhow, I was getting calls about every third night and the person on the other end would say, "Bobby, we're going to fire our coach. What would it take for you to be interested in the job?"

Now, it wasn't the university president calling me. It wasn't the athletic director calling me. It was just boosters. I was cordial and always listened to what they had to say. And the truth was I was interested, but at that time I didn't know if anything would come of it.

I want to emphasize again that I wasn't all that unhappy at West Virginia. I had survived that bad year, and we'd just won a bowl. And like I said, four of our children were in college there. If we left, we'd have to leave those kids. I didn't want to run off and leave them. And we had been there ten years and were used to it. We weren't all that much interested in picking up and moving.

Then a couple of things happened, a couple of things that once again showed me how God works.

After our West Virginia team got back from the bowl game, I got invited to go to Tampa and be one of the coaches for the North team in the now defunct All-American All-Star game.

When Ann and I arrived in Tampa John Bridgers, then Florida State's athletic director, called. John was from Birmingham and I had known him for years—not well, but I knew him. I liked him and think he liked me. He said, "Bobby, we'd like to interview you. Would you be interested in letting us do that?"

I said, "OK."

It's funny how the media finds out about things—they must have a heckuva grapevine.

I figured I might as well hear what John had to say. He was the first official representative of the school to contact me. So, he and the university's president, Stanley Marshall, flew down and got a room at a hotel out near the Tampa airport and I drove out to meet with them.

It's funny how the media finds out about things like that. That must be a heckuva grapevine. There were some Florida sportswriters who already knew that someone from Florida State was interested in talking to me because when Ann and I arrived in Tampa, we were met by some writers. The first thing they asked was, "Coach, has Florida State offered you the job?"

I said, "Naw, I haven't been offered any job." And at that time that was true.

Anyhow, I met with the president and Bridgers, and we must have talked for more than two hours. They didn't offer me the job, but I think they were trying to sell me on it.

The conversation went like this:

I said, "If I come, will you increase the football budget?"

They said, "Yes."

I said, "If I decide I want AstroTurf on the field. Will you do that?" (Fortunately, we stayed with natural grass. Today we know that AstroTurf causes too many injuries.)

They said, "Yes."

And it continued on like that; they agreed to everything I asked for. I was feeling them out and they were feeling me out. When the meeting was over, Bridgers asked me if Ann and I could stop by Tallahassee on our way back to West Virginia to look the place over and meet with the athletic council.

I said, "I don't know. We might, but I've got to talk it over with Ann." I was interested, but not enough at that point to leave West Virginia. And I wasn't at all sure how Ann would feel about it. I sure wasn't about to take any job unless she went along with it.

So, when I got back to my hotel I told Ann everything that had gone on and added, "They didn't offer me the job, but they made it sound mighty interesting. And they want us to go by Tallahassee on our way home. Why don't we go by the place for old time's sake? We ain't been back there in ten years. Why don't we go see what the place looks like and see how it has changed?"

Ann was very reluctant. She wanted to get back home. So, it wasn't like she couldn't wait to get back to Tallahassee. The truth was she couldn't wait to get back to Morgantown and the children.

We finally decided to change our plane tickets and fly home by way of Tallahassee. Bridgers met us at the airport, checked us into a nice hotel, and then drove us around the campus and showed us the new football offices and locker rooms. Now, those weren't the offices and dressing rooms we have now. But I remember at the time thinking, "Golly, these are about a million times better than the ones we have at West Virginia."

The coaching profession isn't anything but a popularity contest, and you're popular only as long as you win.

Since then West Virginia has all new facilities and a new stadium, but at the time I couldn't see that in the immediate future. I think all that stuff came five or six years after I left.

I met with Florida State's athletic council and answered questions. I knew some members of the council from when I was an assistant at Florida State in the mid-sixties. They all seemed very receptive, but still nobody had offered me a job.

But when Bridgers drove us back to our hotel the offer came. He said, "Bobby, we want you as our coach."

I didn't give him an answer. What I did do was agree to give the offer serious consideration. I said, "John, I'll think about it and call you in a day or two."

The next day, Ann and I flew back to Morgantown, and during the flight we discussed everything, all the pros and cons. And the pros outweighed the cons. We talked about our upbringing in the Deep South. We talked about her mother and mine, both of whom lived in Birmingham. We talked about our roots. And I'll be honest, we talked about the warm weather. So, when we landed, I called Bridgers from a pay phone at the Morgantown airport and said, "If you still want me, I'll take the job."

He said, "We still want you. The job's yours."

At my first press conference after taking the job, I joked to the media and said, "The reason I'm here is because I slipped and fell on the ice up in West Virginia one too many times."

Well, like I said earlier, it was true that I had slipped on the ice during some of those winters in West Virginia, but that had nothing to do with me accepting the job. Funny thing, though, I slipped and fell on the ice that very night, right after I called Bridgers.

When Ann and I arrived in Morgantown, my daughter, Robyn, and her husband, Jack Hines, met us to drive us to the house. When we got off that plane it was cold. There was snow on the ground and the roads were covered with ice. On our way to the house, Jack took the back way, which was the way we always went home from the airport. That route included having to go up over a big ol' hill. Jack got the car about halfway up that hill and couldn't go any farther because of the ice. And all at once, the car started sliding backwards down the hill. On one side was a big cliff, and on the other side was the side of the mountain.

Jack managed to steer the car into a ditch. When the car came to a stop, I managed to get the door open and stepped out. I never gave the dad-gum ice a thought. Suddenly, my feet went up and I went down—flat on my face. I thought for a second I was going to slide on down the daggone hill.

After taking the Florida State job I jokingly told writers that was when I yelled to Ann, "We'll take the job! We'll take it!" But that's not the way it happened. I did fall on that ice, but I had already called and accepted the job.

The next morning I called Leland Byrd, who was then West Virginia's athletic director, and told him of my decision. He said, "Bobby, will you meet me for breakfast? If it's a problem with your contract, we can do something about that. And if it's money, we might be able to do something about that too." Remember, at West Virginia I had only a one-year contract and was making only $28,000. I guess he thought those were the main reasons I was going to leave.

I said, "Leland, I'll be glad to meet you, but you can't talk me out of it. It ain't about the contract or the money. Ann and I have made up our minds. We just want to go home."

CHAPTER 14

The 90-Yard Turnaround

When I took the Florida State job back in 1976 I had five goals, and not one of them included still being the FSU head coach today. My goals were to win a home game, to have a winning record at home, to have a winning record—period, to beat University of Florida, and to go to a bowl game. I certainly didn't have competing for the national championship on my list.

I figured we'd accomplish a couple of those goals the first year, maybe one more the second year, maybe one more the third year, and all of them, if we were lucky, after about four years.

Dad-gum, we accomplished them all in two.

Of course, the way things began, it looked like we had about as much chance of achieving those goals as we did of going to the moon.

I remember that first spring practice when I saw the players that were on the team. I thought, "Man, these are good-looking kids." And they were great-looking athletes. I felt pretty good. Then came September, and we opened the season at Memphis State. It was a game I figured we would win. Well, we didn't. We got beat 21-12.

I wasn't worried though. I was new to the players, and they were new to me. Now, I hated to lose, but I figured we'd improve.

Then we had to play at Miami. Miami wasn't a powerhouse then. Oh, those Hurricanes might have been good, but they weren't great like they are today. They were definitely not a Top Twenty team then. Shoot, we played Miami twice when I was at West Virginia and won one and lost one. We beat Miami 20-14 with a West Virginia team that finished 6-5. And we lost 21-20 with the worst team I had at West Virginia. That was in '74 when I had that horrendous 4-7 record.

Anyhow, I'll never forget that second game. We went down to Miami all primed to get our first victory. We won the coin flip and elected to receive. Miami kicked off. We ran one play and fumbled. Miami recovered and scored. It was 7-0.

Miami kicked off again. We made one first down and fumbled again. They recovered and scored again. It was 14-0. Miami kicked off again. I figured we'd better quit playing it so close to the vest, so we came out throwing. They intercepted a pass and scored again. Now it was 21-0, and we were still in the first quarter. By the time the quarter ended we were behind 27-0.

The final score was 47-0, and we didn't have a dad-gum thing to do with it being that close. It could have been 100-0, except that Miami's coaches took pity on us and called off the dogs.

I went into the locker room after that loss and said to myself, *Lawh, we ain't gonna win a game, not a single one. This is gonna take a lot longer than I thought.*

Our next game—the third away game in a row—was at Oklahoma. I figured if we couldn't beat Miami, those Sooners just might run us clean out of the stadium. They were probably having a pool to see who could guess the final score of that one.

Like I said, we had some great-looking players physically, but the thing I didn't take into account was their mental condition. After that Miami game, I figured out that our players didn't believe they could win. And, folks, I don't care how big, or strong, or fast, or whatever else an athlete is, if a man doesn't think he can win, he is not going to win.

Folks, I don't care how big, or strong, or fast, or whatever else an athlete is, if a man doesn't think he can win, he is not going to win.

Well, we had a bunch of guys living up to their expectations, and those expectations weren't very dad-gum high.

I use a statement every now and then, and it didn't originate with me. It came from Ara Parseghian, the former Notre Dame coach. He said something like, "You don't play players who have potential. You play the ones who are doing the job for you." In other words, potential ain't worth a hill of beans if that's all it is. Potential is what you should have done. I go by what a player does. It's performance, not potential, that counts.

So, after that Miami embarrassment, I sat down with our coaches the very next morning and said, "When you grade that game film, I want every boy you see on that film who looked like he didn't think he could win put on the bench. Let's put freshmen in their place. It don't look like we're gonna win any games anyway, so let's teach them younger players how to play, and build on that. At least those freshmen don't know how to lose yet. Those other guys sure do."

We ended up putting six true freshmen in the lineup. These were guys who were in high school four months earlier. I remember their names. We had Kurt Unglaub and Jackie Flowers at wide receiver. We had Mark Lyles at fullback and Mike Good at guard. And we had Scott Warren and Walter Carter at the defensive tackles. And if you count our kicker, Dave Cappelen, then we really had seven freshmen in the lineup when we took the field against Oklahoma.

We kicked off to start that game and on Oklahoma's first play from scrimmage—Bam!—they gained 50 yards. They had a back named Kenny King, and he took it right up the gut—up the middle of the field. He didn't bother to go around the end because that would have taken too long. I thought, *Uh, oh, this is gonna be awful. Lawh, it's gonna be a track meet, and we ain't gonna provide much competition.*

King didn't go all the way, but I know his long run probably made Oklahoma overconfident. Anyway, those Sooners fumbled a couple of pitchouts, and darned if we didn't hold them to a field goal on that drive. Then we took the kickoff and started from our twenty. In twelve straight plays—boom, boom, boom—we drove 80 yards to score and went ahead 6-3. And it was still 6-3 at the end of the first quarter.

I was really proud of those boys.

I'd like to say we won that game, but we didn't. Oklahoma beat us 24-9, but it was only 17-9 with seven minutes left in the game. We'd had three drives halted by fumbles. One of those fumbles came when tailback Larry Key was going in from the 1-yard line for a touchdown. The ball rolled out of the end zone for a dad-gum touchback.

However, those freshmen we put here and there in the lineup did all right. If there is such a thing as a moral victory, that was one. However, I'm not much on moral victories. I always say, "A moral victory is like a six-foot man drowning in three feet of water. He's still dead."

We wound up losing by only fifteen points when I figured we would lose by fifty or sixty. During that game I began to see a glimmer of hope, because we had some kids in there who didn't know they weren't supposed to win.

We did win our next two games though. We won our home opener the next week over Kansas State 20-10, after spotting Kansas State a 10-0 lead. This was my first home game as the new coach, and it felt pretty good to get that first win in front of the home folks. Like I said, the Seminoles had played sixteen home games the previous three seasons and had won only one of them.

When I took the Florida State job, I said, "When I was at West Virginia, all I heard was 'Beat Pitt!' When I got here in Tallahassee, all the bumper stickers on the cars read 'Beat Anybody!' "

The following week we won on the road at Boston College. It was a rainy, windy day, but we came away with a 28-9 win. But after that we lost to Florida by seven (33-26), Auburn by twelve (31-19), and Clemson by three (15-12).

We went into our last three games 2-6, which wasn't anything to write home about. I wasn't sure we'd win another game. But what happened in those three games was something I don't ever expect to see again. I called what happened "divine intervention." At least, it was somebody's intervention.

At that time I had been a head coach for fourteen years and an assistant for nine. None of the teams I had been associated with had ever had scoring plays from scrimmage of ninety yards or more. I mean, those aren't your normal scoring plays. Golly, I think in all the history of Alabama football, they've had only two or three scoring plays that long.

In those three games we had four daggone scoring plays from scrimmage that covered distances of ninety-one, ninety-five, ninety-six, and ninety-seven yards. Two of them came in the closing minutes to win games.

It all began against Southern Mississippi at home. It was homecoming and we certainly weren't impressing our fans, because with less than twelve minutes to play we trailed 27-10. We rallied, but with about five minutes left we were still behind 27-23. We had the ball on our 5-yard line and it was third down. If we didn't make it, school was out.

I called a screen pass, and quarterback Jimmy Black hit Rudy Thomas, and he ran ninety-five yards for the winning touchdown. We won 30-27 when it seemed we had no chance.

It was the beginning because I think it finally proved to our players that if they worked hard and kept the faith, something good would eventually happen.

Potential ain't worth a hill of beans if that's all it is. It's performance, not potential, that counts.

The next week we went to Denton, Texas, to play North Texas State, and the night before the game the place was hit by a blizzard. The field was covered with five or six inches of snow. It was freezing cold, and, man, the wind was really howling out on those Texas plains.

Now, we had Florida boys. They ain't used to snow. I said, "Lawh, I'll bet 80 percent of our players have never seen snow." I was pretty sure none of our players had ever played a game in snow. I don't think I had ever seen that much snow. (Well, maybe once or twice up in West Virginia.)

Frank DeBord, our equipment manager, went out that morning and bought up all the gloves, stocking caps, and long underwear he could find. I've often laughed when folks refer to that game and ask me if I was worried about any of my players freezing to death. I answer, "Naw, I was just worried about ol' Bobby freezing." That wasn't exactly a joke either.

We went out to "warm up" before the game and all you could see were the goal posts sticking up at both ends of the field. If it hadn't been for the goal posts, we wouldn't have had any dad-gum idea where the field was. You couldn't see a yard line anywhere. All you could see was white stuff. They started shoveling the snow away. They'd find a yard line, and then they'd put down one of those orange-colored highway cones that road crews use for road construction. Eventually, they were able to get those cones down about every twenty yards. It kind of looked like a football field, except it wasn't green.

It was North Texas State's homecoming, and I think about ninety-eight of their fans showed up. Ann and some of our really loyal fans made the trip with us, and I think they stayed on the bus and watched what they could of the game from the bus windows. I didn't blame them.

Before the game I said to my players, "Men, I know most of you have never played in weather like this. So, I just want you to go out there and have some fun. We'll consider it like a sandlot game and have a good ol' time. And don't any of you freeze because I don't know how I'd explain it to your mommas and daddies."

I laugh when I think of that game, because at one point I asked the officials for a measurement for a first down.

I said, "I want a dad-gum measurement. You say you think we haven't made the first down. What do you mean 'you think'? I want to know."

One official, who looked colder than I was, said, "Coach, we can't measure it. There ain't no way. We can't see the yard line. We'll have to dig to find it."

I said, "Then dig. I want to know where the ball is, and if we haven't made it, I want to know how far we got to go."

It must have taken them ten minutes to shovel off the snow so they could try to measure it. You know, I can't even remember if we made that first down. I'll bet those officials said a few choice words about my ancestry after that one.

The game went about like I figured—a sandlot-type game. We blocked a couple of their punts. They blocked one of ours. Each team scored a touchdown off a blocked punt. I don't remember how many times we punted, but it must have been a bunch.

I'm not much on moral victories. I always say, "A moral victory is like a six-foot man drowning in three feet of water. He's still dead."

Anyway, in the third quarter Black connected with Unglaub on a 91-yard scoring play. The guy covering Unglaub slipped and fell down, and Unglaub, who couldn't break five seconds in a 40-yard dash, was off to the races like a cross-country skier. He couldn't see the goal line because of the snow and must have run 110 yards. I thought he was going to run clear out of the stadium. We won that "blizzard" game 22-21 on a halfback pass for the two-point conversion from Key to Unglaub. Afterward, our players were rolling in the snow and throwing snowballs at each other. It was a fun game, one of my favorites of all time.

Our final game that year was against Virginia Tech at home. It rained all day and a lot of fans stayed home. They missed something they'll probably never see again: two 90-yard-plus scoring plays.

Key went off the left side, broke about two tackles, and went 97 yards on one, and Unglaub, our speedster, went 96 yards on a pass from Black for the winning score on the other. That last one came after Tech, which was leading 24-20 with two minutes to play and was going in for an insurance touchdown, fumbled at our 4-yard line. I mean, I was standing there on the sideline hoping they would fumble and we'd recover and somehow win, and that what's happened. It was almost like some unseen power willed it.

Florida State had never had a 90-yard scoring play before—not one from scrimmage, and we haven't had one since. We finished the year with a losing record, but we finished it with a dad-gum flourish. Despite being just 5-6, which is the only losing year we've had here, we did accomplish two goals. We won a home game and had a winning record at home (3-2).

Now, the only difference in our team at the end as opposed to the beginning was the players finally knew they could win. I continue to use that team as an example when I talk to my teams today. I tell them, "That team is the greatest example of what can happen when you are enthusiastic and disciplined. In other words, if you live a disciplined life that's full of God and keep a positive attitude, then you've got it. Men, you got it."

Those three games were unbelievable. It was like some power took over and what happened was beyond our control. Now, it may not have been divine intervention, but all I know is that's what happened. And it didn't stop there. Counting those three wins, we went on to win forty-two of the next fifty games over a four-year span.

Wally
Jim
Jordham

Three players had as much to do with the resurgence of Florida State football as any individuals I could name. They were quarterbacks Wally Woodham and Jimmy Jordan and linebacker Ron Simmons.

Simmons was the missing link on our defense and Wally and Jimmy . . . well, what happened with them was unbelievable.

Ron was a player who came into our program as a freshman in 1977 and was mature when he arrived. It was hard for him to get any better, because he was great from day one. He was about 6'2", 225 pounds, could run 40 yards in 4.5 seconds, could bench press over 500 pounds and was built like Superman.

The year before Ron arrived we had a defense that I don't think was ranked in the Top 100. (If it was, it was just barely ranked.) We didn't stop very many folks. And we had eight of those defensive starters back. We took those eight guys and added Simmons, who was just out of high school, at nose guard, and in '77 our defense was in the Top Ten.

That one player's presence, along with the added experience of our veterans, was the difference. Ron was named defensive freshman of the year and made All-American as a sophomore and junior. He didn't have a great senior year because he was hurt most of the season.

Now, with Wally and Jimmy, an odd thing happened. What I did with them I didn't set out to do, and I'll probably never do it again. I sure wouldn't recommend what I did to any coach.

What I did was turn those two into a starter-reliever pair. I'd start one, and if he wasn't on his game, I'd bring in the other to save it. And then I'd start the other, and if he wasn't doing it, I'd bring in the other and he'd do it. Writers started calling them "Wally Jim Jordham."

When I came to Florida State, Wally was already in school. He enrolled in 1975 and had played only junior varsity ball. Jimmy came in 1976 and played some as a freshman. I red-shirted (that means holding a player out of competition) Wally that year. So, in 1977 both were sophomores eligibility-wise.

Both had attended Leon High School in Tallahassee. Wally set a national high school passing record with 3,560 yards passing, and Jimmy broke Wally's record the next year with 4,098 yards. They could both throw it, but had different styles. Wally was kind of like a little fat butterball and wasn't a runner at all. He was too heavy. But he could throw a pretty pass, and was great at finding the seam in a zone. Plus, Wally really slimmed down his last two-and-a-half years. Jimmy looked like a quarterback. He had a great arm, one of the best I've ever seen. He could really stick the ball in there against man-to-man coverage.

Now, Jimmy did have trouble taking something off the ball and floating it in the gap in a zone. Not that he couldn't do it, but it was just that Wally was better at it. And Wally didn't handle man-to-man coverage like Jimmy did.

In my thinking, Wally was never going to play for us. I figured nobody was gonna unseat Jimmy once he got in there. Shows you how much I know.

Anyhow, in '77 Jimmy was our starting quarterback, and Wally was his backup. One day Wally came by my office and said to me, "Coach, I'm gonna hang it up. I don't see any future for me here, and I don't enjoy it. I'm not gonna play anymore."

I said, "Wally, you ought to stay on the team. You don't know what will happen. You've got a long career ahead of you. Don't quit."

I tried to talk him out of it, not because I thought he would help us, but because I always try to talk all of my players out of quitting. I don't want boys to quit, because if they quit on football they might quit on something else down the road. I know something about quitting, because like I said earlier, I quit my freshman year at Alabama and have somewhat regretted it ever since.

Wally stayed.

We played our first game and beat Southern Mississippi 35-6. Jimmy had a great day; he threw two touchdown passes. Wally came in late, when the game was wrapped up, and threw for one. Then we played the next game against Kansas State and won that one too. This time, though, Jimmy wasn't all that sharp and we won by only 18-10. Our third game was against Miami. We had them beat by about four points when we got called for a roughing penalty late in the game. That penalty enabled them to keep a drive alive and they barely beat us 23-18.

About two days later, Wally, who was a class kid, came to see me again. This time he didn't talk about quitting. He said, "Coach, I just want you to know I'm not happy sitting on the bench. I think I can do a better job than Jimmy." And he walked out.

I almost choked on the cigar I was chewing. (I used to chew a lot of those things. Never put a match to one though.)

But what Wally said really meant something to me because up until then I really didn't think he cared all that much. Wally was an assertive-type person, while Jimmy was the quiet type.

Our fourth game was at Oklahoma State, which had tied Oklahoma the year before and won the Big Eight Conference championship. We started Jimmy again, and he started off bad and didn't get any better. He couldn't do anything right. We got behind 10-0, and if we hadn't gotten a couple of breaks it would have been worse than that.

A "big" game is the one you just lost. Our fans just plain don't like to lose to them Gators, and they don't cotton much to coaches who do.

So, we took Jimmy out and put Wally in. I said to myself, *It's not happening with Jimmy in there; why not put the other boy in and see what he can do?*

Wally went in and moved the team right down the field for a field goal. And in the second half with him still at the controls, we came back to win 25-17. The next week we started Wally against Cincinnati and won 14-0. And we started him the following week against Auburn. Wally engineered another victory. This one was 24-3 and was our first win over a Southeastern Conference opponent in five years.

Then Wally started doing badly. So, I took him out and put in Jimmy. Jimmy did well, and we won. Then I made Jimmy the starter again, and after a while he started doing badly, and I put Wally back in and he did well.

It went that way for three years. Jimmy the starter and Wally in relief, or Wally the starter and Jimmy in relief. I've never seen anything like it.

Somebody asked me after those two were gone if I would ever do that again. I said, "Naw. That just happened. What happened with Jimmy and Wally is not the ideal situation. No coach likes to juggle his quarterbacks around. I like to have a first-team quarterback and a second-team quarterback—period. If number one goes down, you go to number two. But you don't jerk your quarterbacks in and out of a game."

Whenever I hear a coach say, "Boy, I got me three great quarterbacks," I wonder if that coach is going to play his games with three footballs. An old coach once said, "You show me a team with two quarterbacks, and I'll show you a team without a quarterback."

I used to believe that too—until Wally and Jimmy. Anyhow, with Wally and Jimmy, or Jimmy and Wally, at the controls, we went 10-2 in '77, and that included a 40-17 win over Texas Tech in the Tangerine Bowl. It was the first time ever that Florida State had won nine or more games in a season. And it was Florida State's first bowl win since 1964.

But the really important thing we did that year was go to Gainesville and beat those daggone Florida Gators 37-9. I remember the big play in that game came in the third quarter when we were leading by only 17-9 and were backed up on our 12-yard line with a third-and-thirty. We ran a draw play with Larry Key and he ran for 38 yards. It was a situation where everybody in the world knew we had to throw it.

So, I figured, *Let's run it and see what happens.* Now, I sure didn't expect a first down, but I discovered a long time ago that this game is full of a lot of surprises, and most come when you least expect them.

Florida State hadn't beaten Florida in nine years, and when we got back to Tallahassee after that win, you would have thought we'd won the dad-gum Super Bowl. About 5,000 fans turned out to welcome us home.

Now, I knew the Florida game was big, and I knew it was bigger for Florida State than it was for Florida. Florida was "THE" school. We were the poorer cousins up in the state capital. Florida had dominated the series, which stood at 15-2-1 at that time. But I really didn't realize the importance of it.

Remember, I had been at West Virginia for ten years, and before that I was only an assistant at Florida State for three years. And like I said, I wasn't all that happy in those three years. So, I wasn't aware of how much those losses to the Gators were sticking in a lot of Florida State folks' craws.

After that win over Florida, writers asked, "Is that the greatest game you've ever won?"

I said, "No, it isn't. When my West Virginia team beat Pitt 17-14 in 1975 was better. That was a game we won on a field goal with no time left on the clock when our kicker, a boy named Bill McKenzie, booted it right down the pike. That's as exciting a win as I've ever been involved in. You see, up there West Virginia vs. Pitt is what they call the 'backyard brawl.' " I suppose I hurt some of those Florida writers' feelings, but they asked me a fair question and I gave them an honest answer.

We beat Florida the next year, and the next, and the next. So we were beating Florida consistently. I knew it was a big game, but it wasn't any big deal to me. We would just go play them and win. It seemed like any other big game.

It took six straight losses to Florida (1981 through 1986) before I realized the significance of it. A "big" game is the one you just lost. Our fans just plain don't like to lose to them Gators, and they don't cotton much to coaches who do. I wasn't too happy about it either. I don't like losing to anybody six times in a row, not even in Ping-Pong.

I remember after we lost to them one time . . . well, we didn't exactly lose, we got annihilated, 53-14. That was in 1983, and it was a game where everything went wrong. We would make a great play and fumble. Then we'd make another great play and fumble. All we did was fumble. We didn't have anybody who could hang onto the dad-gum ball. All we heard was, "Their ball! Their ball!"

I know I say it's just a game, but when it's going on, it's more than that. It's a serious game. And if I didn't think so, I'd get out tomorrow.

After that loss I said something to the effect that "maybe I ought to hang it up." Well, the media got wind of it and some writers called me when I got home and asked, "Bobby, were you serious when you said you thought you ought to quit?"

I said, "Well, I would if I could find someone better to take my place, but I can't find anybody any better." I was trying to be cute, but it sounded like a smarty answer. What I should have done was answer the question with a question. I should have said, "If you were a head football coach and your team had just been beaten 53-14 by a big rival, how would you feel?"

Actually, the truth was when I made that answer I was really saying, "I stuck my foot in my mouth, and I'm just trying to get it out."

We did come back and beat Florida four more times in a row after those six straight losses. And through 1993, our record against them is 10-8.

In 1978 we went 8-3. We beat Florida and Miami and won at Syracuse. We lost by four points at Pitt and by six at Houston. But the one loss that was really disappointing was when we lost at Mississippi State 55-27. If you've never taken a team to Starkville, Mississippi, you have to realize you're not in New York City. You're in Starkville. Those folks have a tremendous home-field advantage. Also, there was a tremendous wind blowing the day we played them. I don't think we've ever played in a worse wind.

Our Florida kids didn't know how to handle it. They weren't accustomed to playing in wind. Also, Mississippi State had a great passer, and he led his team to 596 yards total offense against us. That was a lot of yardage and it disappointed me until I heard where that quarterback gained more yards than that the next week against Alabama.

We were down by only 21-20 at the half. They scored twenty-one points with the wind at their backs in the first quarter. Then we got the wind and scored twenty. In the second half they had the choice and they were smart. They took the wind and scored two more times. In the fourth quarter I figured we had to gamble. It backfired, and they ended up beating the tar out of us.

The 11-0 season of '79 didn't begin in spectacular fashion. In fact, if it hadn't been for our defense, it wouldn't have begun at all. We opened at home against Southern Mississippi and trailed in the fourth quarter 14-3. We held Southern Miss and forced a punt, and defensive back Monk Bonasorte broke through to block it. We recovered at their 15-yard line and four plays later scored when Jordan hit Jackie Flowers in the end zone.

Then we held them again and forced another punt. This time defensive back Gary Henry, who had fair-caught every dad-gum punt all day, took this one and raced sixty-five yards for the winning touchdown. We won, barely, 17-14.

When that season was over, someone asked me if I was worried that our 11-0 season was in jeopardy in that opener. I said, "Eleven-and-oh!

How could I be worried about that? I was worried we were gonna be oh-and-one."

We rolled along after that with impressive wins over Arizona State 31-3 and Miami 40-23, and then managed an unimpressive 17-10 squeaker over Virginia Tech. I said after that one that "it wasn't pretty and we had a lot of dad-gum junk calls on our part, but it was a win."

LSU was our seventh game, and believe me, I was worried about going over to Baton Rouge. Up until then, we had started Woodham in every game, but we played a hunch in this one and started Jordan. I figured, "LSU's coverage was made to order for Jimmy's bullet-like passes. Jimmy ought to pick them to pieces." And that's what he did. He completed fourteen of thirty-one for 312 yards and three touchdowns, and we managed to come away with a 24-19 win. Now we were 7-0.

Our final game that year was at—yeah, you guessed it—Gainesville, against those Gators. Florida hadn't won a game (0-9-1) and we were 10-0.

Boy, did we struggle in that one. We were ahead by only 20-16 with about two minutes to play. Fortunately, we got a call when Florida didn't allow us to fair catch an onside kick. That gave us the ball in good field possession and we scored as the clock ran out for a 27-16 win. Those Gators sure didn't play like a winless team, and we didn't play like an unbeaten one. However, we made it, even though it wasn't pretty—11-0. It's the only 11-0 regular season in Florida State history, and it's the only one I've ever had.

You know, every coach sets out every season to win them all, but every coach also knows how much luck is involved. That year we were good and experienced, and we had a lot of luck.

We finished in the Top Ten in both wire service polls (number six in the AP poll and number eight in UPI) for the first time in school history, and we were picked to play number three Oklahoma in the Orange Bowl. I thought, *We haven't arrived yet, but we're about to crash the party*.

It was our first New Year's Day bowl, and we probably weren't ready for all the stuff that goes on at a major bowl. But we went ahead of Oklahoma 7-0 early in that game, and could have made it even more when Bobby Butler blocked a punt and we took over at the Sooners's 17-yard line. We got to the 2-yard line and then got penalized. And on the fourth down, we botched the snap on a field goal attempt. After that, Oklahoma's wishbone just wore us out, and we lost 24-7. But it might have been different if we had scored after that blocked punt.

That was the game where I agreed to let NBC-TV wire me up with a portable microphone.

That whole game I was worried about what I might say. I remember once, one of our players was chasing down an Oklahoma runner right in front of me and I screamed, "Kill him! Kill him!" And as soon as the words were out of my mouth, I thought, "Lawh, everybody in America just heard me tell one of my players to kill somebody."

I didn't really mean kill him. I meant, "hit him as hard as you can." I meant, "put that runner *on* the ground, not *in* the ground." But I didn't have time to say all that. Most of the time I'm so wrapped up in the game I don't know what I'm saying anyway.

Fortunately, the network announcers were talking at the time and they had me turned off. Somebody "upstairs" was taking care of ol' Bobby again.

NBC asked Oklahoma Coach Barry Switzer to let them put a mike on him. He was smart enough to say no. I wasn't. Those network folks sure wouldn't want us coming into their offices and letting millions of folks hear everything they say. Anyhow, I don't think I'm ever going to agree to do that again because sometimes words slip out in the heat of battle. But the truth is I did enjoy every minute of it.

I know I say it's just a game, and it is. But when it's going on, it's more that. It's a serious game. And if I didn't think so, I'd get out tomorrow.

Surviving Murderer's Row

I remember back when I made up my mind to take the Seminoles' job, I looked at some of the future games on the schedule and almost choked when I saw what we were facing down the road. I thought, *Lawh, somebody must think we're in the National Football League. Oh, well, it won't make any difference. I ain't gonna be here long anyway.*

My plan was to stay at Florida State for four or five years and then move on. I honestly took the job with the idea—or hope—of moving on to the University of Alabama or Auburn University. I was just hoping to do good with the Seminoles so I could get back to Alabama. My target was to be gone before all those tough future games, especially the ones on the schedule in 1981.

And my departure nearly became a reality several times, but it never happened. I've had opportunities to go to other schools, and even had opportunities to go into professional football. I won't name the pro teams, because when I got the feelers from them they phrased them in such a way that they wouldn't be embarrassed if and when I turned them down. I just never said I was interested. As I look back, I'm convinced it worked out for the best.

In 1980, we had consecutive games against Miami, Nebraska, and Pitt, two of which were away. But what I saw on the schedule in 1981 was enough to make any coach say, "There ain't no way. Nobody in his right mind would schedule those teams that way."

What I saw was an unbelievable stretch of five straight away games: at

Nebraska, Ohio State, Notre Dame, Pitt, and LSU. That's right, five on the road, in a row. And those teams we had to play weren't exactly the weak sisters of the poor. That was not only going to be impossible, it was going to be murder—probably mine.

Before I talk about that five away-game stretch, let me say something about big wins. We've won some mighty big games here at Florida State. We've won at Notre Dame, at Miami, at Ohio State, at Michigan, at Florida, at Clemson, at Auburn, at LSU, and you-name-it. But if anybody ever asks me what were the two biggest games we ever won back-to-back, I can tell 'em. It was at Nebraska and at home, against Pitt, in 1980.

We went out to Lincoln and beat those Cornhuskers 18-14 when they were ranked number three in the nation. The next week we outlasted Pitt 36-22 when the Panthers were number two. Both teams had their sights set on winning the national championship.

Nebraska had a tailback named Jarvis Redwine, who was a Heisman Trophy contender. I think we "held" him to 145 yards rushing that day.

And I still believe that Pitt team with Dan Marino at quarterback and Hugh Green at linebacker, and Lord knows who else, was the most talented college team I've seen in my forty years of coaching. Man, they were good.

Our kicking game—with punter Rohn Stark and placekicker Bill Capece—played a big role in that Pitt win. Stark, who was a phenomenal punter, averaged over 48 yards on seven punts, and Capece kicked field goals of 50, 44, 43, 30, and 24 yards. We haven't had kicking like that since.

A lot of folks forget that the week before we played those two, we played at Miami and lost a 10-9 heartbreaker. We scored late in that game and went for two and the win and didn't make it. It was a loss that would keep us from a second straight 11-0 season. I didn't know it then, but it would be the first of a bunch of tough losses to those dad-gum Hurricanes.

That was when we were at our peak, and Miami with Jim Kelly at quarterback was just coming up. We were coming off that 11-1 season in '79 and had won our first three games over LSU, Louisville, and East Carolina. I think we were averaging forty-four points and had allowed only one touchdown.

The problem against East Carolina was we lost both first-team and second-team centers. When our first-teamer went down, we put in John Madden, who married our baby, Ginger, and is now my son-in-law. John went down on the very next play. So now we don't have a center. You ever try playing a game without a center? Well, if you think a quarterback is important, try it without a center.

It's like old baseball manager Casey Stengel said when asked how important a catcher was. He said, "Well, if you ain't got a catcher, you'll have a lot of passed balls."

Well, if you ain't got a center, you'll have a lot of fumbles. And sure enough, when we had to move a guard over to play center, we fumbled ten snaps against Miami. I think they recovered five. And we lost to them by one dad-gum point.

Anyway, we managed to win at Nebraska, and did it without a regular center. We had a little luck in that one. Nebraska had a quarterback named Jeff Quinn—I think that was his name—and he fumbled late in the game, and that fumble kept us from getting beat. When we got back to Tallahassee, I wrote him a letter and told him what a great job he did against us, and not to get discouraged because things like that happen in the game of football. I felt I had to let that boy know that making a mistake isn't the end of the world. I just felt I needed to give him a boost because he might have gotten some criticism over that fumble.

I'm always reminded of the expression that "the player who never fumbled, never played." If you play, every once in a while you're going to fumble. And it always amazes me how mad fans get at some kid for dropping the ball. I wonder if they ever think of how that kid feels?

The thing that really impressed me when we beat Nebraska was the Nebraska fans. After we upset their team and came off the field, I expected them to throw things and cuss us out. To my complete surprise, those fans on the end of the field where we went off stood up and gave us a dad-gum standing ovation.

Now, don't misunderstand, those fans love their Cornhuskers and can probably get pretty mean when they play Big Eight Conference teams. But with us being from Florida, they knew us beating them would have nothing to do with them winning a conference championship. It was almost like they said, "Those Florida boys are visitors. Let's be nice to them." I thought they were the greatest fans in the world. Since then we've played them three more times out there and twice in bowls, and our record against them is 4-2. They've never beaten us in a bowl. Oh, by the way, we've always had to play at Lincoln. They have never played us at our place.

A stronger opponent can't hurt you if he can't catch you. There ain't no substitute for speed.

I still get calls from people in Nebraska. I've had folks come through Tallahassee and call me and say, "We're just passing through on vacation and thought we'd say hello. Saw your game recently on television. Your team looked great." Those fans amaze me.

After we beat that talented Pitt team, we went on to finish the season 10-1-0, and we beat Florida again 17-13 and got another bid to play Oklahoma in the Orange Bowl. Now, this game was maybe the biggest game in my first five years at Florida State. We went into the game ranked number two in the nation behind Georgia. Oklahoma was number four. If Georgia lost its bowl game, we could win the national championship by beating Oklahoma.

We scored with just forty-nine seconds to go in the first half to take a 7-0 lead, but Oklahoma somehow managed to move the ball just past midfield, and they sent in their placekicker to attempt a 53-yarder. The kid got all of it and hit it right down the middle. And we led by only 7-3 at the half. I said to myself, "That dad-gum field goal just might haunt us." And sure enough, it did.

We were still ahead 17-10, but we were playing without Simmons, the key man in our defense. He didn't play at all. Oklahoma drove down and scored with just seconds left on the clock, and went for two points and made it. On that drive, we had them third-and-nine at their 23 and their quarterback, J. C. Watts, completed a 42-yard pass. A few plays later, Watts threw a pass right into the hands of one of our tackles, who dropped it. After both those plays, my first thought was, "Uh-oh, something's gonna happen, and I don't think it's gonna be good for us."

It was a game we had won, but we lost 18-17. We finished number five in both polls. And even if we had won, we wouldn't have won the national championship because Georgia won its bowl game and the title.

And now we had that 1981 schedule staring at us. We had to face what writers down here started calling "murderer's row" (that stretch of five consecutive away games). I sure had hoped to be gone by then, but that season arrived and ol' Bobby Bowden, who never won any prizes for being real smart, was still around. And since I was, I figured we might as well strap it on and see how far our program had progressed.

If we could somehow manage to survive against Nebraska, Ohio State, Notre Dame, Pitt, and LSU, all on the road, I knew we could line up against any dad-gum team in the country.

I don't think any team in the history of modern-day football has ever had to play a stretch like that, certainly not against that caliber of competition. Those teams weren't exactly your sissy teams of college football. You might have to go all the way back to 1900 or 1901 when Sewanee had those great teams. I think they once played something like five games in two weeks. That would be impossible today because of the way the game is played with such high-speed collisions. Players couldn't survive. You would kill them.

Anyhow, we went to Nebraska 2-0 after beating Louisville 17-0 and Memphis State 10-5. Believe me, I was worried, because we struggled against two teams that weren't even in the same league with the teams we were about to face. And we got a sound beating by those Cornhuskers. They ran through our defense like it was a sieve. They gained 472 yards on the ground, which is the most rushing yardage we have ever allowed. Final score was 34-14.

We got a week off to lick our wounds, and then we headed for Columbus, Ohio, where those Buckeyes, ranked number seven nationally, were waiting. We blocked a punt and ran it in for a touchdown, got a 52-yard field goal by kicker Mike Rendina, pulled a trick play—a fake field goal—for another touchdown, and hung on for a 36-27 win. That was despite Ohio State's Art Schlichter throwing for 458 yards against us. I think that's the most ever passed against us too.

We had played two of the "murderer's row" and were 1-1.

But Notre Dame was next. Now, I'll have to say this, those Fighting Irish weren't having one of their better years, but it was still Notre Dame. And believe me, it is worth getting Notre Dame, no matter what kind of team they have, on your schedule. We played them again in 1993 at South Bend (FSU lost 31-24), and then we will play them in 1994 at Orlando.

Someone asked me why we weren't playing the Irish in Tallahassee in 1994. I jokingly said, "Well, Notre Dame wanted to play the game in Rome, but we didn't figure we'd have many fans over there." The fact is they wouldn't come to Tallahassee. And whatever Notre Dame says, that's what you have to do. I know one thing, that game in Orlando is probably going to be the biggest game Florida State has ever played. They won't be able to print up enough tickets for that one.

Anyhow, it was a thrill to go to South Bend that first time and dress in the same dressing room where so many legends of the game have dressed and then walk down that hallway out onto the field. It was just the tradition, the tradition of Knute Rockne, George Gipp, the Four Horsemen, Angelo Bertelli, Johnny Lujack, and on and on. So, from the standpoint of the tradition, it was a big personal thrill for me.

But to be honest, we've played in places that were a lot louder. Notre Dame's crowd is loud, but it's what you would call a coat-and-tie crowd, and I guess the crowd only gets excited according to how the team is doing. And the team wasn't doing very well.

It wasn't anything like walking onto the field at Auburn, or Florida, or LSU, or Miami, or for that matter, at our place. Man, those crowds almost overwhelm you with noise. You feel like your life's in danger. Well, it ain't quite that bad, but that noise can sure cause you to have some daggone crucial penalties, and they'll kill you. A crucial penalty can cause you to lose a game. And we've had some crucial ones called at all those places.

Anyway, we broke a 13-13 tie with a touchdown in the fourth quarter and beat Notre Dame 19-13. We had now won at Ohio State and Notre Dame and lost at Nebraska. I thought, *Dad-gum, maybe we will survive after all.*

Our kids were on an emotional high, but the problem with that was we knew they couldn't sustain it week after week. And the next week we went to Pitt and Dan Marino picked us apart. We got clobbered 42-14.

We bounced back in style, though, at Baton Rouge. We jumped on those Tigers 17-0 early and went on to win 38-14. Freshman tailback Greg Allen rushed for 202 yards, which I think was the highest single game performance by a running back in school history at that time. Allen bettered that a couple of weeks later against Western Carolina with 322 yards rushing, which at that time was an NCAA record for a freshman.

So, we didn't get murdered in "murderer's row." We won three of those five road games.

The problem was, we still had four games left on our schedule, two of which were against rivals Miami and Florida, and a third against always dangerous Southern Mississippi. Southern Miss was even more dangerous because they were unbeaten and ranked number ten. And I was worried about those last three games because before heading into them we had played Western Carolina and gave up thirty-one points. Oh, we won the game, all right, 56-31. But the fact that our defense gave up that many points to a team like that wasn't a good omen.

We promptly lost to Miami 27-19, Southern Miss 58-14, and Florida 35-3. Oh, it was awful.

You could say the FSU program started growing some whiskers in 1979 and 1980, and it started shaving every day in 1981.

We finished 6-5, and I believe it was due mainly to that unbelievable dad-gum scheduling. It's amazing how some athletic directors will schedule games just to make some money. (The ones who schedule them don't have to play 'em.) I still can't believe we played those five away games and won three of them. Imagine, Nebraska, Ohio State, Notre Dame, Pitt, and LSU back to back to back to back to back!

I wouldn't even wish that on those Gators and Hurricanes. (Well, maybe I would. Naw, I take that back. I'd better be nice because we have to play those guys every year.)

Now, we had gone 11-1 and 10-2 and finished in the Top Ten the previous two years, but I don't think folks around the country believed we were for real. I think the "experts" just figured, "Oh, that's just one of those Florida teams. You know, those tanned boys who just romp and play in the sun. They're just flashes in the pan."

After playing that "murderer's row," though, I think we finally got respect and moved into the upper echelon.

The next year we went 9-3. It was kind of disappointing because we went into our last two games 8-1, including a 24-7 win at Miami. The last two games were at LSU and at home against Florida.

We went to LSU and got murdered 55-21, and that loss cost us a bid to the Orange Bowl.

Florida beat us, too, 13-10. So, instead of going 10-1 and getting another Orange Bowl bid, we settled for 8-3 and a Gator Bowl bid. Our opponent was to be my old team—West Virginia.

All the so-called experts picked West Virginia. The Mountaineers were ranked number ten and had a 9-2 record, which included big wins over Oklahoma, Maryland, Boston College, Virginia Tech, and Syracuse. And they had Jeff Hostetler at quarterback. If you recall, Hostetler took the New York Giants to a Super Bowl win a few years ago.

We put in the shotgun formation for this one. It was just something to get our kids excited because they were really down after the way the regular season ended. West Virginia was much stronger than we were, but we had too much speed. A stronger opponent can't hurt you if he can't catch you. They couldn't catch us, and we won 31-12. There ain't no substitute for speed.

After the game I was asked if I had any mixed emotions about playing West Virginia, a place where I had spent ten years of my life. I said, "If you're asking me if I enjoyed it, no, I didn't. I did not get a big thrill out of winning this one. Now, I'm glad we won, but as far as 'we showed y'all,' naw, it wasn't anything like that. I liked it too much at West Virginia."

Three things happened the next year. Two were really wild. The other was weird.

We opened the 1983 season against East Carolina at home. Now, in case you don't know about East Carolina, let me tell you that East Carolina is one of those mighty dangerous teams without a big reputation.

Late in the fourth quarter of that game we had forty-one points on the board. Problem was East Carolina had forty-six. We had to score with just a few minutes to play, and then recover a fumble to keep them from scoring again. We won 47-46. It wasn't one of your classic defensive struggles.

The next week we went to Baton Rouge to play LSU. We promptly got behind 14-0 and then scored thirty-one straight points and managed to get out of there by the skin of our teeth 40-35.

So, in two wild and crazy games we scored eighty-seven points, but our opponents scored eighty-one. You might say I was a little worried about our defense.

In our third game we had to go back to Louisiana, this time to New Orleans to play Tulane in the Superdome. This was the weirdest trip any team of mine ever took. Nothing went right, including the game.

For some reason, we were nationally ranked. I think we were about number nine or ten. Those pollsters must not have been looking at our defense. Anyhow, we were heavy favorites over Tulane. We flew to New Orleans and went out to get on the buses that were supposed to be at the airport to take us to the hotel. They hadn't arrived. We waited a while and then called the bus company to find out where the buses were. They said they sent them, and they didn't have any more available. We finally had to get a couple of city buses to come after us. We must have waited around in that airport for close to two hours.

When we finally got on those city buses and headed downtown on the expressway, there was a big wreck. An eighteen-wheeler (an over-the-road truck) had done a flip-flop and was upside down across the highway. Traffic was backed up for miles. So we sat on those buses for another hour-and-a-half.

I was beginning to get upset. My coaches were getting upset too. And I know our moods rubbed off on the players.

When we finally got to the hotel, something had happened to the hotel computer, and our room assignments were all fouled up. At least that's what they told us. They didn't have any rooms for us, and we had to stand around in the lobby for another hour while they got everything straightened out. I don't think they ever did get it straightened out right, though, because some of our players were assigned to honeymoon suites.

To make matters worse, the dining room they gave us for our team meals was a place where people in the hotel could walk right through while we were eating. We had folks walking into our meeting rooms and everything. People just walked in one door, strolled through the rooms, and walked out another door. It was like Grand Central Station.

Now, I think I'm pretty easy to get along with, but I'll be dad-gum if I hadn't just about run out of that easy-to-get-along-with stuff. The big thing on my mind was, "What happened to the stinking buses?"

What happened was Central Florida was playing some team just out-side New Orleans that same weekend. They had arrived at the airport just a little before we did. And the drivers of the buses sent to pick us up went up to them and said, "Are y'all the team from Florida?"

Naturally, Central Florida said, "Sure are."

And the drivers said, "Well, climb aboard and let's go."

So Central Florida got on *our* buses and was driven to *our* hotel. I think they got all our rooms too. And I'm sure those bus drivers took them to some nice place to eat. I'll bet they didn't eat their meals in a dad-gum three-ring circus like we did.

Anyhow, we didn't go into that Tulane game in the best frame of mind. We were upset over all the stuff that had happened, and we got upset 34-28. I don't know whether all that pregame mess caused us to lose the game, but it sure didn't help.

Oh, yeah, a nice ring given to me by some of our fans turned up missing too. I reckon somebody in New Orleans wanted a nice gold and garnet Florida State ring. If the person wanted it that bad, I might have given it to him if he had asked.

On top of that, Tulane's quarterback was ruled ineligible and the NCAA later said they had to forfeit the win. A forfeit! Those things don't mean a dad-gum thing. I was just glad to get out of there without losing more than a game and a ring.

Our record over the last dozen years is proof positive that we don't have to take a backseat to nobody.

Fortunately, we managed to bounce back and finish 8–3 for the regular season, and then beat North Carolina 28–3 in the Peach Bowl.

I'm not going to go into all the seasons from then on because all that's happened since has been triggered by what happened before. You could say our program started growing some whiskers in 1979 and 1980, and it started shaving every day in 1981. What I hoped to do when I came to Florida State was establish a solid program. I didn't want one that had to be rebuilt every dad-gum year; what I wanted was one we just had to reload. In my opinion, that's where our program was then and is now.

And the fact that we've gone to twelve straight bowls (1982 through 1993) and haven't been beaten in any of them, have finished the last seven seasons (1987 through 1993) ranked in the Top Five (number one in '93), and have joined the Atlantic Coast Conference is proof that we don't have to take a backseat to nobody.

I know folks are saying we ought to go into the ACC and win the thing every year (Florida State did win the ACC championship its first two years in the conference). And when you look at where we've been ranked the last few years, you can see where those folks are coming from. Frankly, we want to win it, but it's not going to be easy like some folks think. Playing Clemson at Clemson isn't easy. Playing at Virginia isn't easy either. And Georgia Tech has its program going pretty well too. We're not going to be shoo-ins.

I'm partial, though, because I think the Seminoles are for real. And that's the dad-gum truth.

Trick Plays

The reputation I seem to have acquired for running trick plays isn't really true, in my opinion. Sure, we use some once in a while, but not all that much. It really isn't smart football. The odds on a trick play working aren't all that good. When you run them and they work, people think you're a genius. But there have been times when they haven't worked. Then folks question your sanity.

It's just that sometimes I do things because I have to. And it's not because I get a kick out of pulling off trick plays either. It's because when our backs are to the wall, I will try anything I can think of to win the game. And you better watch out because we might throw it from our one-yard line, or we might fake something and run something else.

I guess the most famous (or I should say "infamous") trick play we ever ran was the "punt-rooskie" in 1988 against Clemson. We were truly in a dogfight. It was in front of 82,500 screaming Clemson fans and a national television audience. If you're going to run a trick play, you might as well do it—and pray it works—in front of the biggest audience you can get. That's how a reputation is acquired.

The punt-rooskie is my favorite and the one I remember the most because of the way it turned out. I remember it, too, because it was also the dumbest play I've ever called in my entire career. And I've never admitted that to anybody until now.

I say that because there were only about ninety seconds left in the game. The score was tied 21-21, and we had fourth-and-four from our own 21-yard line. What we should have done was punted. What I did was tell our quarterback to "run the punt-rooskie." That's where our punter fakes the punt, and instead he gets the ball to our "up back" and he takes off. Now, it wasn't very smart on my part because if it hadn't worked, Clemson would have taken over deep in our territory and kicked a field goal to win the game.

But it worked.

Our "up back," cornerback LeRoy Butler, got the ball, broke a tackle, and streaked down the sideline seventy-eight yards to the Clemson one-yard line. He would have gone all the way, except he ran out of gas. From there we kicked a field goal to win 24-21.

I looked like a genius, but it was really a stupid call. And I don't know why I did it, except I wanted to win the dad-gum game. I could have settled for a tie and probably should have. But at times I'll try anything to win.

We also picked the right time to run a couple more trick plays. That was in 1991 at Michigan in front of 102,000 fans and another national television audience. We beat those Wolverines 51-31, but in the first quarter it was tied 7-7. That's when quarterback Casey Weldon tossed a lateral to reserve quarterback Charlie Ward, who threw back to Weldon for a 29-yard gain to the Michigan 11. Three plays later, we lined up for a field goal. Instead, the ball went to holder Brad Johnson, who threw a shovel pass to fullback William Floyd for a touchdown.

I guess I now have a reputation for running trick plays. That's all right with me. It keeps our opponents on their toes. The funny thing is, though, every trick play we've ever put in, somebody else has done. It's just that we've had more success and gotten more publicity running them.

I've sure received a lot of credit for things other coaches have come up with. For instance, we had some success with a thing we called a middle-screen pass. But I got that from Notre Dame. I think Notre Dame got it from Penn State. I don't know who Penn State got it from. There aren't any secrets in this game. And it's not so much what you do, it's when you do it.

Folks call me an innovative coach. I would describe myself as an innovative copier. We will play some team and they will run a play that I like. Unfortunately, when I like a play, it usually means our opponent has run it against us with some degree of success. So, I might incorporate it into our offense, or I might change it a little bit and it will become a new gimmick. But what we all do is steal—maybe borrow sounds better—from somebody else. All coaches do it. That's the way it is in this business.

When you run trick plays and they work, you're a genius. But when they don't work, folks question your sanity.

Assistant coaches don't really like trick plays. They always say, "It takes time away from real practice. We don't have time to work on no dad-gum gimmicks." Sometimes I almost have to insist. And when I do, my coaches hate to see me coming. They'll say, "Look out, here he comes with another one of his tricks. We're going to have to waste time on one of his fumble-reverse-lateral passes, or a fake whatta-ya-call-it."

Since I know how they feel about my tricks, I always say, "OK, I know y'all don't want to waste the time, and you don't think it's gonna work. If it doesn't work, somebody is gonna look like mighty stupid. So put my name on it. Then if it doesn't work, everybody will know who the stupid guy is." So, my name always goes on some of the trick plays. My assistants call them "Bowden-rooskies," or "rooskie this" and "rooskie that."

The first time I ever heard the term "rooskie" was from Nebraska. They ran a play they called the "fumble-rooskie" against somebody. I don't know where they got the term "rooskie" from. It was about the trickiest play I ever saw. Their center moved the ball up to the quarterback's hand. Then instead of the quarterback taking the snap, the center brought the ball back down and laid it on the ground between his legs. His legs hid the ball. Then the guard came along, picked it up, and took off running. Technically, the officials called it a fumble. You know, I'm still not sure that's a fumble. I kind of liked that term "rooskie."

I remember the first trick play I ever ran. It was in 1972 at West Virginia when I put in a flanker reverse. We had a wide receiver named Harry Blake, who is still one of the fastest players I ever coached. Now, you have to understand that nobody ran reverses back in those days.

I had my coaches put the play in and we practiced it for a couple of weeks. We ran it and ran it, and it worked pretty daggoned well in practice. The next thing was to get up nerve enough to run the thing in a game. We finally ran it against Stanford at Palo Alto. At least, I think it was

Stanford. Anyway, it was a game we were losing and I wanted to try something to get us some momentum.

I said to my offensive coordinator, Frank Cignetti, who replaced me when I left West Virginia, "Frank, run the reverse." I don't think Frank was too keen about it, but he did what I told him to. We ran the reverse.

I'll never forget it. The dad-gum play lost seventeen yards. Seventeen yards! We also lost the game, 41-35.

It took me about two years before I got up enough nerve to run it again. That was when we had a receiver named Danny Buggs, who went on to play in the NFL and Canada. He was born to run the reverse. I think one year he averaged something like twenty-five yards every time he touched the ball. You know, there are certain players who are just made to run the reverse. They know exactly when to cut and head up field. And there are players who can run like the dickens on ordinary plays, but ain't worth a dime at running the reverse because they make the wrong decision about when to turn it up field.

Danny was one of those runners who could run it. When he got up a head of steam, nobody—and I mean nobody—caught him. He was one of those runners who would just sort of glide over the ground.

On a punt return once in the final minute at Maryland, Danny went about seventy-five yards to break a 13-13 tie and win the game. He fielded the ball, started one way, and got hemmed in. One tackler even had hold of the back of his jersey. Danny reached back and yanked the guy's arm loose, backpedaled to about the 15-yard line, and changed direction. He went clear to the other sideline and headed up field. And when he still had eighty yards to go, I said to myself, *Lawh, he's gonna go all the way.* And he did.

There aren't any secrets in this game; it's not so much *what* you do, it's *when* you do it.

We've had some kids at Florida State who were naturals at running the reverse too, guys like Mike Shumann and Jessie Hester. The first time we ever ran the reverse at Florida State was in 1977 in a game at Virginia Tech. It was a rainy day at Blacksburg and the field was a quagmire. Sometimes those are the best days to run the reverse because people have a hard time changing direction in the mud. And remember, the runner knows where he's going. His opponent doesn't.

We trailed in that game 14-3, but came back to win it 23-21. Shumann ran on the reverse three times, and I think he was our leading ground-gainer that day with something like 100 yards. Also, on one reverse, Shumann, who was lefthanded, threw a 29-yard pass to Roger Overby to set up the winning field goal. Shumann went on to play with the San Francisco '49ers and today has a Super Bowl ring.

It got to the point where we were running that daggone reverse a lot, so much so that it almost became a joke.

Every Monday we have a boosters' luncheon where I eat with our fans, and then I have to get up and explain what happened in Saturday's game. A lot of times I'd just as soon skip lunch. Sometimes hundreds of fans show up, especially when we're winning.

When we have messed up a key drive in a particular game, someone at the luncheon might ask, "Bobby, why didn't you run the reverse?"

Someone else might ask, "Why did you run the reverse?"

And someone else might ask, "What happened on that reverse?"

Like I said, sometimes I'd rather skip that ol' luncheon.

We finally ran the play so much that it wasn't a trick play anymore. To me, the reverse is just a regular play now. It's a play we run now for a purpose—to keep defenses from over-pursuing. Everybody runs the thing now.

We've run some fake field goals too. The one I remember most was in 1982 against Southern Mississippi.

I can't take credit for this trick play. That goes to former assistant George "Duke" Henshaw, who played at West Virginia back when I was offensive coordinator there. George joined my staff when I was head coach at West Virginia and came with me when I came to Tallahassee. He designed and taught the execution of that fake field goal.

Anyhow, we played Southern Miss and it was the year after those guys had humiliated us at home 58-14. In the fourth quarter of this game the score was tied 17-17. We had fourth down at Southern Mississippi's two-yard line. We lined up for a field goal and quarterback Kelly Lowrey was the holder.

The thing was, there was too much time left, and I was sure Southern Miss quarterback Reggie Collier had plenty of time to even the score, or maybe win the game.

So, we told Kelly, "Fake it."

And he took the snap, tucked the ball under his arm, and went up the middle for a touchdown to win it 24-17. After that game, writers asked me about the fake, and I said, "Well, you gotta know when to hold 'em, and know when to fold 'em." Like I said, those statements just pop out of my mouth. I don't know where they come from. It's not that I'm trying to be cute. I'm trying to somehow convey that it's just a dad-gum game; that you gotta have some fun now and then.

Now, we always have one or two gimmicks up our sleeve. I am never going to go into a game without a few tricks. Golly, a coach never knows when he might want to break the monotony. Honestly, though, it depends on how the game goes as to whether or not we use them. We might go four or five games sometimes without ever running a trick play.

I run into people from all over the country and they say, "We love your brand of football. Your offense is so wide open. We love it."

Now, I don't know what our brand of football is. I think those folks think we throw the ball on every play. We don't do that. Sure, we'll throw it, but really what we do—most of the time—is take what the other team's defense gives us. That's what we base our offense on. We might play a whole game and not throw the ball much at all. If we play a team that's going to play pass coverage all day, then we might run it all day.

It's just a dad-gum game; you gotta have some fun now and then.

In 1991, when we were number one all those weeks, we ran the ball 507 times and threw it 390 times. And in 1992 we ran it 464 times and threw it 387 times. I wouldn't exactly call that an offense that's wide open. What we try to do is keep our offense balanced. We're not a run–and–shoot team. We're not nearly as wide open as most people think.

People talk about the tricks and the passing because for about ten years we've had teams that have scored a lot of points. We've averaged nearly five touchdowns a game. But we've also had a defense that allowed opponents less than eighteen points over the same span. And remember, we've played some pretty darned good teams.

Basically, when we play a great team we have to try and stop that team from doing what it wants to do. And that's what we stress, because I firmly believe if we're going to win and win consistently, we have to do it with defense. And I include the kicking game when I talk about defense.

We can't just swap touchdowns with a tough opponent. The other guy just might have more guns. If we're going to win, there reaches a point in every game where our defense has to stop the other guy and get the ball for our offense. The defense has to make a big play. We've won a lot of games with defense. Defense is more consistent because it's physical. Offense is inconsistent because it is timing and execution.

In 1991, we had an offense that averaged more than five touchdowns a game, but when we got in our really tough games against Miami, Florida, and Texas A&M, they all ended up defensive struggles. In those games, both teams averaged less than two touchdowns. The game of football boils down to defense. It always has.

The National Championship— Finally!

A lot of folks equate winning and losing with success and failure. They think that if you win, you succeed and if you lose, you fail. When we played Nebraska in the Orange Bowl on January 1, 1994 for the national championship, some writer for a Miami newspaper inferred in an article that if my team didn't win this game and win the national championship, then I would never go down in history as a great coach (whatever a great coach is).

It was like my whole career was wrapped up in this one game and if I didn't win it, I would always be a failure. Can you believe that?

Well, then I guess that guy would figure I'm a great coach because we won, 18-16—and got our first national title—when Nebraska missed a last-second 45-yard field goal try.

I kind of chuckle at that because, truthfully, I believe I did one of the poorest jobs of coaching in my entire career. It certainly wasn't one of my better performances. I don't feel like I'm a great coach—if I am one—just because we won that darned game. It was just one football game. In this business there's always another game to play later on.

What about Nebraska coach Tom Osborne? Is he a failure just because his field goal kicker missed that field goal? The truth is, Osborne did a better job of coaching than I did and probably deserved to win the game. I really felt sorry for him because he is such a great Christian man and such a great coach. He deserves a national title too.

I guess it was just Florida State's time. I think it was just meant to be.

Now don't get me wrong; I'm mighty happy to have finally won that championship because it was important to me. But I have to repeat, I was never obsessed with getting that national title. I don't think people ever understood that. I mean, those writers and broadcasters kept asking me, "Coach, ain't it driving you crazy because you've been so close to winning it all, but never have?"

It wasn't. What was driving me crazy was people continually asking me about it. What was bothering me was those labels those writers and broadcasters kept sticking on me—the labels like "Bowden couldn't win the big one" or "Bowden couldn't do it under pressure."

I mean, doesn't the fact that we've won an NCAA record nine bowl games in nine years mean something? Doesn't the fact that we've gone 11-1, 11-1, 10-2, 10-2, 11-2, 11-1, and 12-1 in seven consecutive seasons mean something? It does to me. It means we've been pretty daggoned good and pretty daggoned consistent at being good.

One day at a press conference in Miami prior to our game with Nebraska I said to the writers, "Men, just let me ask you something. What is the highest honor in y'all's profession?" Somebody threw out the names of a couple of awards. I forget what they were. Maybe one of them was the Pulitzer Prize.

Anyhow, I said, "How many of you have ever won one of those awards?" I didn't see any hands go up.

Then I added, "Well, is the fact that you've never won driving you crazy? Does the fact that you've never won mean you're no good at your profession? Are y'all failures? Are you obsessed with winning one of those awards? I'll bet you don't give a darn whether you ever win one of them or not. Now, if you win one, good. But I'll bet it ain't driving you crazy. That's about the way it always was with me about winning a national championship: it was not driving me crazy."

Then one of the writers said, "Yeah, but we haven't been in the runoffs every year like you have."

Well, we have been close a few times. We were predicted to win it a couple of times and didn't get it done. But if things had gone right, we could have won national titles in 1979 and 1980. And we really could have won it all in 1987, 1988, 1989, 1991, and 1992. I guess you call that being "close but no cigar."

In those five seasons, Miami figured in knocking us out of a chance at the title four times. Two of those losses were by a single point, and another was by three points. So, we've lost at least three national titles by a grand total of five points.

Folks would ask, "Bobby, aren't you just devastated because you've never won a national championship?"

When you get in a national championship game, the pressure is unbelievable. If all of us coaches had that much pressure every week for every game, we'd all be dead.

I would say, "Naw, I'm not devastated. I am disappointed because I'm a competitor. Sure, I want one. I want one bad, but I ain't gonna cut my wrists just because we've never won a national championship. I'd much rather have a program that goes 11-1, 10-2, 10-2, and maybe 9-3 every year, than I would have one that goes 12-0 and wins it all one year, and then goes 5-6, 6-5, and 7-4 after that. I'd much rather be consistent because when you're consistent you win a lot more than you lose."

I will say this, when you get in a national championship game, the pressure is unbelievable. We couldn't play under that kind of pressure if we had it every game. If all of us coaches had that much pressure every week we'd all be dead.

Look at what happened in that Orange Bowl game. We did not play well offensively in the first half. Charlie Ward, our quarterback who won the Heisman Trophy, was exhausted. I can see why Heisman winners have trouble playing in bowls after winning the trophy. There are so many distractions, so many demands on their time during the weeks leading up to the bowl game.

Anyway, late in the fourth quarter we led 15-13. Then Nebraska kicked a 27-yard field goal to go ahead 16-15. There was 1:16 to play. We took the kickoff and marched sixty yards and (freshman kicker) Scott (Bentley) kicked a 22-yard field goal to retake the lead 18-16 with twenty-one seconds left. I thought that was the game.

The problem was our players ran onto the field to celebrate. I think some of them were the walk-ons we had brought with us. They knew they weren't going to get in the game. I reckon they thought they could get their pictures on television, I don't know. Anyhow, I was angry—and had to ask for a little forgiveness after that—because I knew we'd be penalized fifteen yards on the ensuing kickoff. And with twenty-one seconds to play,

Nebraska still had time to get the ball back in field goal range. Why they won't let kids celebrate, especially when they think they've won a national championship, I don't know. But that's the rule.

I know I was chewing on my gum like mad. Yeah, I know that doesn't look good on television. I probably shouldn't do that, but I forget about it. What I was really doing was hoping our defense would stop Nebraska. Then I was hoping Nebraska would fumble or throw an interception. I was saying to myself, *Please, Nebraska, turn the ball over.*

What happened was they completed a pass down inside our 30-yard line. I mean, those Nebraska boys never gave up. But I looked at the clock and it read, "Two seconds!" Then, "One second!" Then, "No seconds!"

I thought, "We've got it."

About that time I got hit with a big bucket of ice water. My victory drenching. Talk about cold! It was freezing. That cold went right through my body. I was pushing forward through the crowd to the other sideline to get to Coach Osborne.

I couldn't find him, but one of the game officials found me. He said, "Coach, we have to put one second back on the clock."

I said, "Why? Ain't the game over?"

The official said, "No, they called a timeout."

So, there I stood dripping wet and cold from that victory drenching and I found out the game wasn't over. Nebraska was going to get one more play. I went back to our sideline and my main concern was where the officials were going to spot the ball. I saw they had spotted it on our 34. So, I thought, *Well, that's 34 yards, plus 10 yards for the end zone, plus 7 yards more on the hold of the ball. That's 51 yards. Their kicker can't kick it that far.*

Considering that the Lord might not have allowed my winning the national title for many years, I thought, *I can accept that.* But I felt like adding, *Lord, if it's not in your plan, then why do you keep letting me get so dad-gum close?*

Then the officials said, "Coach, we're not sure where the ball is supposed to be. We're going to have to check with the press box."

After checking the video replay, they decided the ball had to be moved up to our 28-yard line. I thought, *That's 28, plus 10, plus seven, which adds up to 45 yards. Lawh, their kicker just might make that one.*

And my next thought was, *Bowden, you've had a victory drenching and the whole nine yards and that championship still ain't gonna be yours. You and your team are gonna be "almost champions" again.* I honestly thought their kicker would make it. I was hoping he wouldn't in my mind, but I had a terrible sinking feeling in my heart.

And then their kicker hooked it to the left. I knew for sure it missed when I heard the reaction from our fans.

So I got to celebrate again. I might be the first coach to ever get to celebrate winning his first national championship twice.

After the game, the writers asked me, "Are you going to retire now that you've finally won that championship?"

My answer was, "Retire? Heck, no. Now that I've got one, I want two. Next season I want you writers saying, 'Did you know that Bobby Bowden is the oldest football coach who ain't never won two national championships?' "

I was also asked if I favored a national playoff to determine a national champion. Remember, the way the Division 1-A champion is picked now is by the vote of the polls. In that respect I guess you could call it a "mythical" title. But it's still a title we all fight for.

I answered, "I have never wanted a playoff. I've always felt the bowl games were the playoffs. If we had a playoff with the top four teams, then a good number five team would be left out. If we had a playoff with the top eight teams, then a good number nine team would be left out.

"Now, I do think we will have a playoff one of these days. Everything seems to be heading in that direction. I just don't know how they are going to come up with a system that will satisfy everybody.

"I'm just not in favor of extending the season. It's long enough already. I would have hated to see us try to get our kids ready to play another game after that Orange Bowl game. They were emotionally drained, and so were the coaches."

Prior to winning it all in 1993, I will admit I used to think it wasn't in God's plan for me to win a national championship. Considering that, I would think, *I can accept that.* But I also felt like adding, *Lord, if it's not in your plan, then why do you keep letting me get so dad-gum close?*

The plain truth was I was not going to sell my soul to win a national championship. I am not selling my soul for anything—not for a game, not for making money, not for the temporary pleasure of immorality. Bobby Bowden ain't selling his soul for nothin'.

Jesus says in Matthew 16:26, "For what profit is it to a man if he gains the whole world, and loses his own soul? Or what will a man give in exchange for his soul?" So, I ain't selling my soul. No way.

You know, there are some folks who actually hate other folks over football. I'm always amazed that there is so much hate in the world. Some fans are just awful. They act like they actually hate the other team. They take it too seriously. It's just a stinkin' game.

Don't misunderstand, football is a priority in my life, but you'll hear me say more than once that it isn't *the* priority. If I made football my top priority I'd go crazy because there's no way I could win 'em all. It just don't work out that way.

I know some folks think there are times when I put football first. I reckon there are times when I do, but I try hard not to. It's just that I'm human and make mistakes. I'm just a man doing the best he can to be a good Christian, but I'm a man with the same fears, doubts, hopes, aspirations, and expectations everybody else has.

The plain truth is, I am not going to sell my soul to win a national championship. Bobby Bowden ain't selling his soul for nothin'.

Probably the biggest hurt was in 1987 when we finished 11-1, and that one loss was to Miami 26-25. That was a game where we blew a 19-3 lead in the fourth quarter. I still think about that one.

We played Nebraska in the Fiesta Bowl and won, 31-28, but that Miami loss did us in. Miami won the national championship. If we had beaten them, we would have won it. All we needed that year was two more points. So, we finished number two. We had an offense that year that scored 481 points, the second highest scoring offense we had ever had, and we came up two dad-gum points short of winning it all. There is no doubt about it, that loss to Miami hurt.

In 1988 we were picked to win it all. Unfortunately, we played at Miami in our opener and got trounced 31-0. We just didn't have our team ready. Maybe all of us were reading those press clippings. Every once in a while I wish they would do away with those polls. How in the world can anybody know which team is the best when nobody has even played a game yet? Those folks must be a whole lot smarter than I am, and I think I do know something about football.

Every year I can look at our schedule and say, "Well, these six games here we ought to win. Now, these two we can't win. And these three here might go either way." Those "either way" games are the ones that decide how successful your season is.

Winning the close games is the key. I think we've won more close games than we've lost. Now, you're not going to win all those close ones because when you are in a close game, that usually means the other team is about as good as you are. If they get a break, or a bounce of the ball, or a crucial call, they win.

Every year we set out with the intention of winning them all, but the other guy sets out with the same goal. He's not going to lay down and let you beat him. And he probably thinks he's pretty good too. Now, can you tell me how some members of the media can figure out who's number one, or number ten, before the whole thing starts?

Anyway, after Miami skunked us, we didn't lose another game. And we beat Auburn in the Sugar Bowl 13-7. So we were 11-1 again. Notre Dame won it all that year by beating West Virginia in the Fiesta Bowl. Miami finished number two, and we finished number three. Close again.

In 1989, we opened the season in Jacksonville (in the Gator Bowl) against Southern Mississippi and got upset 30-26. We shouldn't have lost that one. In our second game we got beat by Clemson 34-23. So now we were 0-2. However, we won the rest of our games, including a 24-10 win over pesky Miami, and beat Nebraska in the Fiesta Bowl again 41-17 for a 10-2 record. But Miami won the national championship and we finished number two in one poll and number three in the other. Those two losses at the start of the year were our undoing. Close again.

In 1991, we were picked in the preseason to win it all again. We were coming off another 10-2 year. We stayed number one for eleven weeks, and then Miami came to Tallahassee. We were number one and they were number two. That was a big, big game, no doubt about it.

We led most of the game and had a 16-7 lead with about 14 minutes to play. But Miami scored ten points to go ahead 17-16. We got the ball back with three minutes to play and marched to Miami's 17 where it was third down. There were only twenty-five seconds remaining and we couldn't afford to gamble on running another play. So we tried a 34-yard field goal. Gerry Thomas's boot looked good from my angle, so good in fact that I turned around to make sure none of our players rushed onto the field to celebrate. I didn't want us to get a penalty because we still had to kick off. My thought was, "Don't give Miami a chance to come back in those twenty-five seconds to beat us."

But the field goal wasn't good. It missed by about six daggone inches. And we lost another one-pointer to those dad-gum Hurricanes.

I got some criticism after that game because some fans thought we wasted a timeout on that last drive. Writers even asked, "Bobby, did you waste a timeout?"

I said, "Naw, we didn't waste one. We had to call a timeout or get penalized. I don't call that wasting one."

What happened was we had a third down and about six yards to go. We ran a play and made six, or at least I thought we made six. Our runner was knocked out of bounds on our sideline right at my feet. So, I figured, "He's out of bounds. The clock is stopped." I turned away to try and figure out what play to run next. Also, I figured we had the first down.

Suddenly, I heard my quarterback yelling, "Coach! The clock's running. Give us a play! Give us a play!"

I looked out and yelled at the official, "Did we make the first down, or didn't we? Is it a first down? What is it?"

The official said, "It's third down, coach."

I yelled, "Why is the clock running?"

He yelled back, "Your runner was down before he went out of bounds."

I said, "You gonna measure it?"

The ref replied, "Nope. It's not close. He didn't make it."

So, we didn't get the first down; the clock wasn't stopped. And I ain't got no play called because I was yelling at the official. We had to call a timeout to find out what the heck was going on and to decide what we were going to do. It was a mess.

Some folks think it's easy down there on the sideline. Well, it's not. Coaches get excited. I'll admit I do. Sometimes I get so excited I don't know what I'm saying. And remember, we don't have all day to make a decision.

I've been a hero before, and I've been a goat before. I have to admit, I like hero a lot better.

If we had made that field goal, we would have all been heroes. Instead, we were goats. That's the way this game goes. I've been a goat before, and I've been a hero before. I have to admit I like hero a lot better.

After that game, our players were heartsick, and we had to go play Florida at Gainesville next. There was no way we could get our team back up after that Miami loss. That one just took the wind out of their sails. So, we went to Gainesville and lost to the Gators 14-9. But we had a chance to win it because with two minutes to play we had four downs from the 11-yard line and had a fourth-down pass batted down in the end zone.

We got a bid to the Cotton Bowl and beat Texas A&M 10-2 to finish 11-2. To be honest, I don't know how we beat those Aggies.

I will always believe that if we had beaten Miami we would have found a way to beat Florida and would have won the national title. But there was no way we could get our kids fired up again after the Miami loss. They were spent emotionally and physically. They were a bunch of sorry-eyed kids. Golly, the next morning you would have thought everybody in town had lost their dad-gum mommas. It was that bad.

So, we finished number five in the polls and Miami was number one (co-champion with Washington). Close again.

In 1992 we beat Nebraska 24-7 in the Orange Bowl to finish number two in the polls with an 11-1 record. Yes, and that one loss was to those dad-gum Hurricanes (19-16). We missed another field goal by about six inches at the end that would have tied it.

Miami won four national titles in nine years (from 1983 to 1991). This may not make sense, but I honestly think by us getting so close we proved to others it could be done. I think we showed Miami how to do it.

We were the first Florida team to get hot and gain national prominence. Then Miami got hot when Howard Schnellenberger became the coach there. He said many times he copied his program after ours. I think he saw what we were doing and thought, *If Florida State can do it, we can do it.* And Miami did it. Miami was the team of the 1980s. But if Miami hadn't beaten us all those close games, we would have been the team of the eighties.

Since the final game of the 1986 season when we beat Indiana in the All-American Bowl, we have won 76 and lost 10. Six of those losses were by a total of just twenty-one points, and five of them were to Miami. I think Miami is the only team to have a better record over the same span. And I think if I'd been a better coach we would have been about 82-4, instead of 76-10. I reckon I'm the reason we didn't do better.

We've had some bloody battles with Miami, and I've got to add those Gators in there too. We're all Florida teams made up mostly of Florida boys. So, in that respect we're kind of all brothers. Unfortunately, some of the bloodiest battles in the history of the world have been when brother fought against brother.

We've been so close so many times, and I will admit I did get caught up in the national championship hype in '91. We were number one in the polls week after week after week. Nobody would let us forget it. Everywhere we went our fans would say, "We're gonna win it all, aren't we? Man, ain't it great to be number one, Bobby?" And it was.

But I found myself sweating like crazy on the sideline. My face would get flushed. Only the Lord knows what it did to my blood pressure. I didn't like that and didn't think it would happen to me. I tried not to let that happen in 1993, but I'm not sure how good a job I did. You're human and you just get caught up in it.

I've finally figured out that you cannot set out to win a national championship. And you can't roll and kick and moan and scream over losing a particular game. You can't say, "Well, we lost that one and there goes the championship." If you think that way, you're never going to win one. A national championship just has to happen. And it happens when you least expect it.

What you do is set out to win each game as it comes, and when you win that one, you go on to the next one. If you're lucky enough to do that and do it week after week, then you've got your national championship.

So, long before we won it all, we had lost our share of heart-breakers, and we had lost out on national championships. I know I've seemed to dwell on this national championship stuff, probably too long for something that I've said I wasn't obsessed with. However, I honestly felt Florida State would eventually win a national title. I was just afraid it might not happen while Bobby Bowden was still the FSU coach. But like I said earlier, that was not my goal in life.

There has to be more to life—and a career—than one dad-gum championship.

A retired writer friend was asked once if he missed football. He answered, "Yes, but I've found out there *is* life after football." I reckon one of these days I'll have to find that out, but now I won't have to do it without that national title. I can go to my grave and folks won't have to say, "Poor Bobby, he never won the big one.

The
Death
Threat

You've heard me say that there are some fans who actually hate others over football. Well, let me tell you about the time someone had so much hate that he—and I assume it was a he—actually made a threat against me. At the time I didn't worry too much about it, but folks around me did. They interpreted it as a valid threat against my life. I didn't think about it all that much because I just couldn't make myself believe that anyone would get that crazy over a game.

In 1990—it was early November—we played a game at South Carolina and won 41-10 to run our record to 6-2. That season we finished 9-2, and then beat Penn State 24-17 in the Blockbuster Bowl. After that South Carolina game I did my post-game radio show, showered, dressed, and answered all the sportswriters' questions. Then I started toward the locker room door to head up the ramp to the team buses where Ann, the players, and all their families were waiting. They always hang around the buses until time to board.

As the door opened, I looked out and saw state troopers and policemen lined up everywhere. Man, it looked like a gauntlet. I said to myself, *What in the world are all those cops here for? There must be somebody really important at the game today.*

Then it dawned on me. I said to myself, *Lawdy, they're here to protect me! I'll be dad-gum!*

It hit me that earlier in the week, Billy Smith, our security chief, had told me that someone had written a letter threatening to kill me. Billy is sixty-one years young and has been our team security chief since 1964. He retired from the Florida Highway Patrol in 1985 and helps out as assistant director of the Florida Fire Marshall's office. He's an active Baptist like me. You'll see him occasionally on TV, standing near me during every game and escorting me off the field.

The reason Billy knew about the letter, and I didn't, was because Sue Hall, my secretary, always opens all my mail. If there's anything bad in it, she doesn't bother me with it. Apparently, she found this death threat and called Billy immediately.

When Billy told me about it, I didn't take it seriously. I just figured it was a joke, a bad joke, but a joke nevertheless. But when I saw all those police lined up out there, I remembered about the letter. I had been so wrapped up in the game that I had forgotten all about it.

Billy was the one who really took it seriously. Me? I had a game to worry about. If someone wanted to take a shot at me, there wasn't much I could do about it. But I still couldn't believe it, still can't to this day. I'll let Billy tell you, in his own words:

"I've been standing on the sideline to protect Florida State head coaches ever since Bobby was an assistant here in the mid-1960s under Bill Peterson. I've known Bobby a long time.

"I remember that death threat very well. Bobby's secretary called me the week of the South Carolina game and said she wanted to see me. When I went to her office, she said, 'Billy, I've got something here you should look at.' She handed me the letter. It was from someone in Pennsylvania.

"Apparently, this nut had lost a lot of money betting on our game two weeks earlier at Auburn. We lost 20-17, and he blamed the loss on Coach Bowden. The letter said, 'You called a stupid play at the end of your game with Auburn, and that play cost me plenty. I'm going to take care of you at your next game.'

"By the time we got the letter, we had already played LSU and won 42-3. So the next game was South Carolina. I didn't know whether the words 'next game' meant the LSU game, or the one coming up. However, the words 'take care of you' meant only one thing to me. I wasn't about to take that lightly. I had been in law enforcement too long to do that. I know what kind of crazies there are out there.

"So, I went to Coach Bowden and said, 'Tell me what you want me to do, Bobby. There's no way you can hide on the sideline, and there's no way I, or anybody else, can give you total protection. The presidents of the

United States have the best protection in the world and some of them have been shot. If some nut wants to shoot you, he can do it.'

"Bobby agreed to let me take care of the security part of it. I told him, 'Coach, you take care of the coaching, and I'll take care of the rest.' I also told him not to say anything about it to anyone. He said, 'OK, Billy, fine.' I think he just plain dismissed it from his mind after that.

"I got in touch with the South Carolina law enforcement people, and the night of the game we had that stadium sealed about as tight as you could have a stadium sealed. We had troopers, local police, security people, and undercover and plainclothes police all over that stadium. We must have had about 140 law enforcement officers involved in this.

"I wasn't concerned until right near the end of the game when one of the CBS-TV people came up to me and asked, 'What's going on?'

"I said, 'What are you talking about?'

"He said, 'We heard a rumor that someone was going to try to kill Coach Bowden tonight. Is that true?'

"I denied it, for security purposes; if that got out over the air waves we'd have more kooks coming up with crazy ideas. I still wonder how those network people got wind of it.

"When the game was over and Coach Bowden was ready to leave the dressing room, I had a patrol car backed right up to the door. And when he started to walk up toward the buses like he always does, I said to him, 'Oh, no, not this time, Bobby. You stay right here. We're going to put you in this patrol car.' And we put him in the car and drove out, past two lines of about 100 police officers. It worked fine. Nothing happened.

"Now, there probably wasn't anything to it. Maybe it was just a crank, but we couldn't afford the luxury of letting a thing like that slide.

"Afterward, Bobby never said a word about it. You would have thought it was just a normal game. But the newspapers heard about it somehow, and the following Tuesday they made a big deal of it.

"People asked me, 'Who would want to shoot a good man like Bobby Bowden?'

"I said, 'Hey, they shot the pope, didn't they? There are people out there who will shoot anybody for any reason.'

"I've been asked many times what kind of man Bobby is. It's hard to say that he is any one thing, because he is so many things. But, in my opinion, he is a very compassionate man, a father-type figure. He's the type of guy who makes every person at every level feel important. The traits about him I admire most are that he's straightforward and honest, and he's not on an ego trip. He always has time for people. I don't know how he does it.

"He's in his sixties now, and when you get that age, most folks' energy level isn't what it used to be, but he never seems to slow down. He goes and goes. He speaks to all kinds of groups, and he preaches most Sundays in a pulpit somewhere. He does not charge money to speak to church groups, or military groups, or police agencies. He's such a great, giving man.

"And the funny part about him is that he'd rather be in a room by himself looking at film or in his study at home reading a book on military history. He is a very private person. I don't think he's really comfortable in crowds. You'd never know it though. When he's in a crowd and saying, 'Hi, there, buddy,' you'd think he was just the opposite.

"Now, he's not bashful or modest. Those aren't his strong suits. During games, he's totally absorbed in what's going on out on the field.

"I remember an amusing story about him, and it concerns him being absorbed in the game and what he said to Brad Scott, who was then one of his graduate assistants. It was in 1985, and we were playing at Nebraska. It was a pretty important game for the Florida State program. We won, 17-13.

"We were ahead by those four points with about a minute to go and had the ball with a first down. Nebraska was out of time-outs. So, it was one of those situations where all you had to do was snap the ball, have the quarterback go down on one knee, and the clock would run out.

"You have to understand that graduate assistants aren't very high on the totem pole, and this was a big game. Coach Bowden was more than a little excited.

"I don't stand near him during games. But, since it was near the end, I had moved over beside him because you never know what someone might do. There might be some nut who would come out on the field. Coach Bowden was on one side of me and Brad was on the other.

"Brad turned to Bobby and yelled, 'Coach, we don't have to pitch the ball out or risk a fumble; all we have to do is fall on it and let the clock run out. They're out of timeouts.'

"Bobby hollered back, 'Brad, are you sure they ain't got any more timeouts left?'

"Brad replied, 'Yes, sir.'

"Bobby repeated his question a little stronger, 'Brad, are you darn sure?'

I love my players, and I love this game.

That's me in the middle of the front row, on the Howard College track team.

Ryals Lee

We beat Joe Paterno's Penn State team in the 1990 Blockbuster Bowl 20–14; he's one heckuva great coach.

Phil Coale—*Tallahassee Democrat*

This was my sixtieth birthday party back in 1989. I had a good time, but Lord, where did all those years go?

Ryals Lee

"No, I don't think we were tryin' to run up the score; we were just playin hard . . ."

Ryals Lee

Phil Coale—*Tallahassee Democrat*

LEFT: We were lucky enough to get Billy Graham to speak to our players. I'm convinced that a relationship with God is the key to maximum athletic performance. RIGHT: Sometimes the players just don't cut it in practice and I have to give them the look.

LEFT: Man, I love the excitement and adventure of game day. RIGHT: I enjoy spending time with our fans when I can; they make the stadium come alive on game day.

LEFT: I reckon I've spent most of my time being someone else's daddy. Here I've got Jonathon Richt, one of my assistant's son. RIGHT: I try my best to always be available to the news media; hey, those guys got a job to do too.

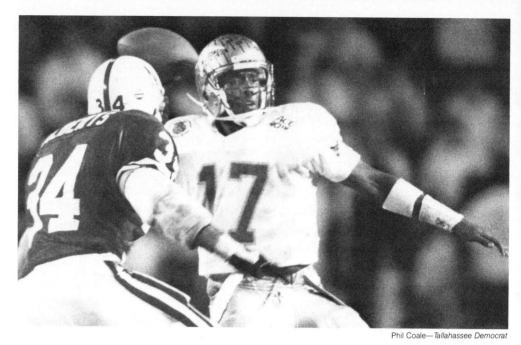

A Nebraska linebacker arrives too late as our Heisman Trophy-winning quarterback Charlie Ward throws a pass in the 1994 Orange Bowl win.

My ice-water dousing (one second too early) as we celebrate our National Championship win over Nebraska.

One of the longest moments of my life . . . the referee tells me that there's one second put back on the clock after we thought time expired.

It was quite an honor for my wife, Ann, and I along with the 1994 NCAA Championship Team to be invited to the White House.

Ross Obley

Ex-Seminole football player Burt Reynolds and I have a laugh on the sidelines.

"Brad said, 'Yes, sir, Coach.'

"Bobby repeated it again, a little stronger this time, 'Are you really for certain sure? Do you know what you're talking about?'

"Brad answered again, 'Yes, sir, Coach. I'm positive.'

"And, Bobby said, 'Well, I'll tell you what I'm gonna do. We're gonna fall on it. But if you're wrong and we lose this dad-gum game, I'm gonna take Billy Smith's .357-Magnum out and shoot you.'

"Afterward, Brad said to me, 'Billy, please, don't ever come to the stadium with that pistol loaded.' Now of course Bobby wasn't serious. Brad still laughs about that incident.

"Bobby might say some things at times in the heat of battle. He doesn't do it 100 percent the way he should all the time. Nobody has, and nobody ever will. But Bobby comes close. They don't make 'em any finer than Bobby Bowden.

"I know he isn't going to coach forever, but I'm thankful I was still around and standing beside him on the sideline when he finally won that national championship."

Dealing with the Media

I f I've learned anything from a lifetime of coaching, I've learned not to show my feelings to the news media, or to take out a defeat on the media. I've always tried to be courteous and respectful to the press.

I remember back in 1988 when all the so-called experts picked us number one in the preseason polls. I couldn't argue too much with that. I thought we'd be pretty daggone good too. But being a preseason number one was like painting a dad-gum big ol' bull's-eye on the backs of our jerseys. When you're number one, folks can't wait to get a shot at you. And all we had to do then was open the season against Miami at Miami, and it was going to be on national television.

Boy, did we ever stink up the place that night. I don't think we could have played any worse if we had tried. We trailed Miami 17–0 at the half, and they got fourteen more in the second half. Oh, it was awful.

Anyhow, like I said, we were trailing 17–0 at halftime. We hadn't even come close to scoring. We never did, the whole game. And as I came back onto the field for the second half, a television commentator stuck his microphone in my face and asked me that great original question, "What did you tell your team at the half, Coach?"

Now, I suppose I could have brushed on past him and refused to answer, but I couldn't do that. I can't be rude to folks. That's not my way. So I just said, "What did I tell 'em? I told 'em if they didn't start playing, we're in a heap o' trouble."

I always try to be friendly, quotable, and accessible. And I am never
going to storm out of a press conference like some coaches do.

Hey, that was as honest as I could be. We *were* in trouble.

I think I do have a certain rapport with the news media. At least, I've
tried to cultivate a good relationship with them. I know I make a lot of
"off the record" statements to sportswriters. I don't make a big deal of it. I
just say, "I'd appreciate it if y'all would keep this off the record. I don't
want to see so-and-so's name in the newspaper. It might hurt him. And I
know it would hurt his momma and daddy."

Most of the time those writers honor my "off the record" requests. I
just try to be fair with them. And maybe I'm naive, but I expect the same
treatment from them. I haven't been disappointed too many times. A lot of
writers are good friends.

I remember one time when I told a writer something "off the record," and he went ahead and wrote the story. It didn't make me mad,
because the writer was honest and up front with me. It was 1975, my last
year as coach at West Virginia. We were in Atlanta to play North Carolina
State in the Peach Bowl. The night before the game I was sitting outside
an elevator in the Hyatt Regency Hotel talking to the writer. We were
good friends.

I reckon he could tell I had something troubling me because he said,
"Bobby, do you have something other than tomorrow's game on your
mind?"

I said, "Naw, not really."

He said, "Well, you don't seem yourself. Something is going on.
You're not thinking of taking another job, are you?"

That was when I had been contacted by some influential folks about
the Florida State job. And to be honest, it *was* on my mind. I never could
lie to folks. So, instead of denying it or evading the question, I said, "How
did you know?"

He said, "I didn't. I was just fishing."

I laughed and said, "Pretty dad-gum good fishing."

And I told him the whole story about what was going on with
Florida State. I added, "Now, this is all off the record."

I'll never forget what he said next. He said, "Bobby, I can't sit on
this. I've got a job to do. I have to write this story."

I understood that. So all I said was, "OK, but do me a favor and write the story in such a way that nobody will know you got it from me." And he did. That writer and I are friends to this day. There's no sense getting bent out of shape when a person is honest and up-front about his intentions.

I hate coach–writer confrontations. I remember a writer told me once what former big league baseball manager Joe Altobelli said about writers. He said something to the effect that "if a writer writes seven good stories about you, he ought to have a free shot coming."

The guys in the media have jobs to do; I've always understood that.
They're trying to earn a living, just like me.

Now, I don't necessarily agree with that, but I think I understood what Altobelli was trying to say. What he was saying was that coaches get hundreds of positive stories written about their programs, and then they get angry when one writer writes one so-called negative story. They've forgotten about all those good stories. You have to take the bad with the good. And you have to be honest with yourself because sometimes you deserve the dad-gum criticism you read in the papers.

I always try to be friendly, quotable, and accessible. And I am never going to storm out of a press conference like some coaches do. If I ever have to leave a press conference early, it's usually because I have something important to do or have another engagement. But I always tell the press, "If y'all need anything else, drop by my office later, and I'll be available."

When we lose a game, there's no sense in me going into an interview room with an angry look on my face and jumping all over the media. Those guys didn't have a dad-gum thing to do with the outcome of the game. Usually, the guy who lost the game is the one standing up there with the microphones, cameras, and tape recorders stuck in his face. When we lose, it's because we out-slopped the other team.

The guys in the media have jobs to do; I've always understood that. They're trying to earn a living, just like me. They just want to report what went on for their readers, many of whom also happen to be our alumni and fans. I try not to wear my feelings on my shoulders even when I'm hurting. And believe me, it hurts and hurts bad when we lose.

However, I honestly think it soothes me to get up in front of the press and explain a defeat. It helps me when I talk about the loss and what we should have done and didn't, or what we shouldn't have done and did. I'm certainly not going to blame the news media. I've never understood coaches who do that.

Those coaches will say, "Y'all wrote such-and-such an article and that cost us the game. I ain't answering your questions." And then those coaches will storm out of the press conference like spoiled babies.

Lawdy, those coaches had their players all week in practice and preparation. They studied films. They had staff meetings. They spent hours getting ready for the game. And then they'll blame some little story written by some sportswriter for losing the game!

I don't think those coaches really believe that. Most of them are just mad at themselves because they know why they lost. When we lose, you can believe that I know why, because I get reminded of it every time I look in the mirror.

I had my writer for this book, Bill Smith, do a mini-poll of some of my more frequent media contacts, and here is what they had to say, both in interviews and quotes from their writings.

When you're number one, folks can't wait to get a shot at you.

Bill McGrotha, the late sportswriter for the *Tallahassee Democrat* and author of the book *Seminoles! The First Forty Years*, said prior to his death, "Coach Bowden gets along with people across the board better than any person I've ever met. Sometimes writers are accused of protecting him. It isn't protection. It is respect. That's because Bobby treats them special.

"As near as I can make out, Bobby treats writers just like he treats everybody else. He's very considerate. When he's being interviewed, he's all yours. There's no looking at the clock, or acting as though he can't wait until you get out of his hair. He gives writers his undivided attention. And his natural sincerity comes across at all times.

"I knew former Georgia Tech Coach Bobby Dodd fairly well, and Coach Dodd came across about the closest to Coach Bowden as anybody I've ever seen. He had some of Coach Bowden's qualities, but he didn't have them all. I don't think anybody does."

Bob Harig of the *St. Petersburg Times,* said of Bowden, "The 1993 season was my seventh year of covering Florida State football. I honestly

think that even though Bobby has been coach of the Seminoles for eighteen years, people are still skeptical of him. They can't believe he's really
that good of a guy. They want to believe it's an act, but they end up
believing that he is just a good person.

"It is no act. That's just the way he is. He is one of the few coaches
who genuinely enjoys being around the news media.

"Most coaches put up with the media because they have to. You
never get that feeling with Bobby. A lot of times the writers will be ready
to wrap up a press conference, but Bobby will be willing to sit there and
talk for another twenty or thirty minutes. He seems to actually have a good
time answering questions and bantering with the writers. That is very
unusual.

"Even after tough losses, when you know he has to be hurting, the
hurt never shows. He always seems to be in a good mood. Most writers
aren't accustomed to coaches acting that way."

CHAPTER 21

Trying to Be Fair and Honest

You know, we've had teams at Florida State that have been able to score a lot of points. In the last six years we've averaged something like thirty-eight points a game and held opponents to about fifteen. We've won some games by forty, fifty, and sixty points. The problem is that whenever you have a team that puts a lot of points on the board, you're going to get accused of running up the score.

What are we supposed to do? You can't put in your subs and tell those kids, "Now don't y'all play too hard. Don't y'all do anything to earn a first-team spot."

Some critics have said, "Yes, Coach, we understand that you want all your kids to play hard, but do you have to keep throwing the ball when you're way ahead late in the fourth quarter?"

My answer to that is simple. I say, "If I put my backup quarterback in there, I want him to really run our offense. I don't want him to just take the snap and hand the ball off. Coaches that have a lead and then are content to go 1-2-3-punt . . . well, in my opinion, that ain't very exciting. If our offense is built around throwing the ball, I want to make darned sure he can do it—and do it in a real live game in front of a big crowd. Plus, the kid wants to show you he can throw."

In the game of football, you never know when someone is going to get hurt. You might have to depend on that backup, and you better make sure he's not going to go out there and wet himself or faint. You've got to know how he's going to react under pressure.

A team that depends on throwing the ball can't shut that baby down, because if you do, you might need to start her up again, and you might not be able to do it. Momentum in the game of football is very mysterious. When you've got it, you don't know why. And when it goes, it's not going to give you any advance warning. It just goes and doesn't even say good-bye.

I think if you put your non-starters in the game and all you have them do is go 1-2-3-punt, you're not being fair to those kids. And you sure aren't being fair to your fans, who spend a lot of money to support your program.

The best way to ensure victory, no matter what your lead, is to keep moving those chains (i.e., keep making first downs, marching down the field) and keep the other team's offense off the field.

So, to the folks who say, "Y'all kinda poured it on by still throwing the ball when you had that big lead," my answer to them is, "If they'll pull out a rule that Oklahoma can't run the ball when they're way ahead, then when we're way ahead we won't throw it. But until they pass a rule like that, we're not gonna stop doing what we're doing."

That rah-rah stuff is superficial. It lasts only until you walk out on the field and an opponent knocks you on your behind. Then you have to get up, shake off the hurt, and go to work.

Oklahoma used to beat people 50-0, 60-0, and 70-0 by running that wishbone offense, but that was all right because they were keeping the ball on the ground. However, if a passing team is way ahead and keeps throwing it, then they are accused of running up the score.

I never have understood that.

I'm not a yeller or screamer. That ain't my way. I very seldom yell at my players and assistant coaches. What I do is stress enthusiasm. I want everybody in our program to be enthusiastic.

When I first came to Florida State, I had the word "ENTHUSI-ASM" printed on everything. I had it painted on one wall in our workout room all the way from the floor to the ceiling. The problem was the players didn't know what it meant. They thought it meant jumping up and down and giving out with a bunch of "rah-rahs."

Shoot, that rah-rah stuff is superficial. It lasts only until you walk out on the field and an opponent knocks you on your behind. Then it's gone. You have to get up, shake off the hurt, and go to work. That's when enthusiasm—plus confidence and preparation—comes into play. And if you don't have it, you're not going to win.

Now, I am firm. I am not going to let my players walk all over me. I don't believe in appeasement either. If you appease your players, the first thing you know the tail will be wagging the dog. This dog ain't gonna let *that* happen. There's only one person in charge, and my contract says I'm that guy. And until that contract changes, my players have to do what I say. It is never going to be the other way around.

The main thing I always tried to do was to be honest with my players.

Now, every kid is different, and sometimes being fair isn't totally possible because each kid perceives you in a certain way. Maybe a kid doesn't think he's had a fair chance, and maybe he's right. But I've never intentionally been unfair to one of my players. Sometimes you just can't be fair to everybody when you're trying to be fair to 100 or more kids simultaneously. It's like life. Life isn't fair. But I try to be fair, and that's all I can do.

I'm not a yeller or screamer. That ain't my way.

The problem with being a coach is that you must be a teacher, a father, a mother, a psychologist, a counselor, a disciplinarian, and Lord-knows-what-else. If all we had to do was coach, they'd have to cut our salaries because coaching is the easiest part of the job.

When you have 100-plus young men, boys who come from all kinds of environments, you are going to have problems. Every year you can count on some boys having grade problems, some getting homesick for their mommas and daddies or girlfriends, some getting into some sort of trouble, some getting girls pregnant, and some getting hurt.

Lawd, these kids have had about eighteen years forming whatever personalities they have. And if some have bad personalities, folks expect a coach to straighten them out in four or five years. We don't work miracles. We're just coaches.

Handling kids today is so much different than it was years ago. Back thirty years ago, if you told a kid to do something, he did it. And if he happened to ask, "Why?" you just said, "Because I said so, that's why." And that was good enough; kids didn't do much questioning in those days. It isn't that way anymore. You have to explain everything. You can't teach kids anything today without telling them why. And you better not be offended when they ask, because they're going to.

You have to have rules too. Folks will say, "Yes, but Coach, you know kids today are going to smoke cigarettes. Some are going to drink alcohol; some are going to experiment with drugs. What kind of rules can you have to guard against all that?"

My answer is, "I wasn't born yesterday; I know what society is like today. But regardless, I'm still going to have rules and will continue to have them as long as I coach."

But you can't have so many rules that the kids feel like they're in prison. They may be football players, but first and foremost, they are kids who are students. You have to give them some leeway. That's part of growing up.

I like to think I'm flexible. Kids used to say, "You gotta go with the flow." Well, I ain't going to do that, but I might bend a little. For instance, I used to have a rule against long hair. That was a silly one. I've changed on that. Heck, I even wear my hair a little longer than I used to. Long hair doesn't have a dad-gum thing to do with a kid's ability or desire to play football. Someone asked me once about long hair and I said, "Well, if short hair and good manners won football games, then Army and Navy would play for the national championship every year."

Before every season I sit down with our players and explain the rules to them. I know some of those kids are going to break the rules over and over. But I want to let them know that if they get caught, they are going to face the consequences.

For example, we have a no-drinking rule during the season.

If you appease your players, the first thing you know the tail will be wagging the dog. This dog ain't gonna let *that* happen.

I would say that out of our squad of 100 players, we probably have 65 percent who drink some alcohol. The other 35 percent might abstain. So, 65 percent of the players break the no-drinking rule. I hate to say that, but I think that's about right. I tell them, "If y'all do it, you better not get caught because we aren't going to turn our heads." What we don't want to happen is for one or two of them to go out and get drunk and tear up something. Alcohol is a terrible thing, but it's out there, and Bobby Bowden can't change that.

We have a no-drug rule.

We test our players, and if one turns up positive, he is put on probation. And he must go to counseling. If he tests positive a second time, he will be suspended from a game. And if he tests positive a third time, he's gone. Drug addiction is horrible, and we try to get the kid back on the right track. Sometimes you just can't do it.

It's sad, but we also have a responsibility to the rest of the players who don't get into that stuff. If a kid can't set himself straight after two chances, then his problem is very serious and he needs more help than we can give him.

I guess the main rule we have—one all teams have—is, "Don't do anything to embarrass the program." That covers a lot of ground, but I don't let it stop there.

All our players must get up for breakfast during the season. And if a player has bad grades, he must get up for breakfast after the season is over. I figure if we make the kid get up for 7 A.M. breakfast, then he's going to make his eight o'clock class. Now, if he eats breakfast and then goes back to bed, I can't do anything about that. But I can do something about it when his grades come out. That's what I call the day of reckoning.

We have a no-profanity rule. And I've got to admit that sometimes I'm not a very good example in that respect. When I get upset, I really have to watch it. That's when I have to ask God for forgiveness. I've done a lot of asking. I'm not proud of that—not one bit. A lot of young folks think profanity is the best way to show toughness. Shoot, that don't make you tough. Talk's cheap. Some of the toughest people I've ever known were Christians, and no bad words ever came out of their mouths.

I remember I spoke at a Florida Evangelist convention once, and the guy who introduced me said, "Coach Bowden never curses. He never swears." And he added a whole bunch of those "never-does-this and never-does-that" compliments.

To be a coach today you must be a teacher, father, mother, psychologist, counselor, disciplinarian, and Lord-knows-what-else. If all we had to do was coach, they'd have to cut our salaries because coaching is the easiest part of the job.

I got up and said, "I wish you were correct about me not using profanity, but I gotta admit I have used some of those words. And I am ashamed and sorry for it."

I'll say it once again: I'm not perfect and never claimed to be.

Now, all those rules aren't hard to enforce when you're winning. But it's a whole new ball game when you're losing. Then you've got problems when you have a bunch of rules.

I have never had a player get seriously hurt or suffer a fatal injury. It would really hurt me if I caused some kid to get hurt bad through conditioning. I'm not sure I could live with the knowledge that I ran a kid to death or ran him so much that it caused him to get hurt.

Now, if it happened during a game, I would still feel terrible. It would be awful, but I could live with that. Everyone who plays and coaches football knows there is contact. Believe me, there are some high-speed collisions out on that field. And there is a lot of risk because football is a dangerous sport. It is a Spartan game and injuries are part of it. Players know that when they come out for football. It's a risk they take. It's a risk I took. My responsibility is to prepare the players and reduce the risk as much as possible.

To me, football is an adventure. Whenever you take a risk, it's an adventure. Why do you think folks race cars, or climb mountains, or go hang-gliding, or go bungee jumping, or go sky-diving? Those folks aren't trying to kill themselves; they are pursuing adventure. It's awful to say, but I think man's greatest adventure is war. I don't know why man is that way, but he is.

The thing I worry about most is subjecting players to excessive heat. We played a game at Nebraska one time and it must have been 120 degrees on that AstroTurf. That helped us win because our Florida boys were accustomed to the heat.

The most a team of mine was ever affected by heat and humidity was the team I had at West Virginia in 1973. We played at Miami and won the game 20-14. I don't think it was all that hot, but the humidity was stifling.

You can prepare players for heat, but you can't prepare them for humidity. We had to play our second team after the first quarter just to survive. Our first team was over on the bench between two big fans that were situated right behind two big chunks of ice. Those boys had their pads off and were just dying. It was a test of that team's character that it won the game.

I admit my Christianity carries over into my coaching. Like I have said many times, I believe God has guided me my whole life and that I'm right where He wants me to be today.

Now, as a football coach at a state university, I know there is a fine line between what you can do, what you should do, and what you can't do. I'm talking about the rules of government. They have so many dad-gum laws now. You can't pray in schools. You can't pray at high school graduations. Sometimes I'm not real sure what you can do.

I know you must "render unto Caesar the things that are Caesar's." But I feel I have a responsibility to expose my players to as much about God as I can. That's why I take them to church twice a year—once to a predominately white church and once to a predominately black church. I want to show my boys that we are all on the same team. But before I do that, I always write their parents to find out if they have any objections to their sons going to church. In all my years at Florida State I've had only one player's parents object. That was their right, and I respect that.

I would never take the players to *my* church. Lawd, I wouldn't do that. I'm not trying to convert them to the Baptist faith. All I want to do is expose them to a church, and then it's up to them to accept or reject it. I would hate to think I would have a young man under my charge for four or five years and he wouldn't hear about God, Jesus Christ, and the Holy Spirit.

We always pray before a game. I never pray for victory; I just pray that they do their best and ask God to take care of our players. God isn't going to win a football game for you; He's got much bigger things on His mind.

I have a responsibility to help shape their lives and help them turn out to be good men and good citizens, in addition to good football players.

I don't preach to our players. At least, I don't think I do. I do pray with them. And I pray with my coaches. Our coaches have a daily devotional session before we begin our morning meetings. Prayer and devotions are just sort of a routine thing.

During practice I'm liable to call the team around me for a prayer. I might do that at any time. I remember once we had a particularly rough practice session. I called the team around me under a shade tree and we had a little prayer. I just asked God to watch out for their safety. It wasn't a big thing.

We always pray before a game. Now, I never pray for victory. I just pray that they do their best and ask God to take care of them. That's all. God isn't going to win a football game for you. He's got much bigger things on His mind. And I don't think one of them is whether Bobby Bowden's team wins a stinking game.

It's like the old story about a baseball player who made the sign of the cross before he went up to the plate. A fan in the stands turned to another and asked, "Will that help him?"

And the other guy said, "It will if he can hit."

We pray after a game too. We thank God for getting us through it without injury. And we pray that by our actions out on the field we glorified Him.

I pray with the team mainly to teach the players about prayer, and to show them that there is a God. And the key point I stress to them is that to receive, they have to ask. I say, "If we aren't going to ask, forget it. We gotta ask."

Jesus tells us, "If you knew the gift of God, and who it is who says to you, 'Give Me a drink,' you would have asked Him, and He would have given you living water" (John 4:10). God gives Himself freely in Jesus to all those who ask. That's what the Bible says.

I always tell the players, "No matter what your religion is, there isn't but one God." Now, I don't try to force my beliefs on the young men I coach. Influence them for Christ, yes; but ramrod them, no. We live in a free country.

Sometimes when we pray before a game or practice that God would protect us from injury, we have no injuries; other times, we do. Of course it's puzzling to some players and to a certain degree, to me too.

So, I'll occasionally give the team a little talk about how everything works out for good for those who love the Lord. I tell them how I believe that God always answers our prayers even though we don't always win or don't always escape injury. We have to trust in Him and His decisions.

And then I tell them how I got a badly broken thumb once and how it changed my whole life.

I firmly believe that when things don't work out for the best, the person with faith, hope, and trust will make the best out of the way things work out. That's not an original statement, but in my opinion it's true.

Now, if Caesar ever made an issue of me taking my boys to church and praying with them, then I suppose I could be stopped from doing that, although I'm not sure I would stop; I believe in my mission too much to just casually change on that one. If it became too big an issue, I reckon they'd just have to fire me.

Like I say, I don't force anyone to believe anything. I simply let 'em know what ol' Bobby thinks and let 'em make their own choice.

■ ■ ■

(Chuck Amato is Florida State's assistant head coach and has been with Bowden for thirteen years. Prior to that, the native of Easton, Pennsylvania, was at Arizona and North Carolina State, his alma mater.)

"I know Coach Bowden has had many opportunities to go elsewhere. I think he worries about us and what would happen to us if he happened to leave. That's the kind of man he is.

To be honest, the system we work in is unfair at times, but that's the way it is. I think every coach in the business knows and accepts that.

"I would hate to see that happen, but I also know that nothing is certain in this profession. It's like sending your team out on the field on Saturday afternoon. You never know what's going to happen, but you have to accept the result because that's the way this game is.

"Coach Bowden is an excellent person to work for because he lets you do your job. When he gives you an assignment, he's not going to stand over you until the job gets done. He simply expects you to do it. He treats all the coaches on his staff like men. Now, if you don't do your job, that's a different story. I don't know of a greater motivator, and he gets it done without all the yelling, screaming, and rah-rah stuff.

"I think most folks know he is very religious, but his religion does not get in the way. He does have a way, though, of getting his faith across to the players. He tries to get them involved in church and to read the Bible. But he doesn't shove it down their throats. He is aware that each person's commitment has to come from within that person. Many of our kids end up in our Fellowship of Christian Athletes chapter.

"How does he get them involved without pushing? The main thing is his example. The players see what kind of man he is.

"We start off every morning staff meeting with a little devotion and prayer. Now, it may last for only three or four minutes, but it's a great way to start the day. I don't think Coach Bowden will ever change that."

■ ■ ■

(Mickey Andrews is Florida State's defensive coordinator and has been on the Florida State staff since 1984. Andrews played football under Bear Bryant at

Alabama (1961-64) and was a second team All-American as wide receiver and defensive back. Andrews, who formerly coached defenses at Clemson and Florida, coaches defensive backs and his most famous pupil was Deion Sanders.)

"Bobby Bowden is not only a great coach, but he's a great man too. And the latter is what stands out about him. There are a lot of great coaches out there, but not every great coach is a great man. Here is a man who has both those qualities. He is a man who has a unique way of drawing people together. He is a guy who has high expectations of himself and the people around him. He isn't a rah-rah coach. He doesn't scream at his players and coaches.

"Coach Bowden just sees life as it really is. And he sees sports for what they are. He knows the game of football plays a certain role in our society. But football is not the most important thing to him.

"He never preaches to anyone. Now, he will preach if he's asked to. I think sometimes that's a very fine line he walks. And I think there have been times when he's battled it. I know there are a lot of times when you know he wants to say or do something to a player or a coach, and yet he restrains himself. But he does have a way of getting his point across.

"What he has said about not being obsessed with winning a national championship is true; it's never been his top priority. If we had never won one, he could have lived without it.

"All those years when we came so close to winning it all and didn't, Coach Bowden just figured it wasn't in God's plan. And he didn't make a big deal of it.

"Do I feel fortunate to have had the opportunity to coach under him? Well, I was fortunate to play at Alabama under Coach Bryant, who in my opinion was the best that's ever been. And now I'm coaching under Coach Bowden. It's been unbelievable to be around him and learn from him. So, yes, I feel very fortunate to have had this opportunity."

■ ■ ■

(Brad Scott was Florida State's offensive coordinator and offensive line coach, but in December 1993, he was named the new head coach at University of South Carolina. He joined the Florida State staff in 1984. Before that, he was head coach and athletic director at DeSoto County High School in Arcadia, Florida. He was interviewed during his last two years at FSU.)

"The coaching profession is such a tough business. It is such an emotional roller coaster. I knew that going in, so I don't worry about it. I'm just glad for the opportunity to be around a man like Coach Bowden. Has he influenced me? That's like asking me if I know the sun comes up each day.

"One of the reasons I took a chance and got into college coaching was because of him. I left a comfortable position as a high school coach and athletic director and came here as nothing but a graduate assistant. And you have to understand, when you're a graduate assistant, you don't get paid. All you get is a full scholarship. At the time, my wife, Daryle, and I had one child and another on the way. So it was a big risk to come here.

"Coach Bowden was the one guy I was willing to take that risk for. And to be honest, he probably tried to talk me out of it because he knew how tough it would be.

"I first met Coach Bowden when I was in college at Missouri-Rolla College. I had been picked to play in the All-American Bowl All-Star game in Tampa. Coach Bowden was coaching the team I was on, so I got to be around him for a week. In that one week I recognized that there was something different about him. He was not your normal coach who was around the team at practice, then was gone, and didn't show up again until the next practice. Coach Bowden was always around.

"He took time to be with us at our hotel. He took a personal interest in us. He'd say to players, 'Hey, buddy, how ya doing? You all right?' He seemed to take a genuine interest in each player. It was a father-type interest. And you could tell it wasn't a put-on.

"I had heard of him and his reputation—that of not only being a great coach, but also being a Christian who was a coach. I was curious to find out what he was like.

"When we go to different places and people find out you work for Bobby Bowden, they will say, 'Is he really as genuine as he seems?'

"My answer is always, 'Yes. That's him.'

"I guess folks have been let down so many times by the so-called great men in coaching that they don't believe a man like Coach Bowden can be so friendly and outgoing and oriented toward people. And there's also his reputation, which is known throughout the country, of being a committed Christian.

"The great thing about him is he lets us coach the players. He coaches us.

"He is very consistent in his faith. He is very consistent in the way he deals with people too. He has been that way through the good times and the bad times.

"I remember once we lost a big game to Miami. We all felt like jumping off a boat in the middle of the ocean. And we still felt that way twenty-four hours later. But as always, when we come together as a staff, Coach Bowden has a unique way of bringing us back together. He will say, 'Men, it's just a game. Now, we know those games are important, and we don't want to lose them. But it's still just a dad-gum game. Ain't you glad that God ain't gonna judge us on the basis of winning or losing a football game?'

"His strength through those rare tough times has really helped mold my character, boost my confidence, and straighten out my priorities.

"Now, don't confuse his faith as a sign that he's an easygoing coach. He isn't. He coaches the heck out of us in those staff meetings. He's a tough coach behind closed doors.

"One thing that has always impressed me, though, is his knack of seeing so many little things. He coaches the little things. He observes practices, and a lot of times he might be thirty yards away, or he might be sitting up in the stands. But believe me, he doesn't miss a thing. And he always has a pencil and a little note card in his pocket. He will scribble on that little card what he has seen wrong, what he thinks we should have done, or what he thinks we shouldn't have done.

"Coach Bowden took a personal interest in us. It was a father-type interest. And you could tell it wasn't a put-on. I got into college coaching because of him."

"We always joke when an assistant or a player messes up in practice. When that happens, we always turn and look for Coach Bowden. And sure enough, he'll be reaching for that pencil and card. We'll think, *Uh, oh, he's getting out the note card. Somebody's gonna get it.* The man can write a two-hour staff meeting on the back of a little 5x7 card. It's amazing.

"He's the first to come down on you if you're loafing too. But he has his unique way of challenging you. He will give you a chance to do things your way until he thinks it isn't working. Then he might step in and say, 'Now I mentioned this to you yesterday, and I think y'all ought to give it a try.' He never comes in and shouts, 'I want it this way, my way!' That's not his style.

"Family is very important to him. And if there's one thing that might drive me out of college coaching, it would be the time away from my family. In most staffs, it's football, football, football. I feel I am so fortunate to work for a head coach who believes family is very important. He does not want us to neglect our families. He says, 'Yes, there is time for family. If there isn't, then all of this ain't worth a dad-gum thing.'

"I am molding my career after Coach Bowden. Now, I don't pretend that I can ever be like him. I'll have to be myself. But, boy, his example has shown me that if you have faith, trust God, read the Bible, treat the news media cordially, have as many friends as you can have, and work hard, then you can be successful.

"I've heard him say many times, 'Men, have class in what you do, how you act, what you say, and how you handle everything. If y'all do that, you will ultimately be a winner, and it doesn't have a single thing to do with winning football games.'

"I have always wanted to be a head coach, so the South Carolina opportunity was welcome, but leaving Coach Bowden was tough. I believe in him so much that I couldn't visualize leaving him. Where else could I go to find another coach who stands for the things he stands for? I know this, there is going to be so much of Bobby Bowden in my style of coaching and administrating at my new job that you will think the ol' boy is standing there looking over my shoulder."

■ ■ ■

(David Van Halanger has been Florida State's strength coach since 1983. He played for Bowden at West Virginia and was co-captain of his 1975 Peach Bowl team. He is credited with starting West Virginia's first organized weight training program. Also, Van Halanger leads FSU's Fellowship of Christian Athletes chapter.)

"When I was recruited by Coach Bowden to attend West Virginia I wasn't a Christian," said Van Halanger. "He is the one who exposed me to Christianity. He got me to go to an FCA meeting my first year at West Virginia. He made all of his first-year players attend at least one meeting. After that, it was up to the players. He doesn't make his players go to a first meeting like he used to, but he does suggest they go. I don't think you could make them go today because of all the laws, rules, and regulations.

"I sat in on that first FCA meeting and it boggled my mind to suddenly realize that there was a coach and players who were not ashamed to stand up and talk about what it meant to them to be Christians. It had such a profound impact on me that I accepted Christ at that first meeting.

"It was because of Coach Bowden that I had the opportunity to hear the gospel, and it changed my life. I am so thankful for that because at age thirty-five I had a heart attack, and I was comforted by God's promise that if I died, I would be with Him.

"I feel that Coach Bowden has started many—well, for want of a better term, I'll call them 'Christian chain letters.' By that I mean he exposed me to the gospel and I got saved. I began witnessing to others. Some players heard me and their lives were changed, and they began witnessing to others. Others heard them and their lives were changed, and they began witnessing. I just wonder how many of those Christian chains Coach Bowden has started?

"There is going to be so much of Bobby Bowden in my style of coaching and administrating at my new job that you will think the ol' boy is standing there looking over my shoulder."

"There are some coaches who profess to be Christians, but they just act that way because they think that's the way the majority wants them to act. When it's convenient they say, 'Oh, yeah, I'm a Christian.' When it's not convenient, they don't say a word about God. Coach Bowden is a Christian who happens to be a coach. It isn't the other way around.

"I know his faith is the reason he never has those extreme highs when we win and those extreme lows when we lose. He knows what is important in this life. He says all the time, 'If I die tomorrow, all the games we've won won't mean a thing, but if through me God has saved some souls, that will mean everything. And if I die tomorrow, I'll know I'm saved.' "

■ ■ ■

(Ronnie Cottrell is Florida State's recruiting coordinator and has been on Bowden's staff since 1989. The Brewton, Alabama, native had been a high school coach for eight years before that.)

Cottrell said, "All my life I was taught that good guys can't win. I was led to believe that abuse, profanity, and roughhouse coaching were the only ways to be successful. Coach Bowden has shown me it can be done the other way.

"I'll never forget my first year at Florida State. We were picked number two in the preseason polls and got beat in our season opener by

Southern Mississippi 30-26. It was a huge upset. Then we lost to Clemson 34-23 in our second game.

"In the staff meeting the Monday after the Clemson loss, all of us coaches were sitting around blaming each other. I was new on the staff, and I thought, 'Oh, my gosh, we're all gonna get fired.' That wasn't what happened.

"That particular morning happened to be Coach Bowden's turn to lead the devotion. He held his hands just a couple of inches apart and said, 'My life is this long.' Then he pointed to each coach and held his hands about three inches apart and said, 'Your life may be this long.'

"Finally, he said, 'Our lives aren't really very much. But compared to what we have to look forward to, you cannot measure. I've already talked to our seniors, and I'm telling y'all right now that I'm more worried about how our players are going to be ten and twenty years from now, than I am about winning the next game. I cannot, and I will not, sell my soul for football.'

"And we went out and won the next ten games, and then beat Nebraska in the Fiesta Bowl, and finished number two in one poll and number three in the other.

"There is so much pressure in big-time football to win that many coaches fall into traps. They get trapped to take shortcuts, to undercut people, to use them, and to win at all costs. That environment does not exist here, and it's because of Coach Bowden.

"When I came to Florida State as recruiting coordinator, Coach Bowden called me in and said, 'Ronnie, I don't want you looking for no loopholes. I want you to understand that we not only play by rules here, we play by the way the rules were intended. I want you to help see that I and all the other coaches abide by the rules.' I will never forget that.

"I remember back when I was coaching at W. S. Neal High School in East Brewton, Alabama. I had taken my team to Pensacola for the Challenger Award Banquet. There were probably 3,000 high school students there, and Coach Bowden was the speaker. After his testimony, twenty-three of my players accepted the Lord. You go through your whole life praying to touch one life, and that night he touched twenty-three on just one team. I wonder how many more of those 3,000 he touched.

"Coach Bowden is a witness for Christ everywhere he goes. The bottom line is that Bobby is a man you can see Christ in."

Ann's Turn

I t's a little difficult for me to talk about myself because I don't think any of us ever see ourselves as other people see us. When we look in the mirror, we see what we want to see. That's not really what we look like. When we talk, we hear our voice, but that's not really what our voice sounds like. I think it's the same when we try to tell folks what we're really like. The person who really knows me is Ann. She knows me much better than I know myself.

It takes a special kind of woman to be the wife of a coach because it is an unstable profession. Early in my career we didn't have too much security. You've got to have a wife who is willing to move because, believe me, most coaches move a lot. Now, we haven't moved at all in the last eighteen years. And before that we were at West Virginia for ten years. So, we have moved only once in twenty-eight years. (Of course before that we did our share of hoppin' around.) Believe me, those twenty-eight years are the exception rather than the rule. We've been very fortunate.

You have to have a wife who is willing to live alone a lot because coaches are gone so much of the time. I'd hate to count the hours, days, and weeks Ann has spent by herself while I've been on the road.

You have to have a wife who is able to stand criticism because I guarantee you, the wife is going to hear all of it. Ann hears a lot more of that stuff than I do. A coach can stay free of criticism. During a game he's down on the field surrounded by his players and coaches. He has a fence, or a wall, to keep fans away from him. And if all coaches are like me, they are oblivious to everything except the game. If fans yell bad stuff at me during a game, they are wasting their breath because I don't hear any of that stuff when the game is going on.

After a game a coach can go home and relax. He doesn't have to watch television, or listen to the radio, or read the newspapers. He doesn't have to answer the telephone. At his office he can have his secretary handle the mail and tell her, "Don't bother me with any of that dad-gum bad stuff. I just want the good stuff." So, a coach can pretty much remove himself from criticism.

The poor wife has to sit in the stands surrounded by folks who might be criticizing her husband and his team. Some of that criticism can be pretty nasty too. Then the children go to school and they hear the criticism there. The wife goes to the grocery store and hears more of it there. She goes to a club meeting, or a social gathering, and she hears it there. She hears it all.

So, a coach's wife has to really be a tough person. If she isn't tough and can't take it, and can't stand the husband being gone all the time, the marriage often ends in divorce. It's either that, or the husband winds up getting out of coaching. More than a few coaches have gotten out of the profession to save their marriages.

As far as I'm concerned, Ann is the perfect wife. She's tough. There is no doubt that Ann Bowden is the toughest one in our family. She's like a rock, and when she thinks she's right, she's not going to back down from nothing or nobody. I know that for a fact.

I remember back in 1966 when we left Florida State to go with Jim Carlen to West Virginia. We had just bought a house there and moved into it. The backyard was bordered by big woods. Up behind the woods was an old cemetery on the side of a hill. Anyhow, our boys at times would get the dogs and go back in those woods to play and let the dogs run.

Our oldest son, Steve, was about fourteen or fifteen then. He got to fooling around an old building back in the woods. It was a cabin, or maybe it was a garage-type building, I don't know. Anyhow, the wife of the man who owned the land the building was on called Ann and said something about "what a sorry bunch of boys" our boys were. I mean, this woman was what you would call in West Virginia a real ridge runner. She really gave Ann "down the road" about what bad kids the Bowden boys were.

Ann didn't take too kindly to that, so she called the lady back and said she wanted to talk to her in person. The lady wasn't too keen on that, but that didn't stop Ann. She got in the car and drove out to the lady's house.

It was way out on this dirt road, up this mountain and down the other side, and all the way to end of the road. When Ann got there, there was the lady standing out in her yard with a big ol' dad-gum rifle in her hand.

There is no doubt that Ann Bowden is the toughest one in our family. She's tough; she's like a rock.

That didn't stop Ann either. She went right up to her and said, "If you don't put up that rifle, I'm gonna call the police." The lady didn't put it up, so Ann shoved the barrel of the gun out of the way, and then pushed right past her. She went right into the woman's house and used her telephone to call the police. And there that lady stood with a gun in her hand. The police came, but they didn't do anything because they figured it was just a family squabble. I think the boys apologized and that was that.

I don't think I would have done what Ann did, not with that rifle barrel pointed at me. I'm not that brave. I'm not that tough either. When I think of tough, resolute people, I put Ann right up there at the top of the list. She won't back down. She'll confront you right quick and tell you off the same way. I won't do that. I'll avoid trouble if I can. I guess I'm like an old bull elephant. I trumpet a lot, but I ain't gonna do nothing.

Another thing about Ann is that she's a worker. When we were raising our six children, we took them to church every Sunday from the time they were born. Ann would wash and iron their clothes, polish their shoes, and have all that stuff laid out for the next morning. She would get up, cook breakfast, get the kids dressed, and we'd head off to church. She did that every Sunday until I became the head coach at Florida State. The only reason she stopped was the children were gone.

She's much tougher than me and has been behind me shoving all the way. I haven't the slightest idea where I'd be today without her. But I think I'd better shut up and let her talk.

■ ■ ■

"I make no apologies for being my husband's biggest booster. There has never been a time when I felt Bobby questioned his Christian faith. Never! Bobby's faith has become stronger as he's gotten older.

"It is a fundamental faith. He's very conservative. He believes the Bible is the inspired word of God—period. I do too.

"Bobby believes that if it's in the Bible, then it's true. He believes when the Bible says Jesus raised a man from the dead, or made the blind man see, or healed the sick, then that's what happened. And he believes if the Bible says the whale swallowed Jonah, then the whale swallowed Jonah.

I guess I'm like an old bull elephant. I trumpet a lot, but I ain't gonna do nothing.

"Now, that's not to say that he's closed his mind. It's just that he doesn't question what's in the Bible. It isn't important to him to try and prove that something happened in a certain way. He believes that the men who wrote the Bible were picked by God to write the Word so it would be applicable for all men for all time. And Bobby is positive the Bible was written in such a way that the uneducated as well as the educated could understand it.

"He believes that Jesus was the son of God, was born of a virgin, walked on this Earth, was crucified, was dead, was buried, and arose from the dead and ascended into heaven. He believes in the Trinity—God the Father, the Son, and the Holy Ghost.

"I've heard Bobby say many, many times that it isn't important to him when God created the universe, the Earth, the animals, or man. And it isn't important to him how God did it. The only thing that's important to Bobby is that God did it. All those other theories—evolution, etc.—don't bother him.

"He believes in life after death, and in a heaven and a hell. I think as Bobby has gotten older, he has realized as each year passes that he is not long for this earth. In that regard, Bobby lives in fear of the Lord. The Bible says that fear of the Lord is the beginning of wisdom. I believe my husband is a very wise person.

"I know some people call him 'Saint Bobby.' I don't care much for that. Well, he's not perfect, and he's not a saint either. He has lots of faults. So do I.

"There are some in the news media who are always looking for something off-color or bad about him. They will say to me, 'Come on, Mrs. Bowden, he can't be as good as everybody says he is. There must be something wrong somewhere. There must be something in the closet.

There must be something bad that goes on behind closed doors. He just can't be all that good.'

"I say, 'Well, he doesn't hang up the towels in the bathroom after using them, and he has a bad habit of eating too much chocolate.' Honestly, though, other than things like that, he is just the way you see him. That's him.

"Bobby has always tried to set a good example for the family. He is a very disciplined person. He has never been a profane person. Oh, he might say something during a game every now and then, but profanity has never been part of his life, not that I know of. Alcohol has never been a temptation for him either. I don't think resisting temptation has ever been a problem. I've never had to worry about such things as immorality because he is a morally good person.

"Now, he is not one to get out and take a fruit basket to a neighbor who might be going through some tragedy or crisis in his or her life. He doesn't go visit a sick neighbor, although he does do a lot of visiting in hospitals. Bobby is so busy and on the go all the time, I'm not even sure he knows who his neighbors are. If that's considered a weakness, then that's one of his.

"My husband has a way of witnessing though. I really believe God has given him the talent to go out and testify. Bobby believes it, too, and he has used that talent in the way God gave it to him, which is in speaking in churches and to youth groups. I don't have that talent and don't know many people who do. I think my talent is in interacting with people.

"I have sat in churches many, many Sundays when my husband has been in the pulpit. I find myself listening to him like I would listen to someone I don't even know. It's funny, because I listen very intently to what he has to say. Sometimes I say to myself, 'Is this the man who is my husband, the man who is the father of our children, and the one I've lived with for nearly forty-five years?'

"I know my husband has many good things to tell people, and I know he feels called to do this. That's why he is seldom at home. It seems he lives more out of a suitcase than he does anywhere else. He's always speaking and witnessing somewhere.

"I do think there has been more of a personal battle inside him than I realized. Bobby is a very private person, and I know there will be many who will be surprised at that statement. People will probably say, 'Bobby Bowden, private? He can't be that kind of person. He coaches his teams in front of thousands of people every Saturday in the fall. He coaches his teams in front of national television audiences. He is interviewed by hordes of the media. He speaks to alumni groups. He preaches in churches. He speaks at national conferences of the Fellowship of Christian Athletes. How can he be a private person?' Well, those folks don't know him like I do.

"I know some people call my husband 'Saint Bobby.' I don't care much for that. Well, he's not a saint; he has lots of faults. So do I."

"We don't sit down together and talk all that much. He never does what you would call 'spill his guts.' So, I guess in that respect, I can't really see inside him and know what's in his heart. But I can see the way my husband lives his life. Being a good example has always been very important to him.

"It's been easy for me. I was raised in a traditional family environment where the man was pretty much the head of the house. It would have been hard for me if Bobby had been another kind of husband.

"He is very organized and strict. And like I said earlier, he is very, very disciplined. He is the leader for me and the children. I was the one who did all the things around the house. I took care of fixing things. Bobby was the provider. He set the example. I know that helped our sons realize they should be the providers and the examples in their own families.

"Too many families end up with the woman being the head of the house. The father just sort of goes his own way. I've seen that too many times. With Bobby, it was never that way. He has always set the moral and religious tone for our family.

"Now, there have been times when I think he has erred. There have been times when I think he should have gathered our children around him and explained more about the plan of salvation. He has spoken to other children more than he has his own. Our children have caught it by observing how he lives his life, more than they have been taught by him, if that makes any sense.

"Our boys love to be with their daddy. He will interact with them in his own way, but he has never been one to go out and play ball with them, or take them to ball games, or take them fishing and hunting, or take them camping. The nature of his job, particularly since he's been a head coach at a major university, demands almost all of his time and energy.

"People see him now as a very successful, well-paid, famous coach. Believe me, it wasn't always that way. We had our tough times, times when we didn't have money in the bank, times when we weren't sure how we were going to pay all the bills. There were plenty of times when we couldn't afford to go places or do things. I remember how tight finances were when we lived in that old Army Air Corps barracks at South Georgia Junior College. I remember what it was like to raise six children on less than $5,000 a year. I know what it was like to rob Peter to pay Paul. Through all those tough times, though, I always believed in my husband.

"Bobby's job and his belief that he has a calling from God have necessitated sacrifices, but I know our children, particularly the boys, have seen their daddy sacrifice so he could go out and use the talent God gave him to give his testimony to others.

"It says in the Bible that you shall know them by their fruits. Bobby is known for going out and witnessing. The boys have been able to see what kind of man their daddy is, and now they are doing the same thing. They are speaking, witnessing, preaching, and following his example.

"You can see the father in the sons."

My Kids' Turn

O ur six children are adults now, out on their own. Robyn, the oldest, is forty-two. Ginger, the youngest, is thirty-one. I can't believe they're that old. Where did all those dad-gum years go? It seems like yesterday Ann and I were struggling to make ends meet, to pay the bills, and to keep them all fed and clothed.

I was asked by a sportswriter one time if I felt I had cheated my family, having to be gone from home so much. I suppose I did cheat them some, but I don't think it was a whole lot. Whenever I could, I always tried to get home even if it was two o'clock in the morning.

I remember one time I took the boys on a recruiting trip to Charleston, West Virginia. We stayed in a Holiday Inn, which was right on the Kanawha River. The kids made me get a room clear up on the top floor so they could have a good view of the river and the valley. Charleston is a city that is built up and down the Kanawha River valley among the mountains. It's a pretty place.

I took Ginger with me on a recruiting trip to Charleston once, and when I was head coach at Howard College, there were times when I would take the boys on the team bus for road games. Man, those were six- and seven-hour rides. I think they have fond memories of those trips. I hope so.

The toughest thing I ever had to do in my life—and, oh, I'd hate to do it again—was when I left Ann and the kids to take the West Virginia assistant's job. I had to leave them all in Tallahassee. Remember, I had been an assistant there under Bill Peterson. It was hard on me being so far away from them, but I'm sure it was harder on Ann because she was the one left alone with all the children.

In Morgantown I roomed with Jack Fligg, who was on the coaching staff with me. He was from Atlanta. When we would get three days off, we'd get in the car and head down the highway. Jack did most of the driving and I slept. I'm afraid I didn't do my share of driving because when Jack would get tired and ask me to take over, I'd get behind the wheel for about thirty minutes and then I'd wake Jack up and say, "Jack, I'm getting awful sleepy. I'm afraid I might run off the dad-gum road." Sometimes I'd even run the car over on the berm on purpose, just to wake him up. And Jack would come flying up out of his sleep and say, "Don't do that! Let me drive!"

Talking about whether I was a good father is something I find difficult to do. I think the best thing would be to ask the kids what kind of daddy I was. They'll be honest. In fact, I might not like some of what they say. All are married now and doing very well. They have children of their own. At last count, we had fifteen grandchildren, eight boys and seven girls.

I think any parent would like to say that he or she was a good one. We all make mistakes in the complicated process of rearing children. The problem is none of us have any experience when we start out. We're all amateurs and just do the best we can.

Lawdy, I made mistakes. Maybe I was gone too much, but like I said, I honestly attempted to give them quality time when I was home. I suppose the term "quality time" covers a multitude of things.

I had a sportswriter friend who traveled all over the country covering sporting events. Plus, he officiated football and basketball and umpired baseball in his spare time. He said, "I had four children and I came home one day and they were all grown, and I didn't know where the years had gone."

It's about like the story of the wife who said to her husband, "You're gone so much you don't even know your own children."

The husband snapped, "That's not true. And just to prove it, I'll go talk to them." And when he walked into his living room where his children were sitting, he looked at them and then turned back to his wife and, pointing, asked, "Is that them?"

I guess a lot of us can ask ourselves the question, "Are we like that?" My children can answer that better than I can.

■ ■ ■

(Robyn Bowden Hines is married to Jack Hines, who played football for Bowden at West Virginia and at the time of this writing was an assistant football coach for brother-in-law Terry at Auburn University. Robyn, prior to moving to Auburn, had been a physical education teacher at Oak Mountain Elementary School in Birmingham.)

"I have no bad remembrances of my father. He wasn't home all that much, but I don't remember missing having him around. I knew he was always doing what it took to move on to the next step in his career.

"We were raised with Dad always being in the limelight. We just thought all kids' fathers were the same."

"Back thirty-five years ago, it was expected that fathers would be gone to earn the living for the family. Mothers were expected to take care of the home and the children. Back then you could buy a home on just the man's salary. You can't do that today. It's a different world.

"I've heard Dad speak at times and tell people how tough he was with the switch when it came to disciplining us children. I smile at that because the first thing I remember about discipline from him was when I was about five. The family had gone to a drive-in movie. Dad had just bought a brand-new station wagon. For some reason, they had let me sit up in the front seat. I think mother was in the back with the younger boys. The movie was probably either a thriller or a scary one. Anyway, during the movie I must have gotten excited, because I bit a hole in the vinyl material covering of the dashboard.

"I remember that Mother was really mad and told Dad to give me a spanking when we got home. I don't know why she told Dad to spank me. Usually, Mother took care of that. He took me into the bathroom and told me to cry and pretend like he was really laying it on. I must have put on a good act. He never did spank me.

"We always went to church; it was just something we always did as a family. But it wasn't a strict religious upbringing. Daddy wasn't strict. I think our religious upbringing was very basic. In my opinion, it was what the average person would choose as moral and right.

"Daddy has always been very disciplined, and he has always been true to his values. For him, being true to himself has always been the bottom line. There are some things he will do and some things he won't do, and there is never a consideration for crossing the line. Never. He's the same today as he was when I was a child. Now, I'm sure he has been tempted. All of us fight temptation. Daddy has fought it very well.

"He doesn't drink alcohol; he never has. But it doesn't bother him to be around where people are drinking. He just doesn't use the stuff and will not judge someone who does.

"As far as his religion, he avoids the gray areas. He will not get into religious conflict. He received his religious training back in the 1930s and 1940s, and has made it as black and white as he can. He has always stuck by that. I don't think he believes that good things always happen to good people, and that bad things happen to bad people. I do think he believes you should try to be as good as it's possible for any human to be, and if good things happen, that's wonderful. If bad things happen, God will be there to give you the strength to deal with it.

"When I was a teenager, Dad was very good at advice. I remember one time Mother and I had what you would call a mother and daughter argument. Well, it was actually a fight. I was seeking my independence, and Mother wasn't ready to give it to me. Daddy was the one who called and asked me to come to his office. We talked, and he helped me clear up things with Mother. He was always very understanding and has always been the one to give me advice when I needed to make a decision. If you asked him, he was there. If you didn't ask, he didn't interfere. I think what he did, and still does best, is listen.

"I have thought about the fact that Dad is becoming a coaching legend. It's been exciting, especially the last ten or eleven years, to watch him be in the spotlight. I know if he coaches a few more years he will be right up there with the most famous men who ever coached. That is really neat.

"I think my daddy is a good man, and good things have happened to him. However, even if they hadn't, it wouldn't have shaken his faith."

■ ■ ■

(Steve Bowden is forty-one and the oldest of Bowden's four sons. He received a Master of Divinity degree and a Doctor of Philosophy degree from the Southern Baptist Theological Seminary in Louisville, Kentucky, and has fifteen years of ministerial experience. He was dean of academic affairs at Flagler College in St. Augustine, Florida. Prior to taking the position at Flagler College, he was an

assistant associate professor of religion and philosophy at Samford University in Birmingham [his father's alma mater, formerly Howard College].)

"My father will probably think I'm too analytical in my observations of him. Dad's faith is more of the fundamental kind. Now, first of all, I've been asked many times if he was the normal type father. My answer has always been that I don't have any other father to compare him to. He was mine, and he always seemed normal to me. We were raised with Dad always being in the limelight. We just thought all kids' fathers were the same.

"As far as church went, our home was not a democracy. My father didn't ask us if we wanted to go to church. We were in church every Sunday morning, every Sunday night, every Wednesday night, and any other night there was a service or function going on. We went to revivals; Baptists have a lot of revivals.

"Mother told Dad to give me a spanking when we got home. He took me into the bathroom and told me to cry and pretend like he was really laying it on. I must have put on a good act."

"When we sat down to meals at home, Dad would read the Bible and then he would pray. Dad holds to a very few basic doctrines about the person of Christ, the nature of God, salvation, and the cross. He has never been interested in any kind of theological controversy, and he will not get into any Old Testament discussion. He believes religion is something to be lived. He believes you live what you believe, not the other way around. So for him, living comes before doctrine. For him living really defines orthodoxy.

"His beliefs are set and are not subject to discussion in terms of questioning them. His religious convictions are the same as they have always been. He has never changed, and I don't think he ever will. There aren't going to be many major revolutions in Dad's religious thinking.

"The most genuine aspect of my dad's life is that he lives his religion every day and never varies from it. He is one of the few men I've known who absolutely practices what he preaches.

"Dad will not go down as the greatest intellect who ever lived, although people will sell him short if they think he does not have an excellent mind. It's just that he has distilled life to some basic premises and lives them out.

"I know he is carving out accomplishments in coaching that few will match. He is handling fame well, but it's not often that I think of my dad from the perspective of being a famous man. When I do, I can't hang onto the thought for long. He's just my dad."

■ ■ ■

(Tommy Bowden is thirty-eight and an assistant coach for brother Terry at Auburn. Prior to that, he was an assistant coach at East Carolina, Duke, Alabama, and Kentucky. When Tommy married his wife, Linda, and set out on his own, he wrote this letter to his parents.)

Dear Mother and Daddy,

Now that I am married and on my way, I wanted to write a small thank-you note. I have wanted to do this for a long time, but when you get right down to it, it always seems hard to find the right words. Plus, that mushy stuff just isn't in the Bowden blood.

I can't begin to list the things I'd like to thank you for, so I'll make it brief. You raised me like I would like to raise my children. Anytime I speak or give my testimony, I tell how much you have influenced my life. I'm just now realizing how important it is to be raised by Christian parents in a Christian environment.

It is because of y'all that I pray that God will remain the Lord of my life and be instrumental in establishing the guidelines of my life-style. (Not bad for a P.E. [physical education] major.)

I love y'all more than anything in my life. I hope I can make you as proud of me as I am of y'all. May God bless you.

—Tommy

"I don't really realize the significance of what my father has accomplished in coaching because I'm too close to him. I know he just passed Bo Schembechler and Woody Hayes on the all-time victory list. That will move him into the upper echelon of coaching greats. It's just that it's difficult to think of Daddy in that way.

"I have tried to think of what Daddy was like as a father, but I can't remember all that much. We didn't see him much because for as long as I can remember, he's been a head coach. Head coaches have a lot of demands on their time.

"He is great at dealing with the news media. I was a college student and played for Dad back in 1974 when he had that 4-7 season at West Virginia and they hanged him in effigy and put those 'for sale' signs in our front yard. I was pretty frisky then and wanted to do something to stop all that negative stuff. Dad? He never acknowledged any of it. He didn't let it bother him, or if it did, he never let on. The way he handled all the criticism of that season was a valuable learning experience for me. He taught me that when you get bad press and criticism, you just suck it up and keep going, and keep doing what you believe in.

"All of us children were exposed to the Christian life and religion from day one, and it was all in a positive way. It is the kind of environment I want to establish for my own family.

"Daddy did not encourage or discourage us to go into coaching. He never pushed us. He just always wanted us to do what we felt comfortable and happy doing. But I was exposed to coaching at an early age, and exposed to it under successful circumstances, which in this profession doesn't happen a whole lot.

"After watching Daddy and his career, I figured I'd get married, go into coaching, buy a home, and that would be that. After all, Daddy has been at Florida State eighteen years and has a lifetime contract there. Before that, he was at West Virginia for ten years. It hasn't worked out that way for me; I've moved nine times in fifteen years. Daddy didn't tell me it might go like that."

■ ■ ■

(Son Terry is thirty-seven and became head coach at Auburn in December 1992 [making father and son the only father-son head coaches in major college football history]. Prior to that, Terry was head coach at Samford and in 1991 took his team to the semifinals of the Division 1-AA championship playoffs. After that season he passed his father's victory total at the school.)

"Dad won thirty-one games (31-6) in four seasons as coach at Samford. In six years I won forty-seven (47-18). I guess I'm copying my Dad." (Also, Terry went 11-0 in his first season at Auburn.)

"I got my first head coaching job at age twenty-six at Salem College in West Virginia. All I ever wanted to do was be like my dad. I've also found out that the best way for me to pursue my career is to try to use him as my mentor. I seek advice from him all the time. We talk on the phone just about every other day, and we've done that ever since I got my first coaching job.

"I can't go anywhere without people saying, 'Boy, you're just like your daddy. You talk like him. You coach like him.' They don't know it, but they are paying me the greatest compliment they could pay me.

"I am lucky to have a father who has not had black moments in his life, moments he's not proud of. He doesn't have skeletons in his closet, or something that would cause a son to have doubts. Sure, I've seen him angry and in moments of weakness, but that makes him all the stronger in my eyes, because that is an example of man with weaknesses and faults trying as best as he can to live a Christian life.

"Now, Jesus was the greatest example of someone being exactly what he preached, but I think I'm honest—and I hope objective—when I say that my dad is the best example of any human being I have ever known when it comes to practicing what he preaches. He's just so true to his faith and principles.

"I know most sons will say that their fathers had the most influence on their lives, so what I'm saying about mine is not unique. I also know that many children aren't lucky enough to have a father like mine. That doesn't mean he has affected, or influenced, all of us the same way. We're all different.

"But I have seen him go out and witness to others. I do the same thing. Daddy has left his mark on me."

■ ■ ■

(Jeff is thirty-three and is currently an assistant on his dad's staff. Prior to that he was coach of receivers at Southen Mississippi. He was a wide receiver on his dad's 1981-82 Florida State teams. He remembers with amusement his last game as a senior, the 1982 Gator Bowl win over West Virginia [31-12].)

"That game was one time when some accused Dad of running up the score, because in the closing seconds Florida State was deep in West Virginia territory and had the game won, and we threw the ball. It appeared to many fans and members of the media that my daddy was trying to score again.

"Dad will not go down as the greatest intellect who ever lived, although he has an excellent mind. It's just that he has distilled life to some basic premises and lives them out."

"I hadn't caught a single pass in my entire college career. They were just trying to get me a pass, and I finally got one. That was a lot of years of hard work for just one catch.

"I'm the youngest son in our family and my only remembrances of the early years are that my dad was gone. He was always busy. However, in spite of him not being home that much, the biggest impact he has made, and is having on my life, is the fact that through it all he has been consistent and strong. In simple terms, he has been the example.

"If I am patterning myself after my father, then I pray that I will have his strengths because I know where he gets his strength: from Jesus Christ.

"Am I a coach because my dad is a coach? I don't know. I was exposed to coaching at an early age. Because of that environment, I learned a lot of things about coaching. I figured that might give me an advantage in the future if I used them right.

"I know I have been lucky to have had a great father. A lot of kids don't have that advantage. The only way I can describe my dad is to say, 'what you see is what you get.' "

■ ■ ■

(Ginger is married to John Madden, a former Florida State football player (not the broadcaster) and is attending law school at FSU. The Maddens live in Fort Walton Beach, Florida.)

"When I try to remember what my dad was like when I was child, I can't remember him at all. He was never there. I don't mean this in a derogatory sense, but being the last of six children, I had no contact with my dad at all. I know he had to be gone a lot because of the nature of his job. So he was not your normal-type father.

"I think he gave up a lot to be where he is today. And for everything a person gets, he or she has to give up something. If I were a man, I don't think I would want to make the sacrifices my dad did. I wonder at times whether a game of football is worth those kinds of sacrifices. It's a bit much.

"I know there have been, and will be, plenty of benefits for me and my family because of what my father has done and will do. However, I have often wondered if the price wasn't too high.

"So, as far as missing my father when I was growing up, I figure you have to have something before you can miss it, and I never had it. I can't describe my father because I really don't know him. The only things I know about him are what I read in books and newspapers, and see on television. I'm a female and am very much outside the circle. I'm sure my brothers have told so much more about him than I have.

"My father is very religious. He always reads the Bible. He always has devotions at the breakfast table every morning. He goes everywhere witnessing for Christ. I know he feels that's what the Lord wants him to do.

"My father has made a lot of money coaching, but I don't think money means anything to him. I know he would coach for $30,000 or $35,000 a year, or even much less than that. Mother gets all the credit for the contracts my father has today. If she hadn't pushed him, he would have left things just the way they were.

"I do remember all the negative stuff that was written and said about him back in West Virginia in 1974. I was about thirteen, and I recall it was pretty bad. I was very much affected by what happened at West Virginia. In that respect, I'm glad my husband is in the hotel business and not in coaching.

"As long as I can remember, my impression of my father was that I thought he was bigger than life."

FCA: The Fellowship of Christian Athletes

I've been asked many times why I'm so involved in the Fellowship of Christian Athletes and why I go out and speak so much to youth groups. My answer to those folks is always this, "Have you ever been in the room when a young person has come forward and turned his life around, turned it in the right direction? If you haven't, then you've really missed something because, man, that's exciting."

I first became involved in FCA back in 1963 when I was an assistant at Florida State, and the man who got me involved was Vince Gibson, my old friend from Birmingham. Actually, though, the realization that someday I would want to get involved in making some sort of witness to young men and women goes back farther than that.

When I was a small boy I idolized a guy named Jimmy Tarrant. Jimmy played football at Woodlawn High School, where I would later play. I think he was about ten years older than me. He was an All-Stater and went on to Howard College and was a Little All-American. I remember seeing Jimmy every Sunday in our church. I thought, *Man, if he goes to church and isn't a sissy, then going to church ain't gonna make me a sissy.* Jimmy was a good influence on me, although I'm sure he wasn't aware of it.

Also, Harry Gilmer, the great All-American at Alabama back in the 1940s, attended our church. I know one of the reasons I used to go to church all the time was in the hope that he would be there and I'd get to see him. Man, I worshiped that guy.

The memory of how I worshiped those guys is enough proof to me of how athletes influence youngsters who look up to them. I mean, when I was young, I couldn't wait until I got old enough to be exactly like Tarrant and Gilmer. And if they hadn't been good role models, I doubt that it would have made any difference. I probably would have tried to be like them anyway. Well-known athletes, or even athletes who are lesser known, have no idea of the influence they have on youngsters.

Then—I think it was 1947—I was in church one Sunday night to hear a special speaker. I must have been about seventeen years of age. In walked a guy named Jackie Robinson. He wasn't the baseball player for the Brooklyn Dodgers, but was an All-American basketball player from Baylor University.

Anyhow, Robinson got up and witnessed that night. I don't remember exactly what he said, but it had to do with how God created man and how man couldn't understand Him. He talked about acceptance, commitment, and salvation. I remember how hearing what this All-American had to say affected me.

I think it's because of those men, particularly Robinson, that I go out every Sunday and speak at different churches and speak to all kinds of youth groups. It's because back in 1947 one man came to my church and spoke to my heart, and stirred something inside me. I am happiest when I'm in front of an audience, particularly an audience of young people, telling them about the love of God.

Back in 1947 an All-American athlete came to my church and spoke to my heart. I am happiest when I'm in front of an audience telling them about the love of God.

When I go out and speak to groups, the first thing I say is, "I suppose y'all wonder why a football coach is standing up here talking to you. It's because I am so thankful for what God has given me. I want to give some of it back to you, especially you young people, because I remember when I was sitting in the back row of my church and that All-American stood up in the pulpit and caught my attention and woke me up."

I spoke in Williamson, West Virginia, in 1991. As I said earlier, it was the week before we were to go and play at Michigan. I went up there and spoke to a young group in a tiny basketball gymnasium. Right before I spoke, a young man got up and gave his testimony. I didn't even know who he was. But as he began to speak, he pointed his finger at me and said, "One reason I am here today witnessing for Jesus Christ is because of that man sitting right there."

Man, it gives you a funny dad-gum feeling when someone points a finger at you.

He went on to say, "Years ago, I was at a Fellowship of Christian Athletes' conference at Jackson's Mill and I heard Coach Bowden speak. What he said really made an impact on my life and I've never been the same since." Now, through me God changed that boy's life and I didn't even know it. The word of God is a powerful instrument, and that's a fact.

I figured a few kids might get up and come forward; what happened was every kid in the dad-gum room got up! For one of the few times in my life, I was pretty near speechless.

Jackson's Mill, which was the boyhood home of General Stonewall Jackson, was a 4-H camp in a beautiful setting in the mountains outside Weston, West Virginia. I've been to many national FCA conferences, but Jackson's Mill, where we used to hold that West Virginia state conference, is still my favorite place. There was just something about it. It was so peaceful there, and it was the perfect setting to put yourself in touch with God. When I was at Jackson's Mill, I always thought, "I don't know how you can get much closer to the Lord than this."

Also, there was such great adult leadership at those West Virginia conferences. There were three men from Charleston who stood out. Their names were John Thomas, Ray McNabb, and Bill Smith (not the Bill Smith who co-authored this book). I think Thomas and McNabb are deceased now. They were great men who did great work for the Lord in their own small way. I'm sure y'all know some men just like them. Those are the ones who really make FCA work.

Now, I'm not going to pretend to think that Bobby Bowden changed the life of that boy who pointed his finger at me. I do believe, though, that through me God helped that kid. That's all I ask for. I never speak to any group without first praying, "God, use me. Speak through me. Give me the thoughts and the words, and give me the wisdom to express them in the right way."

I remember one conference at Jackson's Mill. On the last day of the conference I asked the kids who felt led to come down and make a commitment. I said, "I want to invite any one of y'all who wants to, to come on down here to the front and accept the Lord."

I don't pretend to think that I was responsible for what happened next either. I just happened to be the one on the platform with the microphone. Anyhow, I figured a few kids might get up and come forward. That's not what happened. What happened was every kid in the dad-gum room got up and came forward. There must have been 300, and not one boy hesitated. There wasn't any of this stuff of some kids holding back to see what their buddies were going to do. They all came down immediately. For one of the few times in my life, I was pretty near speechless.

I've been to FCA conferences where maybe one-third of the boys would answer the call. I've been to Billy Graham crusades and have seen him call folks to come forward, and a lot of people do. But I have never seen everyone in the place get up like those kids did that day at Jackson's Mill. When something like that happens, it makes you want to throw your hands up to the sky and shout, "God, how great Thou art!" It's almost like you're watching a miracle.

Now, when you speak to youngsters, you have to be careful what you say and how you act. You never know what kids are going to pick up. I remember one FCA conference I attended. We had some college athletes as counselors for the younger boys. It seems that some of the young boys got a little frisky after lights out. They had some pillow fights and threw a few water bombs. Anyhow, a couple of the counselors got mad at the kids and used some profanity.

That old devil is always out there waiting for another chance. That sneaky guy doesn't give up.

A high school coach, who was one of the leaders of the conference, called all the adults for a meeting, and in the meeting he said, "Listen, next year we're gonna have to screen these counselors better. We have to make sure we don't get any sinners here as counselors."

Someone spoke up and said, "But we're all sinners."

This coach snapped, "Speak for yourself."

That kind of bothered me because I think that coach should have read his Bible again. He missed it somewhere. Shoot, I'm a sinner. You're a sinner. We're all sinners. If we acknowledge the truth of the Bible, we know man is born with the seed to sin.

I know when you're in an environment like an FCA conference it's easy to get kids excited about Christ. But I sometimes use this story as an example of what can happen when the conference is over. I say, "It's like a fire made up of burning coals. The coals burn fiercely when they're all together. If some fall away, though, they will start to go out. Then, if somehow the coals that have fallen can be put back near the fire, they will start to burn again. You see, it helps us to be around other Christians. It reinforces our thinking. However, if we get away from Christian thinking for too long, the fire will often go out."

That old devil is always out there waiting for another chance. That sneaky guy doesn't give up.

I believe that next to a kid's daddy, a coach is probably second in influence. I tell other coaches that we have the responsibility for the souls of the young men under our charge. I've coached thousands of boys and I have never seen a single one fail in life, living it Christ's way. If a young person will put his life in God's hands and say, "Take me and use me," he cannot fail. I know some folks will say that's just fundamentalism, and that most fundamentalists are nothing but religious nuts anyhow. That's their opinion, but it's not going to change what I believe.

I spoke at an FCA breakfast during a National Coaches Association meeting a couple of years ago in Dallas. At that breakfast I said, "There's probably not a single group meeting in this country today that is more influential on the lives of young people than this one, because all of y'all command X number of young men. We are the most powerful group assembled that can help the youth of America in the name of Christ.

"If we were car salesmen, we probably wouldn't have much influence. If we were preachers, we might not have much influence because sometimes preachers have a hard time getting kids' attention. But as coaches, we are in a profession that has high visibility. It gives us a platform to witness. And who knows, one of those kids we witness to might turn out to be a world leader and a greater witness for Christ."

I know God has led me into coaching so that I might serve Him better. Our Florida State teams play in a stadium that seats 60,519, and in the near future it will seat more than that. In 1991, we played at Michigan in front of a crowd of more than 105,000, plus we had a national television audience watching. We have played in front of 80,000 in the Orange

Bowl. We have played on regional and national television many times. Man, you can't find a pulpit any bigger than that. Those are the biggest pulpits in the world, and it is a great opportunity to witness.

We all have an influence on somebody. A daddy influences his child. A momma influences her child. A preacher influences folks in his congregation. And as coaches, we influence many, many more.

In FCA there is a poem about influence that describes it better than any words I could say. Part of it goes like this:

> Their little eyes are upon you.
> And they're watching you night and day.
> There are little ears that quickly
> Take in every word you say.
>
> There's a wide-eyed little fellow.
> Who believes you're always right;
> And his ears are always open.
> And he watches day and night.
>
> You're setting an example,
> Every day in all you do,
> To the little boy who's waiting
> To grow to be like you.
>
> Anonymous

Kids look up to athletes. Whether we want to admit it or not, we're all hero worshipers. We don't have cowboys anymore. We don't have war heroes to admire. So most of the heroes today are athletes.

All those companies who get athletes to do their advertising commercials on television aren't dumb. Those companies aren't doing it out of the dad-gum goodness of their hearts. They know who kids look up to. Athletes have such a tremendous opportunity to be role models. There are millions of kids out there who practically beg for role models.

Whether we want to admit it or not, we're all hero worshipers. We don't have cowboys anymore. We don't have war heroes to admire. So most of the heroes today are athletes.

So, if we can influence just one of our players in the right way, that player will go back home where his little brother, or some little kid in the neighborhood, looks up to him. He's the big hero. Those kids will see it in his actions and words, and just maybe when those little kids grow up, they will influence someone else in the right way. And the circle will continue.

As a coach, I believe I have the responsibility to lead my players to want to be good Christians, good citizens, and good people, and to show them the way that can give their lives meaning. Now, I know all too often a lot of them aren't receptive. They think they know it all. I think sometimes that know-it-all stuff is a cover-up. They don't want to listen to some message from an old man, but I still have the responsibility to try and present it. And I'm going to keep trying to present it.

In my career I've probably spoken to tens of thousands of youngsters. I hope I have influenced some.

But let me say this: If it is true that I have influenced many young men and women, then my life has turned out as I hoped. If I have helped many more than I realize, then I feel very humble because I know I'm inadequate, terribly inadequate. My mortal fear is that I may have unknowingly hurt some.

I do believe that FCA has affected the lives of many youngsters in a positive way. It is such a great place to draw athletes together and motivate them to go out and motivate others. FCA helps youngsters put their lives in proper perspective.

If you have a chance to support or participate in FCA, you can't go wrong with this bunch; I recommend you check it out and consider getting involved.

Pride
and
Prejudice

I have to say something about segregation and integration. When I was growing up in Birmingham, I didn't even know what the words meant. I grew up in the south back in the 1930s and 1940s. Black folks lived in one part of town; white folks lived in another. That's just the way it was. I thought that was the way it was supposed to be. I never thought to wonder "Why?"

I knew there were white rest rooms and "colored" rest rooms, white water fountains and "colored" water fountains, but it never occurred to me to question that stuff. I didn't know the injustice of it and how serious it was. How could I? All I was interested in was playing sports and having a good time.

It's easy for me to say, "Yeah, but I played with the black kids when I was going to school. We used to shoot marbles together all the time. My mother had a black maid and we felt like she was part of the family." But that doesn't quite get it.

I remember when I was a senior at Howard College, and I took a golf class to learn how to play golf. Now, we didn't have access to a golf course. All we did during that class was go out and hit golf balls on the football field. But about two miles away was the Roebuck Country Club, where I still play golf when I go back to Birmingham. Being able to play golf at Roebuck back in those days was a big deal.

I didn't have any money back then, and I sure couldn't afford to pay to play golf. One day I said to a friend of mine named Gene McGee,

"Let's get up about six o'clock in the morning and go sneak on the Roebuck course and play some golf." So, we did.

Gene and I were out there playing golf, and while we were out there playing for free, about five or six caddies arrived at the course to get ready for the day. All the caddies were black guys. And since it was real early, they were out on the course looking for golf balls because if they found some good ones, they could sell them and make extra money. If I'd been smart I would have been looking for balls, too, because I sure could have used some extra cash.

If I could wipe out one thing in this world I think it would be racial prejudice. All we can do is hope and pray for understanding, tolerance, and guidance.

One of the caddies was a guy about fifteen years of age. Apparently, he had caddied a lot and had seen so many good golfers that he had figured out what you were supposed to do with your swing to hit it well. I know this, he hit it pretty well.

He started following us, so I asked him, "You want to hit some balls with us? You want to play?"

He said, "Yeah, if y'all don't mind."

So he started playing with us. And in the meantime, somebody back at the clubhouse must have seen us—two white kids out there playing with a black kid. All I know is that all of a sudden we looked back toward the pro shop and here came a pickup truck flying right down the middle of the fairway toward us. I mean, that truck was coming lickety-split.

I thought, *Oh, Lawdy, they've caught us. I ain't got no money, and I'm married and have two kids. Lawh, they're gonna take us to jail.*

That truck came to a screeching stop and a guy jumped out and yanked out a big gun. It was just a pistol, but it looked like a cannon to me. I flinched because I just knew that guy was going to point that thing at me and Gene and say, "Boys, what are y'all doin'? Don't you know you're breaking the law? You boys are under arrest." Gene and I were scared to death.

But that guy didn't even look at me and Gene. Instead, he grabbed that caddy and put that gun right up against his head and yelled, "What are you doin', boy? You know you ain't allowed to do this. I'm gonna fix you good."

And he grabbed that caddy by the back of the neck and threw him in the truck and took off. He never said one dad-gum word to me and Gene.

I often wondered what ever happened to that caddy. I guess all they did to him was scare him and let him go. I pray it wasn't worse than that, but it might have been.

I really didn't think we were doing anything bad by inviting that caddy to play with us. I thought the bad thing we did was sneaking onto the golf course. But back then blacks weren't allowed to play golf at Roebuck. It's ironic because today when I go back to that same golf course I see about as many black golfers as I do white golfers.

Anyway, that incident showed me for sure that segregation was something big and serious . . . and not good. All that caddy was doing was hitting a golf ball. He wasn't hurting anybody. I certainly didn't think I was any better than him just because I happened to be white.

Racial bigotry is nothing but pure ignorance, not to mention hate; and if my vocabulary was bigger, I could probably come up with some better words to describe it.

Until that incident, I don't think I really understood it all. I had gone to a white elementary school, a white high school, and a white college, and had always attended a white church. That was just what we did back then. When I was young I didn't hear anyone talk about the injustice of segregation. I certainly didn't hear it from the pulpit.

Boy, there sure is a lot of ignorance in this world. Racial bigotry is nothing but pure ignorance, not to mention hate; and if my vocabulary was bigger, I could probably come up with some better words to describe it.

As a Christian, there is no way to justify segregation. No way. All of us have a long way to go as far as prejudice is concerned, but thank God it isn't like it used to be. I don't think bigotry will ever totally go away though. There's too much of this "I'm better than y'all" stuff.

The first black player I ever coached was Garrett Ford, a fine running back at West Virginia from 1965 to 1967. He played two years for the Denver Broncos, and after that I hired him as an assistant coach when I got the head job at West Virginia in 1970. He is now an assistant athletic director at West Virginia in charge of providing educational guidance for the student-athletes.

When I was an assistant at Florida State and left in 1965, the school was segregated. When I came back to FSU ten years later, the school was integrated. Integration wasn't a problem, not for me. It never was and never has been.

I think back at West Virginia it was a little bit of a problem for Ford. I don't think I treated him any differently than any of the rest of the players, but I think he thought I did. I never thought anything about it. But Ford, who was from Washington, D.C., told me one time, "I have a hard time playing for somebody from Alabama." It all worked out, though, and we got past that.

I know that although integration has made strides, we still have miles and miles to go. Sometimes I think we'll never get those miles covered. Prejudice is an awful thing.

I'm always baffled by folks who say, "I'm something special because I'm white, or because I'm black."

Others will say, "Ain't I important? I'm so rich."

Whenever I hear that, I think of myself. I had no control over who my parents were. I had no control over whether they were rich or poor, white or black, or whatever. All I know is that I was born, and one day I was old enough to know who my parents were, and they turned out to be Bob and Sunset Bowden. And my name was Bobby Bowden. I had no control over the fact that I was born with white skin. I had no control over the fact that I was born in the south. I could have been born to black parents or to Chinese parents. I could have been born in Africa or somewhere over near Mongolia. I wasn't. I was born in Birmingham, and my skin was white.

Those folks who believe that they're going to get into heaven on the basis of skin color are wrong, and need to go back and read their Bibles again.

The only thing I know is that we are all born equal. Now, that doesn't mean there is equality in the heart of man. But we are all equal in the sight of God, and we're all going to go somewhere one of these days. I don't think we're all going to go to the same place though. Those folks with hate in their hearts had better be careful.

How can folks in their right minds think that God is going to let them into heaven just because they are white and then turn away good people just because they are black? The folks who believe that are wrong, and need to go back and read their Bibles again.

It all goes back to God's commandments. If we obeyed them, all that other stuff wouldn't be an issue. People make bigotry out of the color of a person's skin.

It's just skin.

There are some who don't like blacks. There are some who don't like whites. There are some who don't like Latins. There are some who don't like Orientals. There are folks who don't like others just because they're different or because they follow a different religion. It goes on and on.

We think we're so civilized. We're not. I remember once when there was a power failure in New York City and all the lights went out for a brief time. Man, there was looting, rioting, murder, rape, and Lord knows what else. Are we civilized just when the lights are on?

It shouldn't be that way. God's commandment is that we love each other.

There is so much prejudice and hate in the world. I don't know if man will ever get past that. It just shows how far we've gotten away from the basics of what God wanted for man. All we can do is hope and pray for understanding, tolerance, and guidance. If I could wipe out one thing in this world I think it would be racial prejudice.

I was always taught that each man has a heart and soul, and the blood that courses through his veins is the same as mine. If he is cut, he will bleed. If he is hurt, he will cry. And when he dies, he will be as dead as I'll be someday.

And I know that those folks who go around with hate in their hearts and treat others so cruel are going to have to do a lot of explaining when they meet their Maker.

I'm going to have enough explaining to do. I don't want to have to explain that too.

I Ain't No Saint

I sort of smile when I hear some folks refer to me as "Saint Bobby." I don't get bent out of shape over it, but I do feel a little self-conscious. I don't put any stock in it. A saint? I definitely know I'm not a saint.

That "Saint Bobby" stuff could be misconstrued that I'm something I'm not. When folks want to put a halo over your head, it can move down around your neck in a hurry. I say, "You know what they say about a halo, don't you? They say if you drop it down about one foot it becomes a dadgum noose."

Once I heard a preacher say, "Many times members of the congregation have a tendency to put me on a pedestal. The air can get pretty thin up there." I kind of feel that way when folks refer to me as a saint. That's pretty tough to live up to.

I can tarnish that "saint" stuff easily by going back to when I was a youngster. Then I was a little bit of a wise guy. I had a smart mouth too. It all had to do with me thinking I was pretty good with my fists; I got a big thrill out of fighting.

One year at Christmas Daddy got me a pair of boxing gloves and a punching bag. Daddy put up that bag down in the basement, and I used to go down there and punch that thing by the hour. I'd hit that bag so long my knuckles would get raw and bleed. I never wore gloves when I hit the bag.

I must have punched that bag for years. And I got to where I could make it sing pretty good. Although I didn't know it, I probably used punching that bag for therapy. If I had any bad thoughts, or if I had something bothering me, I could go down in the basement and bang on that bag and get it all out of my system.

It wasn't long before a lot of the kids in the neighborhood started coming around and we would go down in the basement and put those gloves on and box. As a result of punching that bag I developed pretty quick hands and I usually wound up winning more than my share of those so-called boxing matches. I always was quick on my feet.

Anyhow, I got to where I was pretty cocky. That cockiness led to a lot of fights in elementary school and high school. Shoot, when I was a kid I fought all the time. Man, I got in some trouble.

I always had to be careful about my mouth because it would load me up sometimes. I thought if somebody said something you didn't like, you challenged him. That's what I did, and it always led to fights. And if somebody hit you, that led to a fight for sure. "Hit back and hit often" was my motto. It got to where I just plain loved to fight.

But you know when you do that, you better be careful. There's always someone who's a little quicker, stronger, and tougher than you are. I learned that lesson when I was a freshman in high school. It was the most embarrassing fight I ever got into. I was walking home from school one day with a buddy of mine. And as we were walking across the Howard campus to my house, there was this bigger kid walking in front of us.

I thought, "I'll just impress my buddy. I'll show him I can beat up on this guy." Now, the guy was bigger than I was, but that didn't make any difference. I always liked to pick on bigger guys to show everybody how tough I was and that I could whip them.

You know what they say about a halo, don't you? That if you drop it down about one foot it becomes a dad-gum noose.

So I picked up a rock and threw it at him. The rock missed, but it came close enough that he turned around to see where it came from. He gave us a long look, but didn't say anything. He just continued walking; I guess he thought it must have been an accident. I picked up another rock and let fly again. This time the rock came real close; it might have grazed him. He turned around again, and this time he figured out what was going on.

And ol' smart-mouth me, I said something like, "What are you looking at? If you don't like it, why don't you do something about it, you so-and-so?" I shouldn't have said that. Then I said to my buddy, "Watch me fix this guy."

And we got into it. I hit him first. It didn't even faze him. He didn't even blink. I had never had that happen before. I think that's the only punch I landed. I mean, this guy was so much stronger than I was that it wasn't funny. He proceeded to beat me to a pulp.

My nose was bleeding. My mouth was bleeding. One eye was swollen. And the more I tried to back away, the more he hurt me. I couldn't get away from him and couldn't stop him from hurting me. I sure knew I wasn't hurting him, unless it was his fists. I knew this wasn't the kind of impression I wanted to make on my buddy.

Finally, one of the older college boys came by and pulled us apart. And while this college guy was holding him, I hauled off and popped him a good one. The guy broke away from the college guy and beat me to a pulp again. Man, he dang near killed me. That fight didn't do my pride much good. You might say I learned that being a wise guy could be pretty painful.

I remember one time when I was about thirteen, I was up at the Howard College field playing. Now, the quickest way to get home from there was to crawl through a hole we had made in the fence. That's how all of us kids in the neighborhood would get onto the field to play or to watch football practice.

As I was about to crawl through that hole I spied a magazine somebody must have dropped. I picked up that thing and opened it. Dad-gum, it was full of pictures of naked women. Whooeee! I had never seen a naked woman before. Man, I thought those pictures were about the prettiest things I ever saw.

I'd like to say I put that magazine down and left it where I found it, but I didn't. I took it home and hid it in my room so Momma wouldn't find it. Oh, I was bad. I used to go up there and look at those pictures. I don't remember how long I kept that dirty magazine. Today I am not proud of that, but I was just a kid.

The truth was, though, that even at that age my conscience would bother me. I knew I was getting bad thoughts from those pictures. And I knew if I had to sneak around to do something, then it wasn't right. Eventually, I threw that magazine away.

From where we lived, everything I wanted to do, or everywhere I wanted to go took me through the Howard College campus. So Howard was always in my life. I had to go through the campus to go to elementary school, to high school, to go to a picture show, and to catch a streetcar to go downtown.

My buddies and I would meet at the streetcar station, which was just past the grammar school, and go to movies. One night after a movie we were in a little drugstore near the campus having a milk shake and the Howard College night watchman came in. We didn't like him because he used to run us off campus all the time. Truth was, though, we loved for him to chase us.

This particular night we decided to give him a hard time. We got up and left the drugstore and started walking home across the campus. And on our way, we picked up some rocks and started throwing them at the windows in one of the college buildings. We broke out a couple. And pretty soon, we saw that night watchman's flashlight shining in the distance. We laughed and said, "Here he comes." And we took off, and he chased us. He never did catch us.

But we were so stupid. We forgot he had seen us in the drugstore. And sure enough, the next day the college president called Daddy. Daddy said to me, "Bobby, did you do that? Did you break out those windows?"

And I denied it because I knew if I told the truth, Daddy would have blistered me good. I said, "Naw, Daddy. Huh-uhh, Daddy. I didn't do that. I was in the drugstore all the time. I promise you it wasn't me. I didn't throw anything through any windows." So, I not only did something bad by breaking out those windows, I did something worse by lying about it.

Oh, I was bad.

There was something else we would do. I'm not sure I ought to tell this because I'm really not proud of this one. We would go up to the college on Sunday afternoons when everything was locked up and sneak into the gymnasium and play basketball. Now, breaking into the gymnasium wasn't the worst of it. What we did was take off all our clothes and play basketball—buck naked.

Lawdy, I don't know why we did that. I don't know why kids do what they do. Just having fun, I guess. But can you picture about fifteen kids running up and down that floor playing basketball naked as jaybirds? I suppose we were just daring somebody to try and catch us.

I remember one night Mort Vaserberg (who went on to Auburn on a scholarship and is now a retired U.S. Marine major), Dennis Hudson (the guy who loaned me the money so Ann and I could get married), and I went down to East Lake Park. The park had a nice-sized lake.

It was a nice place to swim. There was a big diving platform out in the middle of it. It was late and everything was locked up. But we slipped over the fence and took off all our clothes and started swimming and diving. (I don't know why we were always taking off our clothes. Maybe we took them off because it was hot. That's the best reason I can think of.)

Anyway, we were having the best time diving off that high dive platform. We figured if anybody came, we were so fast that we could get away before they could catch us.

But we forgot about one thing—lights. The pool had lights around it for when they had night swimming. Somebody, maybe the night watchman, came along and turned on the lights. And there we were, all three of us—me, Mort, and Dennis—up on that platform in the middle of that pool naked as the day we were born. Man, did we ever take off.

They never did catch us.

I remember once I got mad at one of our neighbors. For some reason I thought he had done something. Anyway, I was angry and set about scheming to get even. Why is it human beings waste so much time on hate and revenge? We sure don't listen to the Word, do we? I know I wasn't listening. I was too busy being a wise guy. Truth of the matter was, I was acting like an immature fool.

This neighbor had this beautiful big tree in his yard. And one night I got Daddy's saw and cut it down. I never owned up to what I had done, not to anybody, until now. I think the man knew who did it, though, but he never got me to admit it. To this day, whenever I go back to the old neighborhood and drive past that house, I think of what I did. I'll have to explain that one to the Lord too.

I remember the worst free-for-all I ever got involved in. Well, the truth is I didn't really get involved in it—I started it. It was during my freshman year in college. We were playing Tennessee Tech and I was in at defensive back. Now, this was just a few years after World War II and about half of our players were veterans. I reckon Tennessee Tech's squad was the same. We had guys on our team who were twenty-five, twenty-six, and twenty-seven years old. We even had one who was thirty-two. And I was out there at age nineteen. I was a baby. But I guess I wanted to show them I could hold my own and wouldn't back down from anybody.

It was the second quarter and we were getting beat 14-0. We were kind of embarrassed because we thought we were pretty good. Plus, Tech was fixin' to score again. On this one play, a Tech player came my way and I just hauled off and hit him in the face with my fist. I knocked him flat. This was in the days before players wore face masks. I hit him a good shot, only he was tougher than I thought. He got up and came after me, and we went at it. The first thing I knew both benches had cleared and it was now a fist-swinging melee. And I was right in the middle of it.

When the officials finally got the field cleared, the first thing they did was have a conference to figure out what they should do. And then they all looked in my direction. They knew I had started it by popping that guy. The next thing I knew I had been thrown out of the game.

Two games later we were playing Western Kentucky, and I slugged another player. Yep, another free-for-all. I got thrown out of that game too. This time the coach took me aside and let me have it. He said, "Bowden, you've been thrown out of two of our games in the last month. Do you know why?"

I knew why. It was because I was a smarty and was trying to show my older teammates how tough I was. I didn't say anything, though, because I didn't think the coach really wanted me to answer.

He said, "You're getting thrown out of games because you're just plain scared out there. You're scared those big boys are gonna hurt you. And you're using any excuse to get yourself out of there so you won't have to tackle anybody and get yourself hurt."

I've learned you don't have to go around using bad language and fighting to show others how macho you are. That stuff won't get you anywhere; it just shows lack of vocabulary and character.

That really wounded my pride. But it was good psychology because from then on I was determined to prove him wrong. I never got thrown out of another game.

I did a lot of maturing in the next couple of years. My junior year we were playing Tennessee Tech again. It was at their place. I was at quarterback now. Early in the second half, I had just completed a pass. When the play was over, one of their linemen walked past me and slapped me right in the face. Whap!

I said, "Buddy, I'll see you after the game."

He smiled and said, "I'll be waiting."

Well, I didn't go looking for that boy. Naw. Now, if he had come looking for me, I probably would have mixed it up with him. But I sure wasn't going to waste my time looking for him. I never did get into another fight, thank the Lord. I learned you don't have to do that.

I suppose if you talked to some of my old friends, or guys I played with, they could tell you a few more stories, maybe a few I might not be proud of.

I learned a long time ago that you don't have to go around using bad language and fighting and trying to hurt people to show others how macho you are. That stuff won't get you anywhere. It just shows lack of vocabulary and character.

I knew of a hockey player who once played in the National Hockey League. His name isn't important, but his story is. I'll call him John. Anyhow, John was perhaps the first professional athlete ever hauled into court for an incident that occurred during an athletic contest.

What John did was hit another player in the head with his hockey stick. He blinded the player in one eye, made him deaf in one ear, and ended his career. And he was charged with criminal assault with a deadly weapon. Now, he wasn't found guilty in court, but when the trial was over he was so sorry for what he had done that he spent the next couple of years going to churches and FCA conferences.

The man who told me this story about John said he met John at an FCA conference at Shippensburg State College in Pennsylvania. He said that one afternoon John came up to him and asked if he would come to his room that evening. The man said he would. When he went to John's room that evening, John began to talk.

He said, "Have you ever done anything you were sorry for?"

The man said he replied, "Yes, probably a million times."

John said, "Well, you know, when I got into that fight that night on the ice I was so mad at my opponent that I wanted to kill him. When I hit him I thought I had killed him. And as soon as I hit him, I stepped back, dropped the hockey stick and said, 'My God, what have I done! What have I done!'

"And it was done, and I couldn't undo it. What makes people want to do things, or say things, to hurt someone?"

The man said he answered, "I don't have an answer for that, John. I wish I did. I think you need to talk to someone other than me. Maybe you need to talk to God."

And the man added that one day later, John packed and left the conference and he never saw him again. The man said, "John was desperately looking for something, but to this day I don't know whether he ever found it. I hope and pray he did."

I've thought about that story many times and have often wondered the same thing the hockey player did—why do people, who are born with the ability to reason, set about to deliberately hurt others? I wish I had an answer to that.

The story meant a lot to me, too, because I'm sure I hurt my share of folks, especially when I was going through my fighting stage. I don't dwell on it, but I know I used to do and say things to hurt people. It's easy to say, "Oh, well, Bobby was just being a normal boy." But that's no excuse.

For a time in my life I had quite a bit of bad in me. I did some bad things. And I've sure asked for a lot of forgiveness.

The key is to go to church, study the Word, and put your faith and trust in the Lord, and He will handle it. He will enable us to control our thoughts. We have to confess our sins and truly and honestly ask God to change our lives.

We all know when we're sinning. And we know sinning will take us farther than we want to go. And the sad truth is it will often keep us much longer than we want to stay. However, if a person will put the Lord first and foremost in his heart and mind, the rest will take care of itself.

So you see, I ain't no saint, not even close. But thank the Lord, I'm not what I used to be.

The idea of people hurting other people is one of the reasons I go out and try to witness to youngsters, especially the young men who come under my charge. They need to know that stepping on folks is not the way to live.

Now, most kids fall into several categories. Some have been raised by good parents, attended church, listened to a good pastor or priest, and were taught right from wrong. Some kids come from broken homes. Some never had a daddy and momma to make them go to church. Some don't even know who their daddies or mommas are. Some were raised by their grandmommas or other relatives. Some were farmed out to foster homes.

And if I happen to get some of these kids on my team, then I might be the closest thing they've ever had to a parent. That's an awesome responsibility. I honestly feel we are going to be judged on how we have treated the young people we come in contact with.

There is one scripture I have used in talking to other coaches and when speaking to adults who put on FCA conferences. It's the scripture in Matthew 18:6 where Jesus called a child to come and sit on His lap while He was talking to His disciples. Jesus said, "But whoever causes one of these little ones who believe in Me to sin, it would be better for him if a millstone were hung around his neck, and he were drowned in the depth of the sea." I don't want that curse on me.

I interpret that to mean woe unto the person who causes somebody else to sin, stumble, and fall. Whether we want to admit it or not, we are influencing the kids we are coaching. We are influencing so many others because of our visibility. And our actions and words can influence them the right way, or the wrong way.

I guess I'm repeating myself, but I have to keep repeating it. I believe coaches could be, and should be, great role models for youngsters. The same is true for athletes, especially professional athletes. And if those people who have such an opportunity to be influencers go out and get into alcohol, drugs, sex, and so forth, I believe they are guilty in the eyes of the Lord. We are the ones He is talking about in that scripture because we are defeating God's purpose by doing bad when we could be doing so much good.

"Bobby was a confirmed chocolate freak even back then; I suspect when Bobby dies it will probably be from chocolate overdose."

I believe a person's actions speak so loudly that you can't hear a word he or she says. If I'm going to stand up and say what I say and try to witness to young folks, but then go out and commit all kinds of disobediences, my words are meaningless. My words have no more impact than me spitting in the ocean.

Some of those athletes who do bad will claim, "We should be judged only by what we do on the field. We shouldn't be judged by what we do off the field." That's baloney. They are role models, whether they want to be or not. What they do and say off the field has more influence on youngsters than what they do on the field.

That's why I have always liked sports like football and boxing. Yes, I know they are violent sports, but for me when I was young, they were good ways to get my bad out of me. I could get it all out. I tell my players that football is a sport where it's legal to hit the other guy. Now, I'm talking about hitting as in blocking and tackling within the rules.

I say to my players, "Men, the rules say y'all can hit your opponent, and hit him as hard as you can. You can get rid of all your aggression and inhibitions out on the field. Just do it within the rules."

Then I tell them, "I want you to be tigers out on that field, but I want you to be kitty cats off that field. You can prove how tough you are in combat. You don't have to prove it anywhere else. I know you aren't saints. Lawdy, neither am I. When you're off the field, I want you to be courteous and polite gentlemen."

Now, a few of my players don't always do that. Most do though.

I reckon I'll close this chapter by giving my childhood friend, Vince Gibson, a short opportunity to comment on this "Saint Bobby" stuff. We played together at Howard College, then coached together later on; he'll tell you the daggone truth about me.

■ ■ ■

"Bobby was gutsy, feisty, cocky, and very competitive. You have to understand, we both came from a tough part of Birmingham. It was the roughneck part of town. And we ran with some tough playground types. If Bobby had been a goody-goody boy, he would have had a tough time surviving in that neighborhood. He wasn't a saint by any means, but he wasn't a bad guy either. However, guys who underestimated him and backed him into a corner discovered they had a tiger on their hands. Bobby would fight.

"The thing that impressed me when I was a youngster—I'm a few years younger than Bobby—is that he always took up for the underdog. One of the first times I remember Bobby making an impression on me was when I was about eleven years old. He must have been fourteen.

"We used to go up to the Howard College football field and play. We

were playing up there on this particular day and there was this bully picking on some of the smaller kids.

"Bobby, who wasn't very big himself, marched up to this guy and got
right in his face and said, 'Cut it out. Leave them kids alone.'

"This bully said, 'You gonna make me?'

"Well, that was all the invitation Bobby needed. He jumped in and
was all over that guy like a pack of fleas on a dog. He beat that bully like a
drum. From that time on, everybody respected and looked up to Bobby.
From then on, he was my idol.

"I know this, we had some fun when I coached with him at South
Georgia College. All we did then was eat, breathe, sleep, and live the
game. We used to go on recruiting trips. And they weren't like the recruit-
ing trips big-time coaches take today. We didn't get on any airplanes.
What we did was hop in the car, stop at a grocery store and get a couple of
Coca-Colas, then stop at a bakery and get a bag of brownies and take off.
Bobby was a chocolate freak even then. I suspect when Bobby dies it will
probably be from chocolate overdose.

"A lot of folks think that because Bobby has that slow drawl and
seems easy and laid-back, that he's soft on his players. Not true. Bobby
was, and is, a hard-nosed coach. His practices are tough, and that's because
he's a tough guy himself. He never did coach with that soft, goody-two-
shoes attitude.

"But his greatest attribute when it comes to his players is that he has
always been fair with them. His players always know where they stand with
him.

"He genuinely cares for everybody the same way. When my mother
and daddy retired, they moved to Tallahassee. Not long after that, my
daddy died. I was coaching out in Kansas at that time. Well, Bobby and
Ann took my mother under their wing. They cared for her just the same as
if she had been one of their mommas. I will always be grateful to them for
that.

"Folks are saying that Bobby is going to become a legend. They're
wrong. In my opinion, he already is a legend, and is very deserving of it.
They don't come any finer than Bobby Bowden."

CHAPTER 28

I Can't Coach Forever

Whenever I get to feeling like I'm somebody important, and I have to admit every once in a while that old devil gets hold of me, I always have the perfect remedy. I go to the ocean or the Gulf of Mexico and sit on the beach, and just stare at all that water and all that blue sky. I feel about as important as a wee little grain of that sand I'm wigglin' my toes in.

Man, I've been on some Caribbean cruises, and believe me, when you're out on all that water, even that big ship seems pretty small. I imagine folks who live in the mountains get the same feeling when they stand on top of a peak and look at all that expanse of land down below.

Once, I heard a man talk about his first sight of the Yosemite Valley in California. He said, "You drive about halfway up a big mountain and then go through a tunnel, and when you come out of the tunnel there is the valley, with all its awesome granite peaks and waterfalls. It's a valley that was carved out by the glaciers years and years ago. It simply takes your breath away. And when I saw it for the first time, all I could say was, "my God."

If you've ever been in a hurricane, a tornado, or a storm at sea, I don't know how anyone in his or her right mind could feel important compared to all that awesome power. I sure don't. I never have.

So, in the scheme of things, we aren't very much at all. And certainly a guy who has won a few games of football isn't much.

Folks dwell on records our teams have set, how many games we've been fortunate enough to win, our bowl record, where my career stands on the all-time victory list and all that stuff. I don't dwell on that. I never have.

(Going into the 1994 season, Bowden was the second winningest active coach in the country with 239 career wins. Penn State's Joe Paterno was number one, with 257. Bowden was fifth on the all-time winning list behind such greats as Bear Bryant with 323 wins, Glenn "Pop" Warner 319, Amos Alonzo Stagg with 314, and Paterno.)

Back when I was coaching at West Virginia, I picked up a newspaper one day and saw where some writer wrote that at that time I was the fifteenth winningest active coach in the country. I said to myself, "Well, I'll be dad-gum. I didn't know that."

All I ever tried to do was win the game we were playing that particular day. All that stuff is nice, I guess, but what I get caught up in is trying to build the best football team I can build, one that wins and wins consistently. When we win, now, I really get caught up in that. That makes me happy. And when we lose, I'm the unhappiest dad-gum guy you ever saw. I don't think my disappointment over a loss shows because I try to hide it as best I can. It's tough to do that sometimes though. To me, the total number of wins just happened. If you stay in one business long enough, you ought to accomplish something.

I guess I could get burned out as a coach, too, but I'm too lazy for that to happen. I'll go and take a nap before I'll let myself get burned out.

I never imagined back when I first started coaching that we'd ever win as many games as we have, or that I'd stay in coaching this long. I can remember when I thought guys like Darrell Royal, Frank Broyles, Bobby Dodd, and General Bob Neyland were old men and still in coaching. Yet, I think Royal, Broyles, and Neyland quit when they were about fifty-three. When they hung it up, I thought, *I'll probably quit coaching when I'm that old too.*

Yet here I am sixty-four and still going strong. I do realize that because of all the pressures nowadays that a lot of coaches get out of the business when they're fairly young. They will say they are "burned out."

I guess I could get burned out, but I don't think I ever will. I think I'm too lazy for that to happen. I'll go somewhere and take me a nap before I'll let myself get burned out. I've always been able to sleep and rest, and when I wake up, I'm ready to go again.

I remember about eight or nine years ago, a guy introduced me at the Orlando Quarterback Club. He said, "Coach Bobby Bowden has won more ball games than Bobby Dodd, Bob Neyland, Shug Jordan, and Bud Wilkinson." He named a few more. I forget who all he named. But he named some pretty famous coaches.

Again I thought, *Dad-gum! Have I been at it that long?*

How long do I want to coach?

That's a good question. Now that I'm getting up there in age, folks ask me that all the time.

I answer, "I don't know. I do know that after you retire there ain't but one big event left. So I ain't in no hurry about retiring."

I just know I want to coach as long as I can, but that will have to be based on two things: 1) my health, and 2) my enthusiasm. As far as I know, I'm healthy. I do have a bulge around the middle. I like to eat. Always have.

As far as my enthusiasm, I know I haven't lost a drop of that. I still have the same enthusiasm I had back in 1953 when I started coaching. I honestly don't feel any different.

I still can't wait to wake up in the morning and get going. I love to be out on the field coaching our players. I love the strategy. I love to study film and find some weakness in an opponent that we might be able to exploit. I love the excitement of game day.

There's no greater high than standing on the sidelines during an exciting game with 60,000 or 70,000 people in the stands. I get goose bumps just thinking about it.

To me, coaching is great fun. I've heard people talk about getting high on some of that funny dust, or high on that goofy weed, or high on alcohol. I've never had the slightest temptation to use any of that stuff. Man, I can't imagine a high greater than the feeling of standing on the sidelines during an exciting game with 60,000 or 70,000 people in the stands. I get goose bumps just thinking about it.

You know, I love to read books on war, particularly World War II. Now, I know I've been lucky in that I've never had to go to war. I know football isn't war, but in my opinion, it's like war in that it's a battle. I think it's just the competitiveness man has in him. It's the competitiveness to go out and perform and whip somebody, and then strut your stuff.

Now, the only thing wrong with that is that you've got to win. There ain't much fun in competing and losing.

In Florida I can coach until I'm seventy. And when I reach that age, if I'm still healthy and enthusiastic, I might try to keep on coaching. Now, all that has to be based on FSU wanting me to stay. I know I have to win enough games so they will want me to stay. But I think if I can keep the right people happy and stay excited myself, I can stay here about as long as I want.

Some people look at me and say, "Boy, ol' Bobby has it made. He has a lifetime contract. He's making so much money. He's a winner. We just love him to death."

Well, the truth is that all it would take would be about two losing seasons, and then they'd be looking for a younger coach. Sometimes I feel like Satchel Paige when he said, "Don't look back, because someone might be gaining on you."

I also know if I started doing a lousy job and some folks started doing things behind my back, I'd just say, "Okay, if y'all want to buy out my contract, I'll just leave." At my age, and with the contract I have, I don't have to worry about it. My financial situation is such that I don't have to put up with much guff from fans. That gives me a little comfort.

It really doesn't matter how bad I want to coach or how good I feel. If we have a few bad years, the pressure would be put on me. Folks would start saying, "Bobby is too old." I think that's a built-in excuse to get rid of a coach once he's in his sixties. That old "the game has passed him by" stuff is a bunch of baloney.

One advantage of being older is that the things that used to bother me don't bother me anymore. There isn't any panic and frustration now in hoping and praying we can win enough games to get us to the Orange Bowl, or the Sugar Bowl, or the Cotton Bowl, or the Gator Bowl, or the Fiesta Bowl, or whatever bowl. The pressure is off.

I know I can't coach forever. And I know when I do have to hang it up that I'll probably go through withdrawal—whatever that is—but I'll handle it. The Lord will take care of me and see me through it. He has never turned His back on me yet.

I could never retire and then hang around Tallahassee and second-guess the guy who replaced me. New coaches don't like the old coaches always being around and looking over their shoulders. That's natural. Besides, if I did that, it would be unfair to the new guy. When I came to Tallahassee back in 1976 there were four former Florida State coaches living here. Maybe it was five. I'm not sure. But I know a lot of times those first few years it felt like my ears were burning.

I know I can't coach forever. When I do have to hang it up, I'll probably go through withdrawal, but the Lord will see me through it.

I won't do that to a new coach. When I quit, I'll leave and let the new guy have it. I'll just go somewhere on the beach or go somewhere where there's a golf course nearby and get on with my life. Also, I'll go visit my kids and grandkids.

Now, I'm not going to say exactly how many more years I'm going to coach because I don't know. Only the Lord knows that.

Now, what would happen if I never won another game? First of all, I'd have to resign. And then I'd just feel like God looked down at me and said, "Well, Bobby, I think that's enough. It's time for you to go on to something else." I'd just figure that God had a bigger plan for me and wanted me to get on with it.

I believe that God speaks to me in a leading type of way. He has led me down the paths He has wanted me to go. Whenever I've made a move in my career, there has been something that swayed me. It was the Holy Spirit, or something.

So, I think when the time comes for me to hang it up, God will whisper to me through the Spirit, and I'll know.

CHAPTER 29

We Have
to Read
the Book

I have heard so many folks moan, "Gee, I don't know what God wants me to do. I don't know what He has planned for me."

I think my mother and daddy had the right idea about how to find out what God's will is for our lives. They would say, "Listen to Him. The best way to get Him to talk to you is to read the Bible because it is the book of life. It is God's book."

I hear folks moan when I say, "If you don't know what God wants, then you haven't read and studied the Bible. Read the dad-gum book! God will talk to you; He'll tell you what to do. He will help you shape your life. How can you expect God to talk to you if you don't give Him a chance? He put all those words in the book so we could know Him. The Bible is God's Word."

I've said before that I was fortunate to have been raised by Christian parents in a Christian environment, and I don't remember a day when I haven't read the Bible. Now, sometimes when I read it, I'm not always listening. I have a King James Bible that Ann gave me some years ago, and I have scribbled down many of my random thoughts on the inside of the front and back covers of it. A lot of it looks like hen scratchings, but whenever I read something that evokes a thought, I grab a pencil and scribble it down before I forget it. A lot of those thoughts I use when I preach, or give a talk.

Here are some of those thoughts:

SALVATION IS GOD'S FREE GIFT,
BUT MAN MUST CHOOSE.

Everyone can be saved. You can be saved. I can be saved. God requires each of us to make a choice. If you choose salvation, God will give it to you. If you don't, He goes on to someone else. God gives man free will. He says to each of us, "It's here if you want it, but you don't have to accept it. You can go your own way. It's up to you."

Christ tells us in Revelation 22:16–17, "'I, Jesus, have sent My angel to testify to you these things in the churches. I am the Root and the Offspring of David, and the Bright and Morning Star.' And the Spirit and the bride say, 'Come!' And let him who hears say, 'Come!' And let him who thirsts come. And whoever desires, let him take the water of life freely."

He tells us right there that it's free. It doesn't cost a thing, not a dad-gum red cent. Now, why man can't figure that out, I don't know. We are always looking to get something for nothing. Well, here it is. It's the greatest gift of all, and it's free. And some folks turn their backs on it.

Now, I believe we really do pay a price. Some aren't willing to do that. By paying a price, I mean that we can't just accept Him and then do nothing. I feel when we accept Him we have the responsibility to serve Him, to be humble, and to be kind toward our fellowman. And we can't go around looking for someone perfect to be kind to. Jesus didn't do that. He was the friend of sinners and of the despised. He loved them.

I've always figured it's easier to love than it is to hate. Love makes you feel good. I heard a wise man say once that love isn't love until you give it away. I believe that. Besides, hating takes too much energy. I don't have time for that. All hate does is destroy you and make you ugly.

To me, paying a price also means that we might be ostracized by others. We might get kicked out of some club or fraternity. We might get looked down on by some folks and be the butt of jokes when we attempt to live the way God wants us to live. That's never bothered me. Heck, Paul paid a price. Peter paid a price. But I know where those two guys are today. I hope and pray that when my time comes, I'll join them.

ONLY GOD SATISFIES COMPLETELY,
BECAUSE THE SOUL WAS MADE FOR GOD,
AND WITHOUT HIM IT IS RESTLESS
AND IN SECRET TORMENT.

I really believe that statement.

We were made for God; He made us for Himself. And we're not going to find the real joy, peace of mind, inner contentment, and happiness we're looking for until we allow God to take over our lives. And without Him, we will be dead spiritually.

It doesn't matter how wealthy we are. It doesn't matter how famous we are. Unless we let God fill that void in our lives, there's always going to be something missing. Unless we find that relationship with Him, there will come a time in our lives when we will get down on our knees and ask Him to come and save us. We will have tried it our way and it will not have worked, and that's when we will say to Him, "God, help us."

If money, nice homes, and all that stuff made a person happy, no millionaire would ever need therapy. From what I've observed, it seems like a lot of those folks sure spend a lot of time and money paying someone to help them straighten out their lives. That's proof enough for me that you can't buy happiness.

Billy Graham told a story once about the late Howard Hughes, who was one of the richest men in the world. He had billions. And yet, when he died, he was not only alone, but he starved to death. Here was a man with all that money, but he couldn't buy friends. He could have bought enough food to feed a small country, yet he died of malnutrition.

Mr. Graham said, "And when Howard Hughes died, a man asked, 'I wonder how much money he left?' "

Graham said he answered, "I know exactly how much he left."

Then the man said to Graham, "You do, how much?"

And Mr. Graham said he told the man, "He left it all."

Amen to that.

God knows what's wrong with each of us. He knows that when we're tormented it is because we have separated ourselves from Him.

Have you ever gone into the kitchen and taken a recipe out to prepare a delicious dish, and when you take it out of the oven and taste it, it tastes dad-gum awful? I bet you have. And the reason it tastes awful is because you forgot and left out the key ingredient. It's the same with life. If we leave out the key ingredient—and many folks do leave God out— our lives are going to be just plain awful and miserable. We aren't going to be happy.

We can go out and play and have fun. We can go out to nice restaurants and eat the most wonderful food. We can go to banquets and be around crowds of people. But when we go home at night and put our heads on the pillow, man, that's when the torment can begin. We can't fool our hearts. When we're alone, our hearts will whisper to us, and that whisper can become a roar, and that roar can become an avalanche of torment. That has to be the worst loneliness man can have.

In Matthew 11:28–30 Jesus says, "Come to Me, all you who labor and are heavy laden, and I will give you rest. Take My yoke upon you and learn from Me, for I am gentle and lowly in heart, and you will find rest for your souls. For My yoke is easy and My burden is light."

I don't care what we do, it will not—and I repeat, will not work without God.

Thank the Lord, I've turned my life over to Him and don't have that torment. And I have found that His promise is true. The yoke is easy and the burden is light.

THE MIND CONTROLS THE BODY.
THE HEART CONTROLS THE MIND.
AND THE SPIRIT CONTROLS THE HEART.

I use this when I'm talking to football players. Now, this doesn't apply just to football players. It applies to everyone. But when I stand up in front of 100 or so players, I know that many of them aren't interested in going to church. They aren't interested in increasing their spiritual values. And they sure aren't interested in becoming better people. All they're interested in is playing football and becoming big, famous athletes.

Where do you get the spirit and desire to excel athletically? From only one place—from God. Only He can motivate you to be the best you can be.

I tell them, "If y'all want to play and become successful, then you have to get the ultimate out of your abilities. To do that you have to become as strong as you can and find that extra power, extra spirit, and extra spark. And that boils down to enthusiasm."

And I tell them that enthusiasm has to come from the heart. It has to come from within. I say, "Men, I can't get it out of you if you're not willing to listen to me and do what I say. And even if you do that, that still won't quite get it. One man can't give it to another. That's why we need God and the great strength, spirit, and peace that only He can give us. If we have that, then we can reach down inside ourselves and find that little something extra when we need it."

Then I bring out the point that everything we do, every move we make, and every movement of each finger is based on our will to do it. It all starts in the brain, and the brain controls the body. Everything begins with the mind.

There are no exceptions. Even when we sit on a hot stove, we may think we didn't have time to think about it. We think we just say, "Yeow! That thing was hot. I jumped off that danged stove so fast, and I moved so quick you'd have thought I was Superman." But even then, the mind controls the body. It even controls what we call a reflex action. Our mind knows, even without us being aware of it, that a hot stove is beginning to burn us.

Now, when we have time to think, we have to have our minds sharp. I tell my players, "You must know the plays. You must know the offense; you must know the defense. You must know what you're doing so your mind can tell your body what to do. That's why you have to be sharp.

"And what happens when your mind isn't sharp? What if your mind knows what to do, but doesn't want to do it? What happens when your mind tells your body, 'I'm tired, and I ain't gonna do nothin' but take today off'?

"That's when you have to dig down deeper than that, and that's when the spirit comes into play. That's where you find the desire to get the body going. If you don't have that desire, then every once in a while your mind is going to let your body 'dog it' (that's athlete-talk for loafing). And where do you get that spirit and desire? I believe it comes from only one place—from God. He is the center of the heart, and He can motivate you to be the best you can be."

I've seen some athletes who had all the talent in the world, but didn't have spirit and desire. They had no motivation whatsoever. What a waste.

God can make a man superior, whether it's in athletics, business, or whatever. If I didn't believe that, I'd get out of the business.

THE CONSCIENCE OF MAN
IS OFTEN BEYOND THE REACH
OF A PSYCHIATRIST.

I am not into going to psychiatrists for counsel, not at all. I'm kind of like the man who said, "I have never seen a psychiatrist who didn't need one."

Now, I know they do some good and help some people. However, to me, I'd rather go to a good minister or pastor. If I had a problem, I'd rather seek out a man of the Bible who could find an answer in the Word of God. I believe no matter what the problem is, God is the answer. If I feel my life isn't right, I always find out it's because I've separated myself from God, and if I can make it right with Him, then everything falls into place.

Jesus wants us to love him and cheerfully give ourselves to Him and His service. Man, I have seen some folks who have professed to accept Christ, and then instead of their faith lifting a burden from them, they go around wearing their Christianity on their shoulders like a heavy yoke. When I see persons like that, I firmly believe those folks haven't read the part about putting their belief, faith, and trust in Him and letting Him remove their burdens.

How in the world can some people profess to love the Lord and then have that love become a burden? It looks like those folks left out the part where God asks us to be dependent on Him. I don't think they believe He will do what He says He's going to do. Maybe those struggling Christians still think they aren't good enough for Christ. I don't know. I do know that somehow they just didn't get the message.

I firmly believe that the Lord will bless us every day if we have faith and trust in Him, and depend on Him. I can speak from my own experience because I have never gone through a single day without a blessing from God.

JESUS IS YOUR SAVIOR, BUT IS HE YOUR LORD?

It saddens me to see Christians, or persons who profess to be Christians, continually disobey God. Now, I don't judge them. We're not supposed to judge anybody. And if I'm honest, there are times when I'm just as guilty as anyone when it comes to disobedience. The easiest thing to do is to say, "Oh, yes, Lord, I'm saved. You are my Savior." The hard part comes when we try to let Him be the Lord of our lives. It says in the Bible that God not only wants to be our Savior, He wants to be our Savior *and* Lord.

Is God the Lord of your life?

I'm reminded of what happened to some television evangelists several years ago. The things they got into weren't about money, and they weren't about the bad things they did with those women. What they really did was they quit letting God be the Lord of their lives. I'm sure all of us can recall lots of folks who stopped letting God be the Lord of their lives. Sometimes the devil gets in our hearts, and we can't get him out. The devil becomes the dictator of our hearts.

The biggest breakdown of modern-day Christianity is that even though we all claim Christ, go to church, and claim to do good deeds in His name, we still disobey God's laws. If we claim Him, we should obey Him. Both should go hand in hand. It makes sense to me.

WHAT IS MORE IMPORTANT IN WITNESSING —THE LIFE I LIVE, OR THE WORDS I SAY?

This simply means that the life a person lives can erase all his witnessing. I've been witnessing in pulpits throughout the South for forty years, and I could wipe out everything I've ever said with one bad action.

I go back to those TV evangelists. They preached and were good. They influenced a lot of folks. They raised millions of dollars to do God's work. And I think in the beginning they were doing a lot of good. But then they started building empires and began to feel so important and so untouchable that they decided *they* were going to play Lord of their lives.

Now, I don't think it's a sin for man to have money, to be independently wealthy, that is, unless it makes him independent of God. The problem is, man equates money with power, and power corrupts. And, those evangelists became corrupted and disobeyed God, and their acts of disobedience wiped out everything they ever said.

God is no respecter of persons. He doesn't care how famous we think we are. He doesn't care how powerful we think we are. He can knock us down in an instant if we disobey Him, and it don't make any difference who we are.

We might say, "Oh, I might have disobeyed God a little, but I reckon He'll let it slide." Oh, no, He is not going to let it slide. He will get our attention. And if you don't think God will do that, you try Him and find out. I don't know about you, but I don't want to find out.

There are times when I feel I'm just as guilty of disobeying God as any man who ever lived. Oh, I may feel that my disobedience may be in lesser degrees, but disobedience is still disobedience.

My mother used to preach to me, and at the time I didn't know why she used to do that. I do now. She used to say, "If one person steals $10,000 from a bank, and another steals a penny from a poor old widow, in the eyes of God each man is equally guilty. The man who took the penny is just as guilty as the man who took the $10,000. God says, 'Thou shalt not steal.' He doesn't say you can steal a penny, or nickel, or a dime and it won't be a big sin because it ain't a large amount of money. He said, 'Thou shalt not steal—period.'

"So, He doesn't give us permission to steal a little bit. He doesn't say you can believe in Me, but it's all right if you sin just a teeny little bit."

We can say all the right things and be a wonderful citizen and church-goer, but it doesn't mean a thing if we don't practice what we preach. Our actions will speak so loudly that no one will pay any attention to the words coming out of our mouths.

AN ALCOHOLIC FATHER HAD TWO SONS.
ONE GREW UP AN ALCOHOLIC FAILURE LIKE
HIS FATHER.
THE OTHER WAS A SUCCESSFUL
NON-ALCOHOLIC. WHY?

I love this thought because I believe that too many times people blame society, or their parents, or coming from the wrong side of the tracks for their problems. That's the easy way out.

There have been many instances where children come from really bad situations. One will turn out bad and end up a drunk, a wife-beater, and a total failure. The other will go to school and graduate with honors, go on to law school, and become a successful businessman and leader in the community.

Now, both had the same opportunities and had to fight the same obstacles. One chose the path to nowhere, and one chose the path to success. One said, "Poor me. I am no good and I can't overcome it." The other said, "Oh, no, I will not turn out that way. I am somebody, and I'm better than that."

And that all goes back to the truth that we are the ones who determine what we will do with our lives. We can't go blaming society, or our parents, or our status in life, or a non-existent bank account, or a lack of education when things go wrong. When things go wrong, we'd better look in the mirror. It doesn't do any good to blame it on other people or bad circumstances. Some folks even blame it on God.

I can sell most kids on life. I can sell them on dying. But when I say, "Then comes the judgment," man, that gets their attention.

I've had kids from all kinds of home situations come into our program here at Florida State. I've had kids from wealthy families. I've had kids from middle-income families. I've had kids from poor families. And I've had kids from no families. You'd be surprised at the kids who make it and the kids who don't.

I wouldn't want to embarrass or hurt any of the players I have, or have had, by mentioning their names, but I've had kids whose parents were so wealthy that money was like a bottomless pit. And I've had kids whose mommas were prostitutes and who came from seemingly desperate and hopeless situations. Some of those rich kids didn't get their degrees. And some of those kids from hopeless situations turned out beautifully.

It all goes back to the will of man.

That's why I use this devotion when I'm standing in front of kids. I want to let them know that no matter what their situations, they can will it otherwise.

A preacher told me once that basically there are two kinds of people in this world: happy people and unhappy people. The happy person will wake up in the morning, get out of bed, look out his window and see that it's raining and say, "Gee, it's raining. What a beautiful day!"

The unhappy person will wake up and look out and see the same rain and say, "Aw, it's raining. What a lousy day!"

And the preacher said, "Either way, it's gonna rain."

That just illustrated once again that it doesn't make any difference how much money we have, or what kind of families we come from, or what kind of environment we live in, whether we're happy and successful comes from the heart and the will. All of us have a little rain fall on our parade at times.

One man will see a glass of water and say it's half empty. Another will see the same glass and say it's half full. It all goes back to mind and attitude.

IT ISN'T IMPORTANT *HOW* GOD CREATED THE WORLD.
WHAT IS IMPORTANT IS THAT *HE* DID IT.

Too many folks get all caught up in the story of creation and Adam and Eve. They get caught up in where the Garden of Eden was, or where Noah's Ark was, or where this was in the Bible, or when that happened in the Bible. That isn't what's important in the Bible.

I believe everything on this earth was created by God. God says in John 1:3–4, "All things were made through Him, and without Him nothing was made that was made. In Him was life, and the life was the light of men."

I don't think that's so complicated. In fact, it's very simple. All things were made by Him. And it's not important to me when or how. Too many of us get caught up in insignificant details and forget God's message.

THREE THINGS MAN MUST FACE:
LIFE, DEATH, AND, FINALLY, JUDGMENT.

If you think about that, it's kind of scary, especially that final thing we all must face. Anyhow, it's scary to me. We all know we're alive. We can see, and feel, and touch, and taste. And we know, whether we want to admit it or not, that we're going to die. Those things we know. However, it is God who tells us that there will be a day of judgment.

Now understand, nearly all my thoughts and talks are geared toward young people in the hope that by my testimony I can help make them better persons. I deal with so many youngsters who have never been taught the right things to do or the right way to live. I can sell most kids on life. I can sell them on dying. But when I say, "Then comes the judgment," man, that gets their attention.

And I add, "The judgment can already be done if y'all have accepted Jesus Christ as your Savior and Lord and have committed yourself to Him. If you do that, then no matter what happens on that day, you will be saved. But if you haven't committed, you ain't gonna make it. I know, because the Bible tells me so. It says in John 14:6 that no man can get to God without going through Jesus Christ. And Jesus says in Revelation 22:12, ". . . behold, I am coming quickly, and My reward is with Me, to give to every one according to his work."

I don't see how God can make it any plainer than that.

I kind of feel, too, that none of us wants justice from God. What we want is mercy because if we got justice, we'd all go to hell. It all goes back to the truth that we can't earn our way into heaven. There's no way we can earn it. We aren't good enough, and can never be good enough.

Thank God, as Christians we're going to get mercy instead of justice. And through God's mercy, we can make it.

AM I AFRAID TO DIE?

Well, to be honest, I ain't looking forward to it. But I don't think I'll be afraid. It's just that I'm not looking forward to the day when I'll have to go. I think once I know I'm going and there's no turning back, I'll adjust and accept it.

I believe that God made us with a desire to live. He didn't make us with a desire to die. That doesn't make sense. There are several innate things man is born with, and one is that desire to cling to life.

The way I look at death is kind of like this:

As a kid, or even now, when I go swimming, if the water is ice cold, I'm not jumping into it. No way. I'll stick my foot in and let it get adjusted to the cold. Then I'll go in up to my knees and let them get adjusted. Then I'll go in up to my thighs, and after that I'll slowly get the rest of my body wet. Once I get adjusted, man, I can swim all day. I think that's kind of like what it's going to be when we die. Once we get adjusted to it and see God, man, there's no place we'd rather be.

You know, when a baby is inside its mother's womb for nine months, that's a mighty comfortable and warm and safe place. There's plenty to eat. There's plenty to drink. The temperature is just right. Everything's perfect.

Then God says, "OK, little one, it's time to get out. You have to get out into the world."

The baby says, "No, I don't want to go. It's too good in here."

God says, "You gotta go."

None of us wants justice from God. What we want is mercy because if
we got justice, we'd all go to hell.

And then the baby goes out, finds out about life, and discovers that
life is fun. I believe that when we die, if we have accepted Christ and go to
heaven, it's going to be even better than it was in that warm, cozy womb.

The Bible says there is life after death, and that life after death is going
to be good. Jesus says in John 14:2–3, "In My Father's house are many
mansions; if it were not so, I would have told you. I go to prepare a place
for you. And if I go and prepare a place for you, I will come again and
receive you to Myself; that where I am, there you may be also."

And He says in John 11:25–26, "I am the resurrection and the life.
He who believes in Me, though he may die, he shall live. And whoever
lives and believes in Me shall never die. Do you believe this?"

I believe it with all my heart.

The problem is I'm about like the sick woman who was asked if she
was anxious to die, because then her home would be in heaven. The
woman said, "No, I'm not in any hurry to die. I'm not homesick yet."

That's about the way I feel. When I get homesick, then I'll be ready.
I'm just not homesick yet.

WE SHOULD NEVER BE ASHAMED
OF THE GOSPEL OF JESUS CHRIST.

I once wrote in my Bible that I am not ashamed, for there is power
and salvation for everyone who believes. You know, there has never been a
time in my life when I was ashamed to stand up in front of people and talk
about God. Now, there have been many times when I have doubted my
worthiness to do that.

There have been times when I've been about to speak about my faith
and I recall some of the things I've done in my life. I'm not too proud of
those things. But I also know those things are in the past. They are behind
me. I have asked for and received forgiveness. I know I'm not good
enough. I'll never be good enough. And if the day ever comes when I
think I'm worthy, then I'll be unworthy.

Ann and I always begin each day with a devotion, a prayer, and a
scripture. One day we were reading about the seven sins that man commits

daily. I don't remember them all, but they were things like greed, lust, gossiping, and so forth. Most were sins you can't be put in jail for. Anyhow, I got to checking which of those sins I committed and discovered that I did about four out of the seven daily. I'm not going to tell you which ones they were, but it sure made me think. I thought, *Bobby, don't you ever get to thinking you're somebody special, because you're not.*

Here I was thinking I was a man who thought he was working hard at trying to be a Christian, yet I'm committing all those sins every day. Man, that put me in my place in a hurry. It showed me that I'm not even close to being perfect and never will be.

Lawh, some of those things—whooeee! I'm sure God will make me answer for them.

What about you? What are you going to have to answer for?

The Death of Pablo

O ne day I was being interviewed by a writer and out of the blue he asked me, "Bobby, what would you do if you knew today was going to be your last day on earth?"

Well, you know me, I had to say something cute. I said, "Well, the first thing I'd do would be to go to a grocery store and buy about five or six big chocolate candy bars. Then, I'd find a chapel and go sit down and pray, and eat every one of those chocolate bars. I'd eat like mad. That definitely would be in the deal."

I said that because I knew this guy knew I was a chocolate freak. I just plain love chocolate. I live in fear of the day when a doctor says to me that if I eat another piece of chocolate I'm gonna die.

If that scenario ever did confront me, I would try to get my family around me—Ann, my children, and their husbands and wives, and their children—and prepare myself to die. I wouldn't want to sadden them; I would do it so I could leave some important thoughts with them.

I would tell them to always keep the faith and to always put first things first. And then I would make sure they knew that we would all be together again. I would try to let them know that everything was going to be all right. And my hope and prayer would be that I would see them later. That would be my last wish.

Some folks think the best way to live is to play around, raise heck, and do whatever they want to right up until just before they die, and then ask God for forgiveness and they'll be saved. They want to do it on their

227

terms, not God's. The problem is not a single person on this earth knows when he or she is going to die. So, if we're going to accept Christ, we'd better not wait, because death might come in the blink of an eye, and we won't have time to get right with God.

I sure ain't waiting.

Jesus says in Matthew 7:23, "And then I will declare to them, 'I never knew you; depart from Me. . . .' " I don't want Jesus saying that to me.

The thought of us not knowing when we are going to die came up in a discussion about the tragic death in 1986 of Pablo Lopez, one of our Florida State football players. Pablo was a senior offensive tackle and a good one. As we went into that season he was easily our best offensive lineman. I honestly felt he was headed for a fine career in the National Football League.

We had opened the season with a 24-0 win over Toledo. Our second game was at Nebraska and we led 14-10 at the half, but ended up getting thumped 34-17. Then we had an open date before playing North Carolina at home.

Most of our players went home on that weekend, when we had no game. But Pablo, who was married and had a child, stayed in Tallahassee. And on Friday night, he went to a dance on campus with his wife.

Apparently one of our players got into an argument with another student and Pablo stepped in to break it up. Anyhow, this student left the dance and after a while came back with a shotgun. He walked across the parking lot and went right up to Pablo and pointed that gun at him. And I guess Pablo must have said something like, "What are you gonna do? Shoot me?" And that's what the guy did. He pulled the trigger and shot Pablo at point-blank range. I learned from the doctor later that Pablo was probably dead when he hit the ground.

One of my graduate assistants called me at home and said, "Coach, you'd better get to the hospital quick. Somebody shot Pablo."

I said, "How bad is it?"

He said, "I don't know, Coach. I think it's bad."

We didn't know Pablo was already dead. So, first of all, before I left the house I called our team chaplain, a Baptist minister named Ken Smith, and asked him to meet me at the hospital.

Ken knew it was serious because I seldom called him when one of our players got in trouble. Most of the time it was the other way around, because when a player got into something on campus or around town, the authorities would call Ken first. He was usually the one who straightened out those things as best he could.

My fear for my immortal soul is that I might have done or said (or not done or said) something that might cause one of my young men to go to hell; there is a hell, just as there's a heaven.

Ken and I arrived at the hospital at about the same time, and when we got there Pablo had already been pronounced dead. I will never forget the feeling of horror that came over me as I looked down at the body of that young man, one that had been so full of life and so strong. He was a young man who had so much to live for. One minute he was alive, and the next minute he was gone forever.

All of our football players who had been at that party, and there must have been thirty of them, were at the hospital. Their girlfriends were with them too. They were all outside the emergency room. I asked Ken, "How are we gonna tell them about Pablo?"

Ken suggested we find the hospital chaplain and see if there was a chapel in the hospital we could use. The hospital did have a little chapel and we were able to use it.

So, we called all the players and girls into the room and broke the news. We told them that Pablo was dead. It was one of the most difficult things I've ever had to do because I hadn't been around death that much, not that kind of a death.

Pablo was Cuban, and most of the players and girlfriends were either Latin or black. They mourn differently than whites do. At most white funerals I've been to, people shed tears, but they mourn in quiet. These kids didn't react that way. Their mourning was verbal and physical. They screamed, cried, moaned and wailed, and fell down on the floor. It was a heart-wrenching experience for me. We prayed with them, but it didn't settle them down. You see, Pablo was one of the most popular guys on campus.

On Sunday night I called a team meeting. There were some television folks there, and they wanted me to let them into the meeting too. I don't know, I guess they wanted to film the team's reaction to the news. I told them, "I'm sorry, but y'all can't come in. This is private." And I shut the door and turned to face the players.

I don't remember exactly what I said. All I know is my thoughts were that we had just lost a fine young man, and it had nothing to do with his talent as a player. I felt I had to tell my players what this life is all about, and tell them how fragile life is.

I didn't know how many of my players were saved. I talked to them about eternal life and the meaning of salvation. And I talked about life after death and why being a Christian is so important. I think I talked to them about how important it is to be ready to die because we don't know when God is going to call us to be with Him. I told them that there was more to life than football. There had to be.

And finally, I think I said, "Men, if we're not ready to die, then football doesn't make any difference at all. Pablo is dead. We're all gonna die. Dying is real. But eternal life is real too, and God has promised we can all have it if we accept Him and follow His commandments."

So many coaches treat football like it's a life-or-death matter; it ain't. I remember in 1972 when I was at West Virginia and we had just lost the Peach Bowl game to North Carolina State. We got beat bad (49-13). After that game a lot of our so-called loyal fans moaned, "What are we gonna do? What are we gonna do?"

I felt like saying, "Well, I don't know what you're going to do, but I'm going to go to bed. And when I wake up in the morning, I know the sun is going to come up. It will be a brand new day, and I'm gonna get down on my knees and thank God for it. And I'll thank Him for giving us the opportunity to have a good season, go to a bowl and play it, and have nobody hurt."

No one knows when he or she is going to die. So, if we're going to accept Christ, we'd better not wait, because death might come in the blink of an eye.

Football ain't life-or-death. What happened to Pablo was life or death. One second he was alive, and the next he was dead. I've always tried to impress on my players that they should know the difference between what's important in life and what's unimportant, and to keep their priorities straight. Like I've said thousands of times, football is important to me, but it's not the most important thing. My faith, my salvation, is what is important.

I don't try to cram religion down anyone's throat. I never have. I don't try to coerce anybody to believe as I do. I don't know for sure if Pablo was saved or not, but I pray that he was. I think he was. But I sometimes wonder if I told him everything I could have told him about the Word.

My fear for my immortal soul is that I might have done or said something, or not done or not said something, and that those actions or inactions might cause one of the young men under my charge to go to hell, because I believe there is a hell just as much as I believe there's a heaven. To put it bluntly, I don't want any of my players going to hell because of me. That's why I always take every opportunity I can to testify to them. And that's why when I called that team meeting to tell them about Pablo, I had to get right down to it and tell them why being a Christian is so important.

Born
Again

When I was growing up in a church-oriented family, I was taught the Baptist way of doing things. I was taught that there comes a time in every person's life when he or she must make a public confession of faith and be baptized. So, it seems from the very first I always knew there would come a day when I would have to get up and walk down the aisle and tell everybody I was accepting Christ as my Savior. I knew my mother and daddy wanted me to do that. Finally, when I was about ten years of age I got up the nerve and walked down that aisle and was baptized.

Now, you have to understand, I was very young and wasn't looking forward to it. I guess the main reason for that was I didn't know what I was doing, and I didn't know what it was all about. Also, most kids are more interested in their buddies and getting into mischief than they are in getting dunked in a pool of water by some preacher.

It was thirteen years later, when I was twenty-three, that I finally realized what being a Christian meant. That's when I walked back down that aisle and rededicated my life. Now, I don't recall a big change coming over me. My growth in my understanding and commitment was a gradual thing. And I had worked my way from the back row up to about the second row. I don't think I ever made it to the front row. Anyhow, the second time I went down the aisle it wasn't too long a walk.

When I was born again—at age twenty-three—I wasn't struck by lightning. It wasn't a single event or a single day that made me rededicate myself to the Lord. It was just that at last I realized how helpless I was. I realized I could never earn salvation. I realized that Jesus' blood washed away my sins, and that it was through His grace I was saved. It wasn't for some good deeds I had done.

I think people I went to college with and all the guys who knew me back when I misbehaved at times would say they noticed that I changed after that. Until that time, I thought being a Christian meant that you joined the church and were baptized, and then you tried to be good. That was it—just be good. I thought you went through each day, and at the end of the day God would put everything you had done down in His book.

If you were good, He'd say, "Oh, Bobby was good here. I'll put this on the good side of the ledger. But, uh-oh, here's something he shouldn't have done. This goes on the bad side of the book." After God got through putting it all down, if the good outweighed the bad, then you had been a good Christian that day. That was my idea of what it was all about. The problem was, as long as I was living with that understanding, the debit side kept getting larger and larger.

And after years of living that way, I finally realized, "Hey, He's already paid it for me."

Now, I'm not going to say that I suddenly started doing all good things and became a saint. Like I've said time and again, I ain't no saint. It's just that being good became easier and more meaningful. I figured if Jesus had died for me, then I owed it to Him to do the best I could (not that it will ever be good enough). It's just that it was no longer a contest of trying to do enough good so it would outweigh the bad.

I know that if there's some person out there who is reluctant to commit himself to Christ, and his reasoning is that if he becomes a Christian he will have to give up things like alcohol, tobacco, drugs, extramarital sex, partying, profanity, and all those other sins, I would say to him, "Jesus won't make you give up anything. But if you put your life in His hands, you will not want to continue doing all that stuff. God will change your priorities and values. He will give those things up for you."

I believe in tithing (i.e., giving one-tenth of your income to God). My mother taught me to tithe when I was a little fellow. I remember when I got my first allowance. It was a dime. Mother said, "This dime is yours, but God is supposed to get one-tenth of it. You can take the dime and do anything you want to with it, but you must remember that one penny is God's.'' And when my allowance went up to fifty cents, I gave a nickel to the church. When it was one dollar, I put a dime in the collection plate. Even today I don't think twice about tithing. I've always tithed. The first one-tenth belongs to God.

People who don't fear God, but instead laugh and joke about Him, are walking in big trouble, in my opinion.

I try to spread my tithing around. I give one-tenth of my salary from Florida State to my church (First Baptist Church in Tallahassee). From all the other money I make from radio, television, and so forth, I give to a Baptist church in Morgantown, West Virginia, to Ruhama Baptist Church in Birmingham, the church I was raised in, to charities, and to the Fellowship of Christian Athletes. I also give money to certain Christian crusades.

Now, there was a brief period of time when I stopped tithing. I'm not proud of that because I forgot what Momma taught me.

When I left Bill Peterson's staff at Florida State and joined the staff at West Virginia in 1966, I owed so much money from raising those six children that all I thought about was trying to pay the bills and keep the creditors away from our door. I got so caught up in poor lil' ol' me that I forgot to give that one-tenth to God. And, buddy, we just kept getting deeper and deeper in debt. That went on for three years.

I knew I was doing wrong, and I knew the money belonged to God, not me. And my conscience was really beginning to hurt me. (You know what they say when a man says he has a guilty conscience, don't you? They say, ''It's because he's guilty.'')

One day Ann and I sat down and talked it over. We decided we had to start tithing again. I said, ''God gave us everything we have. He gave us good health. He gave us healthy babies. He gave us a home. He gave us a job. We gotta start tithing, even if it means we don't have any money to buy food. We're gonna give God His before we spend the rest of it, no matter how much it hurts.'' So we started tithing again.

And it wasn't but about six months later that I got the head job at West Virginia and my salary doubled. It has gone that way ever since. I've tithed, and God just keeps giving it back to me. My salary just keeps going up and up. I know it sounds like a fairy tale, but it's true. When we give God what is His, He gives more than that back to us.

God has been so good to us. How could we not give back to Him what belongs to Him? To me, Christianity is not something you wear on your breast pocket like a badge.

Some of the finest Christians I have ever known didn't preach to you. They simply said, "I am a Christian." Then all you had to do was stand back and observe them. People who are true believers are witnesses simply by the way they live their lives.

I would categorize myself as a fundamentalist because I believe in the accuracy of the Bible. It is the Word of God. I guess I have a very simplistic view of it in that I don't try to read stuff into it. I leave no room for doubt. I feel like I can prayerfully read it and understand it. I don't have to have a dictionary, or a concordance, or some expert, or some philosopher to analyze it and explain it to me. I just think the Bible is something anyone can read and understand. It's pretty plain.

For example, in the last book of the Old Testament, God said, "Behold, I will send you Elijah the prophet. . . . Lest I come and strike the earth with a curse" (Mal. 4:5, 6). God is so angry at His people that He ends the Old Testament by talking about cursing the earth. That's pretty plain to me. I think about that sometimes when I hear on the news about the worldwide epidemic of the AIDS disease.

God requires us to fear Him, to walk in His ways, and to love Him and serve Him with all our heart and soul—always. He commands us to not commit adultery, steal, kill, or bear false witness, to honor our mothers and fathers, and to have no other gods before Him. He didn't say we could do it sometimes and get away with it. In the Ten Commandments, He said, "Thou shalt not. . . ." Now, I may not be too smart, but I can figure that out.

I take all the Bible and build it around three things: 1) the virgin birth of Jesus, 2) the crucifixion, and 3) the resurrection. The rest of the Bible is interesting to me, and I believe it's true. However, for me, it all boils down to this: Do we believe in the birth, death, and resurrection of Jesus Christ? The rest of it? I would just say, "If you want to believe that, son, that's your business."

I tend to major on the New Testament since that tells of the coming of my Lord and Savior, Jesus Christ. I think the rest of the Bible (the Old Testament) was God's way of revealing His plan for man and telling us what was to come in the New Testament. The whole thing is working up to that.

> I feel a little uncomfortable talking about my fear of God because I've never talked about it before—not to anyone.

When I was young I was afraid of God. To be honest, I'm afraid of Him now. I know our God is a God of love, but I just can't imagine what it will be like when I come face to face with Him. I do know there will be some fear in me. We're supposed to fear Him. People who don't fear Him, but instead laugh and joke about Him, are walking in big trouble, in my opinion. And believe me, there have been times when I've been guilty of that myself.

When some comedian gets on television and makes fun of God and puts Him down, well, that scares me. I don't think God goes for that sort of stuff. Jesus said in Luke 6:25(b), "Woe to you who laugh now, for you shall mourn and weep."

Actually, I feel a little uncomfortable talking about my fear of God because I've never talked about it before—not to anyone.

The main thing I believe is that Jesus was the Son of God and He was sent to die for our sins, and by His sacrifice He gave us the gift of salvation. If y'all want to argue whether His grave was in this cave over here, or that cave over there . . . or how big the stone was over the entrance to the cave . . . or whether His mother was, or wasn't, a virgin, I ain't gonna fight you on that. But I do believe she was a virgin.

If y'all want to believe that Jesus didn't stop the wind, calm the waters, heal the sick, raise the dead, and so forth, that's all right with me. I do believe it. I also believe that Jesus didn't perform all those miracles for gratification of anyone's flesh. I think He performed them to lend authority to the words that came out of His mouth. He performed them to get man's attention. But if you don't want to believe that, that's your prerogative. I believe what I believe, and I believe He is the only way to get to heaven. I think as long as a person believes that, the rest isn't all that important.

It's like the "big bang" theory that the scientists have come up with. Those intellects can argue all they want about how the universe and everything in it was created. I'm not going to get involved in that stuff. Maybe it did all happen with a bang. All I know is that everything that happened, happened systematically. There was a plan. I know that my God is powerful enough to do that. I know that the distance the earth is from the sun is just right. If it wasn't, we wouldn't have life as we know it. That wasn't an accident. If the plan was off by one or two dad-gum degrees, well, I don't know what would happen exactly, but I don't think it would be good.

I think the scientists have backed themselves into a corner if they think it was just an accident or chance occurrence. In my opinion, they are wrong. If there was a big explosion, they haven't explained to my satisfaction what caused it. There had to be something that caused the beginning, something that caused the gases, or whatever, to be just right for that big bang to occur and create all the planets in a systematic way. I don't think man will ever be able to explain "in the beginning" the way the Bible does.

I know some of my children think my religious beliefs are too simple. That's fine. I accept that. We raised them to think for themselves. All I know is that I accept the Bible as it is, and will continue to do so until somebody proves it wrong. Nobody has done it yet. The Bible has withstood the test for untold centuries.

I compare reading the Bible to a person having a fresh peach in his hand. Maybe all he wants is the middle of it, the seed. If that's what he wants, then all the rest of that peach is irrelevant. The seed is what's important. Man, my seed in the Bible is the story of Jesus, His crucifixion, His resurrection, and His promise that He has gone to prepare a place for us. And I pray and know that "us" includes Bobby Bowden.

If my view of all that is simplistic, I can't help it. I'm too old-fashioned to change.

I have many, many favorite scriptures. And like I said earlier in this book, my very favorite is the psalm (42:1) my mother taught me when I was about eight years of age. And of course, there are John 14:6 and John 3:16. It seems like I've known them all my life too.

In John 14:6, Jesus tell us that to get to heaven we have to go through Him. He tells us, "I am the way, the truth, and the life. No one comes to the Father except through Me."

And in John 3:16, He tell us why He came when He says, "For God so loved the world that He gave his only begotten Son, that whoever believes in Him should not perish but have everlasting life." That verse is mighty powerful. You see, here He didn't say we *might* have everlasting life. He didn't say we'll *almost* have everlasting life. He said we "will" have everlasting life.

Those three scriptures are probably at the top of the list, but that list has a lot of other ones on it.

Right behind those would be John 1:1–2, where God says, "In the beginning was the Word, and the Word was with God, and the Word was God. He was in the beginning with God."

There are three verses in the gospel of John and four in Romans that mean a lot to me too.

In John, we are told, "There was a man sent from God, whose name was John. This man came for a witness, to bear witness of the Light, that all through him might believe. He was not that Light, but was sent to bear witness of that Light" (John 1:6–8).

And in Romans, God says, " 'The word is near you, in your mouth and in your heart' (that is, the word of faith which we preach): that if you confess with your mouth the Lord Jesus and believe in your heart that God has raised Him from the dead, you will be saved. For with the heart one believes to righteousness, and with the mouth confession is made to salvation. For the Scripture says, 'Whoever believes on Him will not be put to shame' " (Rom. 10:8–11).

These verses are the main reasons why I rarely turn down a chance to go out to speak and witness. I believe that is what God wants me to do, to witness for Him, especially to young people. I gotta do it.

Witnessing isn't all that big a deal; it's just one person telling another. And Jesus says that whenever two or more are gathered in His name, He will be there too. Don't you see? If the one who hears the Word tells two others, and those two tell four, and those four tell eight, and those eight tell sixteen . . . man, you only have to do that about something like a few dozen times and you've told the whole world.

I firmly believe it's better for a man never to have been born, than never to have been born again.

Jesus tells us that if we believe in Him, the works that He does, we shall do also. He says He will be with us. He will not leave us comfortless. He will come to us. And to me, that means He will come to us in the invisible, unlimited power of the Holy Spirit. It means that He will always be with us and never leave us, even to the end. He says in John 14:19, "A little while longer and the world will see Me no more, but you will see Me. Because I live, you will live also."

There are some powerful words in Matthew 16:25, too, where Jesus

een to a picture show in years. There weren't but about eight
e whole theater.

we started to sit down, the eight folks in the theater started
hought, "Lord, I didn't know they knew me up here." And so
und and gave them a couple of those "thank you" bows. And
ue seat behind us nudged me and said, "Buddy, I don't know
, but thanks for coming. You see, they won't start the movie
t at least ten people in here."

at a church in Parkersburg, West Virginia, one time, and
to the church I couldn't find a place to park. I must have
d the place three times. So, I finally double-parked right in
church. And I put a note under the wiper blade on my

on the note:

officer, I am Bobby Bowden, football coach at West Virginia
I have a very important engagement here at the church. I
l a place to park, so I double-parked here. Please don't tow my
us our trespasses."

I was through speaking, I came out of the church, and sure
car was still there. It hadn't been towed, but it was ticketed.
vas a nice little note on the windshield. It read:

Coach Bowden, I have been patrolling this block for three
a very important engagement too. It's my job. If I don't do it,
. Lead us not into temptation."

n't ever think you're famous or important, because it doesn't
g. Somebody will always slap you down to size. And I always
red that someone slapping you down is God. He will look
e how you're acting and say, "Well, that ol' boy is getting too
ritches. It's time to take him down a notch or two. It's time he
le bit about humility." And believe me, God can take all of us
h or two in an instant.

ly, I couldn't act pretentiously if I tried because I don't like
can tolerate a lot of things, but I don't care much to be around
y to be something they're not.

m is a guy from the East Lake section of Birmingham, who
e Howard College, wound up at Florida State, and was fortu-
u to be surrounded by fine coaches and players and win some
es. I'm a guy who knows that he was very lucky to have come
right time, and for some reason, good things have happened.

says, "For whoever desires to save his life will lose it, and whoever loses his
life for My sake will find it."

Man, that's powerful stuff. It's scary too. Jesus is talking here about
losing our immortal souls. If those aren't strong words, then I don't know
any that are. I firmly believe it's better for a man never to have been born,
than never to have been born again. When you're born again, you're born
again in your soul, and you have the promise that your soul will never die.
I really believe that.

The Bible talks about where we should put all of our energies in
Matthew 6:19–21. Jesus said to the multitudes, "Do not lay up for yourselves treasures on earth, where moth and rust destroy and where thieves
break in and steal; but lay up for yourselves treasures in heaven, where
neither moth nor rust destroys and where thieves do not break in and steal.
For where your treasure is, there your heart will be also."

And then, later on in the chapter, Jesus talks about folks who worship
material things, things that get in the way of them believing in God. In
Matthew 6:24, He makes it pretty dad-gum plain. He says, "No one can
serve two masters; for either he will hate the one and love the other, or
else he will be loyal to the one and despise the other. You cannot serve
God and mammon." (*Mammon* means riches or wealth.)

Jesus means that we cannot make worldly gain our god. That's a false
god. And if we worship those things, we cannot serve Him. We can't do it
because we're not strong enough. And Jesus explains that God doesn't
want us to put any other gods before Him. In 1 Corinthians 10:21 it says,
"You cannot drink the cup of the Lord and the cup of demons; you
cannot partake of the Lord's table and of the table of demons." That's
pretty plain to me.

I think about all the people in the world who are troubled and depressed, and can't find peace and contentment in their lives. If they would
only read the Word, they'd find the answers to their problems. Jesus tells us
in there to trust Him. He says in John 14:27, "Peace I leave with you, My
peace I give to you; not as the world gives do I give to you. Let not your
heart be troubled, neither let it be afraid."

What more can a person want than the promise of peace in his or her
heart? Nothing in this world can buy that, and if we all believed that,
maybe all those pill companies, psychiatrists, and psychologists would go
out of business.

Finally, Jesus tells us God's two greatest commandments in Matthew
22:37–39. He says, " 'You shalt love the LORD your God with all your

heart, with all your soul, and with all your mind.' " This is the first and great commandment. And the second is like it, 'You shall love your neighbor as yourself.' "

We gotta love God, and we gotta love people. We can't love cars, houses, nice clothes, swimming pools, jewelry, money, or none of that stuff. Now, I think it's all right to *like* that stuff. Just don't *love* it, because that's not where happiness comes from.

It's like the old saying, "Money may buy you a good dog, but only love can make it wag its tail."

I'm No Dad-gum Legend

I t's hard for me to visualize th□ is coach a dad-gum football□ surgeon or someone who fou□ seem all that important to me. I really □

Now, I do remember how I felt □ coaches that I was really in awe of. So I a□ in awe of me, although I don't know □ people at ease on that score. I've never □ around thinking, "You're over there, an□ y'all." That's not me. I couldn't live with□ I was some big shot.

And I really have a hard time answ□ "What's it like to be a legend?"

I say, "Legend? I'm no more a dad-□ moon."

I tell a story sometimes about how □ down to earth when we get to thinking w□ this way:

Once Ann and I drove up through □ were just trying to get away from people□ ended up in a little town of about 5,000□ After we checked into a motel and had di□

We hadn't □ people in t□

And a □ clapping. I □ I turned ar□ the guy in □ who you ar□ until they □

I spok□ when I go □ driven arou□ front of th□ windshield.□

I wrot□ "Dear □ University. □ couldn't fir□ car. Forgiv□

When□ enough, m□ And there □

"Dear□ years. I hav□ I will lose □

So, d□ mean a thi□ kind of fig□ down and □ big for his □ learned a li□ down a no□

Hone□ phoniness. □ folks who □

All I □ went to lit□ nate enoug□ football ga□ along at th□

Sometimes I'll go play golf at some Seminole function, and at nearly every one of those things they will pair me up with somebody I've never played with. It will be somebody I've never met, but he will be a big booster, and I guess they think they'll get a big contribution out of him if they let him play with Bobby Bowden.

And after we've played about four holes and the guy has hit the ball all over the lot, he'll say, "I don't usually play this bad, but I'm so nervous about playing with you."

I'm almost at a loss for words, which is rare for me. I can't understand that. I'm just an ordinary guy like he is. I hit bad shots all the time. In fact, I've probably played worse than most of the guys I ever played with.

> As far as being some sort of dad-gum coaching legend, I find that ridiculous.

I don't think of myself any differently than I did when I was a young coach at South Georgia College, or at Howard College, or at West Virginia. I haven't changed any, except maybe to put on a bunch of pounds around the waistline.

When I think of change, I'm reminded of the story about the old husband and wife who were riding down the road in the car. The husband was behind the wheel and the wife was sitting over by the door on the passenger's side. She said, "Honey, what's happened to us? We don't sit close like we used to be."

The husband said, "I haven't moved."

And that's how I feel. Somebody may have changed, but it's not me. I know what I see when I look in the mirror. All I see is just ol' Bobby, the guy who is trying as hard as he can to be a good Christian and a good example for his children, his grandchildren, his players, and any other youngsters he might have an opportunity to influence.

As far as being some sort of dad-gum coaching legend, I find that kind of ridiculous. I know this, if being driven to succeed makes a person some other folks might look up to, then I might be that kind of person. I've always wanted to win every daggone game I've ever coached. I've never been able to enjoy what I have done because it's not over yet, and I ain't looking back.

When I get through coaching, then I might sit back and say, "Well, let's look back and see what all we did." But I can't honestly say how I'll feel about it. I might say, *Gee, Bobby, you should have done better than that. Some of those teams at Florida State might have won a few more national championships if you hadn't got in the way.*

I know my weaknesses and know how I have failed. So, I'm not going to be the one to gloat or brag. I couldn't do that even if I wanted to. I'd be scared to do that. It says in the Bible in Proverbs 16:18 that "Pride goes before destruction, and a haughty spirit before a fall." I know what can happen when a person gets to feeling he's somebody important.

If some folks think they can describe me, I'll let them do it.

■ ■ ■

(Ken Smith was Florida State's team chaplain from 1979 through 1987 and is now an itinerant Baptist Bible teacher and traveling evangelist. Smith, a big man at 6'5" and 248 pounds, said he always laughs when he hears people say that Bowden is a gambler and one of the luckiest coaches in the country because his teams have a reputation of pulling trick plays and seem to make a habit of pulling out so many victories in the closing minutes.)

"When I first started hanging around team practices, I used to watch Bobby run those trick plays and I'd say to myself, 'Where does he dream up those dumb plays? They won't work against anybody.' But Bobby would just smile and say, 'You gotta have faith. It ain't nothin' but a dad-gum game.' And I slowly came to the realization that the people who called his coaching style gambling and luck were just talking trash. I suspect they wish their coaches had the courage to do the same thing.

"He's as fierce a competitor as I've ever known. I remember back in 1983 when we drove back to Tallahassee after a game at Florida when Florida had beaten Florida State 53-14. Bobby said, 'Florida may beat me again, but they'll never outphysical a team of mine again.' That's when he hired Dave Van Halanger, who had played for him at West Virginia, as strength coach and they really went to work on the weights. Florida has never outmuscled his team since. I don't think any team has.

Legends don't understand their footprints.

"I remember in the winter of 1984, when a pastor called me from Quincy, Florida, and said his congregation was trying to raise money for a little girl in the community who was dying of cancer. They were going to have a fish fry with all the proceeds going to help the girl's family with hospital expenses. Bobby, even though he always has a full schedule, agreed to go to help her out.

"Now, neither one of us paid any attention to the date of the event, which was scheduled on a Saturday. But on Monday of the week we were supposed to go, it dawned on me that the day of the event was also the Saturday when Florida State had its big recruiting weekend of the year. It was when all the major prospects Bobby was recruiting would come in. I knew how important that day was to Bobby and his program. So, I did what I always did when a conflict came up. I got about thirty of his athletes to go in his place. I figured that the players, since they had beaten North Carolina 28-3 in the Peach Bowl about a month earlier, would be good substitutes for Bobby. I knew there was no way he would have time to go.

"So, I made those other arrangements and went to the football office and said to him, 'Bobby, I'm going to get the players I've lined up and head on over to Quincy for the fish fry.'

"Bobby said, 'Wait a minute, Ken. I thought I was gonna go.'

"I said, 'Coach, you can't go. You've got all these recruits here. You have to be here.'

"He said, 'Naw, I have to go to Quincy with you. That's more important than me signing some high school football players. If I'm supposed to get those players, I'll get them.'

"And he got in the car with me and we drove the twenty-five miles to Quincy. You would have thought it was the only thing Bobby had to do that day. He spoke and then signed autographs until there weren't any more to sign. He stayed around after the affair was over and chatted with folks. He acted as if he had all the time in the world.

"That is the side of this man that nobody ever sees. And there are so many times when he does this sort of thing. If ever a man had his priorities straight, it's Bobby Bowden.

"Once we went over to play at LSU. This game was important because this was a time when Bobby was beginning to turn the program around. When we landed at the airport in Baton Rouge, we were met by a car driven by a Louisiana state trooper. It was the same trooper who had met us and drove us to the hotel the year before.

"When we got in the car, the trooper turned to Bobby and said, 'Coach, I did what you told me to do.'

"Bobby looked at him and said, 'What was that?'

"The trooper said, 'Remember last year, when I told you how I was having problems in my marriage and that my life was all messed up?'

"Bobby said, 'Yeah, I remember.' I don't really think Bobby remembered.

"Anyway, the trooper said, 'I'll never forget how you witnessed to me and shared Christ with me. Well, after that I changed my life. I started reading the Bible and going to church, and I accepted Christ. And now everything is straightened out.'

"Apparently Bobby had preached that trooper a powerful sermon on the way from the airport to the hotel the year before and didn't even remember it. Bobby has said many times that he takes every opportunity he can to give his testimony to people. That was one of those times. Oh, yes, Bobby won the game, too, 38–14.

"The death of football star Pablo Lopez was probably the most profound incident in Bobby's entire career. I will never forget the look on his face when he looked down at that dead young man. It was as if part of him had died. He changed that night.

"When Bobby called a team meeting a night or two after Pablo was killed, I was fortunate enough to be in the room. I've been a preacher for more than twenty years, and that night Bobby Bowden preached the best sermon I ever heard.

"I believe at one time Bobby really wanted the Alabama job. I used to kid him about it. I'd say, 'Bobby, you're going to be the guy who replaces Bear Bryant.' Bobby would say, 'No, I'm not. I don't want to be that guy. But I wouldn't mind being the guy who replaces the guy who replaced Bear.'

"Once, when we were in Birmingham to play Indiana in the All-American Bowl, it was rumored that Alabama was going to get rid of Coach Ray Perkins and hire Bobby. Bobby said to me in a half-joking manner, 'Ken, can you get a church in Tuscaloosa?'

"I said, 'Sure, if somebody will call me and ask me to come up there and pastor. Why?'

"And Bobby said, 'We just might end up there.' Bobby didn't get the job, and although he's never said it to me, I think that's the one job he might have left Florida State for. After that bowl game I had to go over to Mississippi for a speaking engagement, but I fully expected to hear the next day that Bobby had been hired as the new coach at Alabama. I believe the man's integrity was so great that he said to Alabama's president, 'If says, "For whoever desires to save his life will lose it, and whoever loses his life for My sake will find it."

Man, that's powerful stuff. It's scary too. Jesus is talking here about losing our immortal souls. If those aren't strong words, then I don't know any that are. I firmly believe it's better for a man never to have been born, than never to have been born again. When you're born again, you're born again in your soul, and you have the promise that your soul will never die. I really believe that.

The Bible talks about where we should put all of our energies in Matthew 6:19–21. Jesus said to the multitudes, "Do not lay up for yourselves treasures on earth, where moth and rust destroy and where thieves break in and steal; but lay up for yourselves treasures in heaven, where neither moth nor rust destroys and where thieves do not break in and steal. For where your treasure is, there your heart will be also."

And then, later on in the chapter, Jesus talks about folks who worship material things, things that get in the way of them believing in God. In Matthew 6:24, He makes it pretty dad-gum plain. He says, "No one can serve two masters; for either he will hate the one and love the other, or else he will be loyal to the one and despise the other. You cannot serve God and mammon." (*Mammon* means riches or wealth.)

Jesus means that we cannot make worldly gain our god. That's a false god. And if we worship those things, we cannot serve Him. We can't do it because we're not strong enough. And Jesus explains that God doesn't want us to put any other gods before Him. In 1 Corinthians 10:21 it says, "You cannot drink the cup of the Lord and the cup of demons; you cannot partake of the Lord's table and of the table of demons." That's pretty plain to me.

I think about all the people in the world who are troubled and depressed, and can't find peace and contentment in their lives. If they would only read the Word, they'd find the answers to their problems. Jesus tells us in there to trust Him. He says in John 14:27, "Peace I leave with you, My peace I give to you; not as the world gives do I give to you. Let not your heart be troubled, neither let it be afraid."

What more can a person want than the promise of peace in his or her heart? Nothing in this world can buy that, and if we all believed that, maybe all those pill companies, psychiatrists, and psychologists would go out of business.

Finally, Jesus tells us God's two greatest commandments in Matthew 22:37–39. He says, " 'You shalt love the LORD your God with all your heart, with all your soul, and with all your mind.' " This is the first and great commandment. And the second is like it, 'You shall love your neighbor as yourself.' "

We gotta love God, and we gotta love people. We can't love cars, houses, nice clothes, swimming pools, jewelry, money, or none of that stuff. Now, I think it's all right to *like* that stuff. Just don't *love* it, because that's not where happiness comes from.

It's like the old saying, "Money may buy you a good dog, but only love can make it wag its tail."

I'm No Dad-gum Legend

I t's hard for me to visualize that I'm somebody special. All I do is coach a dad-gum football team. It's not like I'm a heart surgeon or someone who found a cure for some disease. I don't seem all that important to me. I really mean that.

Now, I do remember how I felt when I was young. There were coaches that I was really in awe of. So I am aware that some folks might be in awe of me, although I don't know why. I have always tried to put people at ease on that score. I've never tried to be a big dog; I don't go around thinking, "You're over there, and I'm over here. I'm better than y'all." That's not me. I couldn't live with myself if I went around thinking I was some big shot.

And I really have a hard time answering some folks when they ask, "What's it like to be a legend?"

I say, "Legend? I'm no more a dad-gum legend than the man in the moon."

I tell a story sometimes about how quickly we can be brought back down to earth when we get to thinking we're something we're not. It goes this way:

Once Ann and I drove up through New England on vacation. We were just trying to get away from people for a little peace and quiet. We ended up in a little town of about 5,000 population in New Hampshire. After we checked into a motel and had dinner, we went to a picture show.

We hadn't been to a picture show in years. There weren't but about eight people in the whole theater.

And as we started to sit down, the eight folks in the theater started clapping. I thought, "Lord, I didn't know they knew me up here." And so I turned around and gave them a couple of those "thank you" bows. And the guy in the seat behind us nudged me and said, "Buddy, I don't know who you are, but thanks for coming. You see, they won't start the movie until they get at least ten people in here."

I spoke at a church in Parkersburg, West Virginia, one time, and when I got to the church I couldn't find a place to park. I must have driven around the place three times. So, I finally double-parked right in front of the church. And I put a note under the wiper blade on my windshield.

I wrote on the note:

"Dear officer, I am Bobby Bowden, football coach at West Virginia University. I have a very important engagement here at the church. I couldn't find a place to park, so I double-parked here. Please don't tow my car. Forgive us our trespasses."

When I was through speaking, I came out of the church, and sure enough, my car was still there. It hadn't been towed, but it was ticketed. And there was a nice little note on the windshield. It read:

"Dear Coach Bowden, I have been patrolling this block for three years. I have a very important engagement too. It's my job. If I don't do it, I will lose it. Lead us not into temptation."

So, don't ever think you're famous or important, because it doesn't mean a thing. Somebody will always slap you down to size. And I always kind of figured that someone slapping you down is God. He will look down and see how you're acting and say, "Well, that ol' boy is getting too big for his britches. It's time to take him down a notch or two. It's time he learned a little bit about humility." And believe me, God can take all of us down a notch or two in an instant.

Honestly, I couldn't act pretentiously if I tried because I don't like phoniness. I can tolerate a lot of things, but I don't care much to be around folks who try to be something they're not.

All I am is a guy from the East Lake section of Birmingham, who went to little Howard College, wound up at Florida State, and was fortunate enough to be surrounded by fine coaches and players and win some football games. I'm a guy who knows that he was very lucky to have come along at the right time, and for some reason, good things have happened.

Sometimes I'll go play golf at some Seminole function, and at nearly every one of those things they will pair me up with somebody I've never played with. It will be somebody I've never met, but he will be a big booster, and I guess they think they'll get a big contribution out of him if they let him play with Bobby Bowden.

And after we've played about four holes and the guy has hit the ball all over the lot, he'll say, "I don't usually play this bad, but I'm so nervous about playing with you."

I'm almost at a loss for words, which is rare for me. I can't understand that. I'm just an ordinary guy like he is. I hit bad shots all the time. In fact, I've probably played worse than most of the guys I ever played with.

As far as being some sort of dad-gum coaching legend, I find that ridiculous.

I don't think of myself any differently than I did when I was a young coach at South Georgia College, or at Howard College, or at West Virginia. I haven't changed any, except maybe to put on a bunch of pounds around the waistline.

When I think of change, I'm reminded of the story about the old husband and wife who were riding down the road in the car. The husband was behind the wheel and the wife was sitting over by the door on the passenger's side. She said, "Honey, what's happened to us? We don't sit close like we used to be."

The husband said, "I haven't moved."

And that's how I feel. Somebody may have changed, but it's not me. I know what I see when I look in the mirror. All I see is just ol' Bobby, the guy who is trying as hard as he can to be a good Christian and a good example for his children, his grandchildren, his players, and any other youngsters he might have an opportunity to influence.

As far as being some sort of dad-gum coaching legend, I find that kind of ridiculous. I know this, if being driven to succeed makes a person some other folks might look up to, then I might be that kind of person. I've always wanted to win every daggone game I've ever coached. I've never been able to enjoy what I have done because it's not over yet, and I ain't looking back.

When I get through coaching, then I might sit back and say, "Well, let's look back and see what all we did." But I can't honestly say how I'll feel about it. I might say, *Gee, Bobby, you should have done better than that. Some of those teams at Florida State might have won a few more national championships if you hadn't got in the way.*

I know my weaknesses and know how I have failed. So, I'm not going to be the one to gloat or brag. I couldn't do that even if I wanted to. I'd be scared to do that. It says in the Bible in Proverbs 16:18 that "Pride goes before destruction, and a haughty spirit before a fall." I know what can happen when a person gets to feeling he's somebody important.

If some folks think they can describe me, I'll let them do it.

■ ■ ■

(Ken Smith was Florida State's team chaplain from 1979 through 1987 and is now an itinerant Baptist Bible teacher and traveling evangelist. Smith, a big man at 6'5" and 248 pounds, said he always laughs when he hears people say that Bowden is a gambler and one of the luckiest coaches in the country because his teams have a reputation of pulling trick plays and seem to make a habit of pulling out so many victories in the closing minutes.)

"When I first started hanging around team practices, I used to watch Bobby run those trick plays and I'd say to myself, 'Where does he dream up those dumb plays? They won't work against anybody.' But Bobby would just smile and say, 'You gotta have faith. It ain't nothin' but a dadgum game.' And I slowly came to the realization that the people who called his coaching style gambling and luck were just talking trash. I suspect they wish their coaches had the courage to do the same thing.

"He's as fierce a competitor as I've ever known. I remember back in 1983 when we drove back to Tallahassee after a game at Florida when Florida had beaten Florida State 53-14. Bobby said, 'Florida may beat me again, but they'll never outphysical a team of mine again.' That's when he hired Dave Van Halanger, who had played for him at West Virginia, as strength coach and they really went to work on the weights. Florida has never outmuscled his team since. I don't think any team has.

Legends don't understand their footprints.

"I remember in the winter of 1984, when a pastor called me from Quincy, Florida, and said his congregation was trying to raise money for a you're going to hire me, hire me today because if you stretch this thing out, it will not only kill Alabama's recruiting, it will kill Florida State's too.' It didn't work out, and that was Florida State's gain and Alabama's loss.

"I have done a lot of speaking for Billy Graham's ministry. And I was vice-chairman for his crusade when it came to Tallahassee in the mid-1980s. Bobby asked me if there was any way I could get Mr. Graham to come and speak to his players. Now, I really love Mr. Graham, and if anybody else in the world had asked me to try to get him, I might have said, 'I can't bother Mr. Graham. He's too busy.' But when Bobby asked me, I went and got Billy Graham. And Mr. Graham came to the football building and spent three hours with the players. I respect Billy Graham, but I respect Bobby Bowden more. I love Bobby and firmly believe that he is unique. I am proud to call him my friend.

"I'm not sure what a legend is, but I kind of have a hunch that Bobby is one of those men who has all the ingredients to be one. The truth is that legends don't understand their footprints. I know Bobby Bowden doesn't understand his."

I've Been Blessed

Why have I been blessed?

I don't have an answer to that one. I wish I did. All I know is I have tried to live a good life, but have failed miserably at times. I have seriously tried to be a good witness for Christ by my words and actions as much as humanly possible. But like I said earlier, I know a lot of folks who are better Christians than I am, and they haven't been blessed like I have. The way I feel is that God has to have something else planned for them. Maybe it's something better.

I know some other coaches who have more faith and trust in the Lord than I do, but they haven't been blessed like I have. There are coaches who are just as dedicated, who believe much more than I do, who go out and are better witnesses than I am, who might work harder than I do, and yet they have trouble winning. Some of them have even been fired.

Folks will say, "Bobby, don't worry about it. You've paid your dues. You've been through the bad times, now enjoy the good times."

That don't hold water. A lot of folks have paid their dues. I saw coal miners when I coached in West Virginia who had really paid their dad-gum dues. I have seen people in all kinds of professions who have paid 'em. These are folks who have worked hard all their lives and tried just as hard as I have to be good and do good. And none of them come close to having what I have today.

I don't know why some good, hard-working Christian folks never have lots of money and have to struggle, or why some die at an early age. I don't know why a good person gets a bad illness and dies. I lost a close friend in 1991, a man named Dan Merck. He played with me at Wood-lawn High School and at Howard College. He became a medical doctor and was a missionary over in Thailand. He was a great Christian, but he died of cancer. The Lord called him home. I don't understand that.

I've walked through children's wards of hospitals and seen little babies dying of leukemia. I've seen little tots who have been horribly burned. I've seen youngsters in wheelchairs paralyzed from the neck down. It breaks your heart. I don't know why all that happens to those babies, who are innocent and have never harmed a single person in this world. I don't understand that either. That's when you have to just stand there and try to believe.

Life isn't fair, because if it were, God would strike me dead where I stand, and no innocent baby would ever die.

I wish all the bad folks in the world could visit just one of those children's wards, and visit it with their eyes open. Of course, I know that wouldn't cause man to change. Jesus performed miracles and it didn't cause man to change. Man didn't change when he saw the dead raised to life right in front of him. All man did was nail Jesus to a cross.

Man says to God, "Show me, and then I'll believe." God says to each man, "You cannot believe by seeing. You must believe in order to see."

Many, many persons turn their backs on that, and that's where we get into a lot of mighty big trouble. Like I said, we want to live our way in God's world. The Bible says if we do that, we are fools.

I read once where a daddy shot and killed his son over an argument about which television show they were going to watch. Can you believe that? I've read stories about young gang members who go out and shoot and kill innocent bystanders just for the fun of it. I've heard about mommas and daddies who go off and leave their children. They'd rather go out and do drugs. I've read about drunk drivers who get in horrible accidents and kill innocent people, and the drunk comes out of it with hardly a scratch. Whenever I read or hear about those things, I think, "Lord, why does man do that to man?"

A friend of mine said once, "Every time I read in a newspaper about a child dying, it tears me up, especially when I think of all the sins I've committed. Life isn't fair, because if it were, God would strike me dead where I stand, and no innocent baby would ever die."

So, I do wonder why it's me and my family that have been blessed. The only thing I know is I've always asked God for things in my prayers. A lot of folks don't ask. I've asked for good health. And for some reason, God has given me good health. You know, I never took a physical examination from the time I was twenty-three until I was about fifty. I wouldn't go to doctors. I was scared they might find something wrong. I don't care for doctors, and I don't want them fooling around with me. I hope that don't hurt some doctors' feelings. I think that dislike goes back to when I had rheumatic fever. That doctor scared me to death, and I haven't liked to go to a doctor since.

My wife is healthy. All our children are healthy. All our grandchildren are healthy, as far as I know. We've really been blessed, and I don't know why the Lord has taken care of us.

I've been asked what the future holds for Bobby Bowden. I don't want to know. Life is an adventure; I wouldn't want to know what's next.

God has all our days numbered. Mine just haven't run out yet. And in the meantime, all I can do is lean on my faith and trust in Him and His plan.

In regard to death and God's plan, I heard a true story once about a young junior high basketball coach in Charleston, West Virginia. The coach, whose name was Frank Martin, had been a tremendous athlete and could run like the wind. He came down with Lou Gehrig's disease. The doctors gave him something like five years to live. The years went by, and the coach's body gradually deteriorated until he couldn't walk, talk, or use his hands. He was confined to a wheelchair.

In the last couple of years of his life, one of his junior high players, one who was headed for trouble with the law if he didn't change, began to take care of the coach. The kid lifted him in and out of the wheelchair and pushed him around. By then, the coach didn't weigh but about eighty-five pounds. The kid bathed him, dressed him, and fed him.

And here's the amazing part of the story. In the last year that man coached, even though he couldn't walk and couldn't talk, his junior high team went undefeated.

Anyway, the coach died, but the kid who took care of him went on to attend college on an athletic scholarship. And today he is a fine upstanding citizen. Don't you see? One man's death changed another person's life, and the coach now lives in the heart of the one who was changed.

And that's just one example that points out that when we are told by God that all things work for good for those who believe (Rom. 8:28), we have to believe that. We don't know God's plan. All we can do is put our trust in Him.

I've been asked what the future holds for Bobby Bowden. I don't know that. I don't want to know. I think if I knew, it would ruin my life. Life is an adventure; I wouldn't want to know what's going to happen next. I wouldn't want to know that our teams were only going to win so many more games. I wouldn't want to know I was only going to coach so many more years. And I certainly wouldn't want to know I was only going to live so many more years.

I will admit that football is a labor of love.

And I sure don't want to know how many more times we're going to lose to those Miami Hurricanes.

To me, it's exciting not knowing.

Folks will ask, "When you gonna retire?"

I say, "Hey, I might not be able to retire. I might not be around."

If I could map out my future, I could map me out a pretty darned good one. But I feel like if I tried to do that and say, "This is the way I want it to go," it would be sacrilegious. I mean, me try to determine which way the rest of my life is going to go? No way. God controls my life. He is in charge, and I just try in my humble way to do His will.

And if it's not in His will that I die tomorrow, I'm not dying.

If it's not in His will for me to get cancer, I'm not going to get cancer.

If it's not in His will for me to coach five or ten more years, I'm not going to coach five or ten more years.

It would be so easy for Ann and me to retire. We could do it right now. We could have done it some years ago. I don't have to travel all over the place and go here, there, and everywhere speaking and testifying. I don't have to put myself under the pressure of this dad-gum game of football. I do it because for me testifying is what I feel God wants me to do, and football is the instrument He has given me to do it with. Also, I will admit that football is a labor of love.

Ann and I could just retire to our condominium down on the Gulf of Mexico and spend our time going and watching the grandchildren play. We could have a pretty nice retirement. But I don't want to do that. Life is too much fun. I'm just going to live every day like it was my last, and enjoy each day that God gives me.

And I sure don't want to know how many days I have left. Do you?

The Most Important Message of All

(The following is a composite of sermons that Bowden has given over the years, coast to coast. He wanted readers to have the opportunity to "hear" one here, even if they didn't get to hear one "live.")

First of all, I want to thank y'all for inviting me here today. I come as a believer, and not as one who is good enough to stand before you. And I'm thrilled to death to be here.

I'll tell you right off that I'm a Southern Baptist. Now, it's not that big a deal. Recently, I spoke two times at a big Methodist rally in Pensacola, Florida. They must have had about 7,000 people at that thing. Anyway, a minister said to me, "Bobby, you aren't self-conscious about being a Baptist and speaking to us Methodists, are you?"

I said, "I'm sure not. After all, we're all trying to get to the same place. We believe in the same things. We just practice and worship differently. And y'all can just keep doing it your way, and I'll continue to do it *His* way." (In case y'all didn't know it, that was a joke.)

I suppose some of you know I'm a football coach. I love football. I can't stand to be away from it. And one time my wife said, "Bobby, you love football more than you do me."

I said, "Yeah, but I love you more than basketball." Shoot, she can't have everything. What does she expect?

One time I spoke at a church that had two pastors. Can you imagine that? Two pastors. They had it made. When something isn't going right, one can blame it on the other. I said to the congregation, "That's what

I'm gonna do when I get back to Florida State. I'm gonna hire me a co-head coach. And when we lose, guess who's gonna go out to face the news media?"

First of all, I have to tell you that I'm not an authority to come in and tell y'all how you should live. I won't try to do that. I just want to tell you some of the things I believe. And what I'm going to express is simply Bobby Bowden's beliefs, nobody else's. I will tell you why I am a Christian. I don't come here today as a pastor. I'm not a pastor, and I'm not a preacher either. I'm a layman. I am a man who believes in God. I am a coach who has accepted Jesus Christ as his Savior, and I do not apologize for that. I am not ashamed of it.

Now, I know some of y'all will sit back and say, "Well, who does he think he is?"

Like I said, I don't claim to be a good person. I said I am a Christian. I didn't say I was perfect, because I ain't. Lawh, I'm not even close. I remember I spoke at a church once, and there was one of my former players sitting right in the front row. I thought, "Well, he's seen me. He knows how I act at times. He knows there are times when I haven't done right. He knows the times I have failed. Lawdy, I hope he hasn't told anybody in this congregation."

We played Auburn in the Sugar Bowl one time and the game was on national television. Late in the game we got what I thought was a bad call. And I yelled some bad words, those s.o.b. words. I was so excited I didn't know what I was saying, but even if I had known, I didn't think anyone would hear me. After all, it was so loud in that New Orleans Superdome you couldn't hear yourself think.

About a week later I got a letter from a big Florida politician. He congratulated us on our win, and then he said, "But Coach, I don't see how you can go out and speak at churches and witness to young people when you use the language you did in that game. I know what you said, because the camera was on you, and I read your lips."

I wrote him back and said, "I want to apologize, and I have already asked God to forgive me for what I said. But in regard to going out and witnessing, if I wait until I'm good enough, I'm never gonna get to go because I'll never be good enough."

I didn't say I didn't sin, because I do. Can't stop. Now, I see some of you smiling because you can relate to that sinning part, right? Well, I do sin, but not like you think I do. The good news is that I am forgiven.

Do I deserve Christ, and eternal life and salvation? No way.

All I said was I have committed my life to God, and I have asked Him to take me and use me.

I spoke at a small church one time in Pinetta, Georgia. There were probably less than 150 people there for the service. But it was an old country service and they had these four girls get up and sing. It was a quartet, or do you call four girls quartet-ettes? Anyhow, they got up and sang an old favorite of mine. When I hear the songs of the Lord, especially old favorites, it really fires me up.

It's like when we play football at Florida State and our band comes marching down the center of the field. And Chief Osceola, a student dressed up like a Seminole chief, comes riding out on that Appaloosa horse and jams that flaming spear into the ground at midfield. Man, I get so fired up I want to turn around and hit the first guy I see, especially if he's smaller than me. Trouble is there isn't anybody much smaller, so I don't get to hit nobody.

Anyway, the song these girls sang was, "Yes, I'll rise again. No power on earth can tie me down. Yes, I'll rise again." And here's the kicker: "No power on earth can keep me in the ground." Amen.

To me, that's the fundamental cornerstone of what I believe. The core of Christianity is not ethics and doctrine that we get caught up in. It is simply the crucifixion and resurrection of Jesus Christ.

I worship at an empty grave. How many religions do that? They killed Him, but He ain't in that grave. He's not there because He's still alive. Praise the Lord.

People don't understand God. They will whine and moan, "I just don't understand it. It's hard. Will you explain God to me? Right now, I just can't believe in God because I don't believe there is a God." And when you've been around universities like I have all my life, you meet a lot of so-called smart folks, ones who are so smart they don't know anything about God. Some think they have all the answers.

We don't have to ask, "Who is God?" That's not important. The important thing is who Jesus Christ is. We don't have to go out and define God. If we believe Jesus lives, then God lives. And we are made in God's image. That's what the Bible says.

I know who Jesus is. And when I talk about Jesus, I'm talking about God, because they are one and the same. The Bible tells us that in John 10:30 when Jesus said, "I and My Father are one."

I ask God to give me wisdom, especially in making decisions. Oh, but I didn't appreciate that two-point conversion play He sent me last season where we didn't make it in and lost the game—next year I'm kicking it. (In case y'all didn't know it, that was another joke.)

I do have a personal relationship with Him. He talks to me. And I know if you don't have much faith, you'll say, "Bowden talks to God and God talks back? He's nuts."

Well, He sure does talk to me. And if God doesn't talk to you, folks, I can give you a couple of reasons why He doesn't. One, you don't read the Bible, and, two, you don't go to church.

You know, if we stand around all day waiting for God to talk to us through a burning bush like He did to Moses, I'm afraid we're gonna have a long wait. As far as I know, that burning bush thing hasn't happened lately. And if we wait for lightning to strike and knock us off a mule, I don't think that's gonna happen either.

We have to read the Bible. It will tell us how to live and what's right and wrong. And it will give us strength like we've never had before in our lives.

So if we read the Bible, we'll have God's word. And if we go to church, we'll have it preached to us too. I don't know any other way to know God and get Him to talk to us.

Jesus was such a great teacher. You know, I've been a head coach in college now for thirty-two years, and I've run across a lot of teachers. What a great asset it must be to be able to teach. I feel sorry for some teachers who can't teach. They can't motivate their students. They can't make them listen and want to learn. And then there are those teachers who can make students hang onto every word they say.

Jesus had that ability to teach and make people understand. And it doesn't matter how dumb we are. If we read the Bible, we can understand the teachings of Jesus. Even *I* understand them.

And you young mommas and daddies, where are your children going to be taught how to live right if it's not in church? You think they're going to get it in school? You think they're going to get it in college? You think they're going to get it by hanging out on a street corner?

Folks, you better get them in church and try to get equal time. That's just about the only hope I see for these young people. You parents think you are doing your children a favor by letting them run around and do as they please. Well, you're not, because many of those kids are gonna go straight to hell. If you do that, you don't love 'em.

But if you love your children, you'll discipline them, read the Bible to them, and take them to church. Now, don't make them go to church on their own. Go with them. You have to be the examples. Oh, they might stray, but they will eventually come back because they will have been taught the right way.

I was speaking at a Fellowship of Christian Athletes conference one time at Black Mountain, North Carolina. And I made a statement that I was born with an incurable hunger for Christ. But I said, "I was born," and then I paused. They all started clapping. I guess they were happy I had been born. But I said, "Hold it, boys. Let me finish my sentence."

I said, "I was born with such a hunger inside me that if I don't let God help me with it, it's awful. And you know what? You have that same hunger whether you know it or not. Hunger for food wasn't the only hunger you were born with. And you're not gonna satisfy that hunger, or fill that void, except through Jesus Christ."

Why is it man will give anything he's got for his body, which is gonna die and rot in a grave, but he will abandon his soul, which is gonna live forever?

During that talk to those FCA athletes, I held my hands about one inch apart and told them, "This is about how long your life is. But eternity goes on forever. I can't reach that far. Are you going to abandon eternity for one inch of life? You gotta be out of your minds. You have to keep your priorities in order, and number one has to be God. Jesus said, "For what will it profit a man if he gains the whole world, and loses his own soul?" (Mark 8:36).

I would love to be the greatest football coach that ever lived. And I'm sure you would love to be the greatest in your profession, whatever that profession is. And then when I am gone, folks would say, "Boy, that ol' Bobby was the best, wasn't he?" That would be awful nice because like I said, football is very important in my life. But if I put football first, I'd be selling my soul for a game. I won't do that.

When I was a kid growing up in Alabama, my daddy and my uncle used to take me fishing. I guess I was about nine years of age. Now, they wouldn't let me fish. My job was to keep the worms warm and string the fish after they caught them.

For years I thought my name was "Shut Up Bowden." Every time I'd say something, my daddy and uncle would say, "Shut up! You'll scare the fish."

By the way, I don't fish today because of that. I'm not gonna go anywhere where I have to keep my mouth shut.

Anyway, when they would catch a fish, they would flip it up on the bank. And that was exciting to me. I used to love to watch those fish jump and flop around on the ground. But the thing about that fish, as excitable as it was and as much energy as it was using, was that it was fixin' to die, unless it got back in the water. It couldn't live out of water.

God made that fish for water. And He made man for Him. And friends, if we don't put God in our lives, we don't have a chance of making it. We will live our lives like fish out of water. We'll be just like that fish, unless we get back in the water. Jesus referred to Himself as "living water" in the Bible (John 4:10; 7:38), and He is what we need.

Being a coach, I get to speak at a lot of banquets and functions. And my favorite groups to talk to are those junior high school and high school kids. They are the most fun because they are searching and eager and can be influenced. And when I talk to them, I tell them that God doesn't need their abilities. He needs their availability.

It's just like you. I don't care who you are. God doesn't need your ability; He doesn't need my ability. God could replace me at Florida State —snap!—just like that. And he could replace me with somebody ten times better. (I can imagine some of you nodding your heads—now don't you go agreein' too much there!)

I don't know if I do anything worthwhile. I can't judge myself. But what I try to do is make myself available to God, whether it's football or whatever. It's like speaking here today. I didn't call your pastor on the phone and say, "Hey, can I come over and speak to y'all?"

No, he called me. All I did was make myself available.

But the point I try to get across to young people is, "Make yourself available to God. Let Him use you." And I tell them, "When you do that, do it with enthusiasm."

I tell my players, "Men, we have to have enthusiasm. And we have to have character." I tell that to my coaches all the time too, because we can't win without it.

Ralph Waldo Emerson wrote, "Nothing great is ever accomplished without enthusiasm." It's true. Enthusiasm comes from the Greek word *entheos*, which means full of spirit or full of God. Enthusiasm means God in you.

Did you ever see a team try to play a game without enthusiasm? They got beat, didn't they? Without it, a team, even though it is equal to its opponent physically, will lose every single time. That's why we preach enthusiasm at Florida State. And that's why we talk character to them too.

Character is so important to the type of young men we're trying to bring along.

And don't confuse reputation with character. Reputation is something that's seen; character is being.

Reputation is your photograph; character is your face.

Reputation is something you manufacture; character is grown.

Reputation is something you have when you get a job; character is something you have to have to keep it.

Reputation is something you have when you come to town; character is what you have when you leave town.

Reputation is what man says about you; character is what God knows about you.

Your reputation is what they'll chisel on your tombstone; your character is what Jesus will say about you—before the throne of God!

I want to tell you how God used me one time. This would have been about 1970. Anyway, I recruited a great tackle for West Virginia. The kid was from Akron, Ohio, and was about 6'4", and weighed about 255. He was an All-Stater and a high school All-American. Now, back then freshmen weren't eligible, so he couldn't play his first year. But, boy, I couldn't wait until he became eligible.

The kid came from a broken home, a terrible background. His momma and daddy had broken up when he was very young, and he had been passed around from one member of the family to another. I felt sorry for him.

He had been in college about four or five months when I got a call from the police. They said, "Coach, we got one of your players in our jail. He got drunk and tore up his dormitory. He broke out windows, tore down a door and beat up people who tried to stop him. Come on down and get him."

I said, "I'm not coming down there tonight. I want him sober. If you guys will let him out when he gets sober, I'll see him in my office Monday morning."

Then, the police put him on the phone and I told him, "I'll be in my office bright and early Monday. Don't you be late."

So Monday morning came and he was there. Of course, he was ashamed and repentant. He was so ashamed. I said, "Son, you can't do things like that. You can't break out windows, kick in doors, and beat up on people. If you ever do that again, you can just pack your bags because you're gone. And I won't even waste time seeing you in my office."

After I got through chewing him out, he got up to leave. Oh, by the way, that kid ended up playing professional football for about ten years and had a great career.

Anyway, as he got to the door, I called his name and he turned around and looked at me. I said in a loud voice, "Do you know what you need?"

He said in a sullen voice, "What?"

I reckon he thought I was going to say he needed a good swift kick in the pants, or a good whipping with a switch, but I said, "You need God." That was all I said. And I turned my back to him and went back to work at my desk.

About a month later, I came to my office one morning about eight o'clock and there he was standing in front of the door waiting for me. He said, "Coach, I need to talk to you."

So, we went into the office and I closed the door. He said, "Coach, I found Him."

I said, "You found who?" I had forgotten what I said to him a month earlier.

He said, "I found Christ."

I said, "Tell me about it."

And he said, "You know, when I left your office that day and you said what you said to me, I went back to the dorm and a bunch of fellows were having a Fellowship of Christian Athletes meeting. I walked in and sat down and listened to them. They read scriptures from the Bible. They discussed them, and then they prayed together. I enjoyed it so much that I went back the next week. And Coach, I was converted. I accepted Christ as my Savior."

Wasn't that great? And all Bobby Bowden did was make himself available, and God did the rest. Perhaps that's the way He'll do with you. Maybe He has already. But, my goodness, make yourself available.

I love the parable of the talents in Matthew 25:14–30. Jesus tells the story that a master gave each of his three servants a certain number of talents (money). To one, he gave five. To another, two. And to a third, he gave one.

The servant who got the five talents went out and invested them and earned five more. And when he told his master what he had done, his master said, "Well done, thou good and faithful servant."

The servant who had two talents did the same and doubled his. And his master said, "Well done, thou good and faithful servant."

But the servant who got one talent was afraid of losing it. And instead of trying to earn more, he took his talent and buried it in the ground. When his master found out what he had done, he said, "Thou wicked and slothful servant." And the master took the talent away from him and gave it to the one who had ten and cast the unprofitable servant into outer darkness.

I think Jesus told this parable to emphasize that each of us has a talent. We're not all the same, but we all have a talent of some kind. And we can cheat ourselves, our wives, our children, our relatives, our bosses, and so forth. But when we cheat God, who gave us that talent, that's the greatest cheat of all.

When I read that parable, I know for a fact Jesus is talking to me. He's saying, "I have given you something. Now, won't you use it?" If you turn your life over to Jesus and if you desire Him with all your heart, soul, mind, and strength, you can forget about the other needs in your life. God will fill them up and enable you to use the talent He has given you.

I believe God wants me to coach football. If He didn't, I wouldn't be doing it; I'd be doing something else. I believe God wants me to use football as His pulpit.

I heard a preacher say once, "You know, God has a hard job. Just look what he's got to work with—people like me and you."

That's so true because try as hard we might, that ol' devil gets hold of us at times. I fight that dirty rascal all the time because he's always trying to make me turn my back on God.

I recruited a player once at West Virginia who looked like an All-American. I mean, he was about 6′6″ and 275 pounds, and was all muscle. And he could run. I said, "This guy is gonna make us a winner, and he'll be All-Pro someday for sure."

But when I started him in a game, he didn't look good. And he didn't look good the next time out either. Now, about two "look bads" is about all I give 'em. And a smaller kid who didn't have nearly as much talent beat him out. When this big guy's senior year rolled around and the pro scouts came around in the spring to see who the prospects were, they said, "What about that kid there, Coach? Man, he is really a physical specimen."

I said, "Naw, don't waste your time. He don't have it."

The pros drafted him anyway. He lasted about two weeks and got cut. And about five years later, I picked up a newspaper one day and read a story where this kid had been arrested for dealing in drugs. He was selling cocaine. That was sad. And even worse, he didn't need the money, because his daddy had left him millions.

He had God-given ability, but he hid that ability under a rock. He just didn't have it and didn't want it.

How about you?

Do you have it?

Do you want it?

And if you want it, do you know how to get it?

In order to experience God's best for your life, you must be willing to accept Christ and obey God's rules. I think young people today are starving for discipline. I am guilty at times of being afraid I'm too tough on my players. And at other times, I'm afraid I'm not tough enough. I know they want to be disciplined and I won't discipline them.

One thing I've learned from the Bible is that people who obey God enjoy life. They are blessed and find peace and happiness. People who disobey God are the sorriest folks you ever did see.

If we don't have God in our hearts, we're not gonna be happy. I believe that. God did so much for us. How can we not try as hard as we can to obey him?

Can you really get it through your head what God did for us? The Bible tells us in John 3:16. Were you raised on that scripture when you were young? I was. And, Lord, I believe in that one. "For God so loved the world, that He gave His only begotten Son. . . ."

I couldn't do what God did. I'm not that strong.

Could you lay down your life for a friend? Jesus says, "Greater love has no one than this, than to lay down one's life for his friends" (John 15:13). Could you love somebody that much?

But God took it one step further, didn't He? He went to an even higher degree of love. Can you believe it? He gave His Son to die for us.

Give up your children?

I have six children. If I had to give up my youngest son . . . well, let's say someone wanted me to give up my son so that young fellow sitting there in the front row could live. That would be tough. So, if someone said to me, "Bobby, would you let your son die so that boy might live?"

I'd have to say, "Huh-uhh. No way. My heart don't go that deep." Now, I might give up *my* life. But I could not give up my son. I just couldn't do it; I love him too much.

And yet God loves us so much that He gave His Son. I don't see how people can reject that. Are they crazy?

But then again, I do see how people reject God. They are uneducated and don't know it. Jesus said in John 14:6 that He is the way. And that's why I am a Christian. I accept Christ because He is the open door. He is the only door.

One of the saddest scenes in the New Testament to me is when Paul was in prison. I think it was just before they were going to put him on trial and kill him. They didn't like him because he was a Christian.

And he went before King Agrippa and was permitted to defend himself and talk about Jesus. And after hearing Paul speak, King Agrippa said in Acts 26:28, "You almost persuade me to become a Christian." In effect, that king said, "Paul, dad-gum, you almost got me."

"Almost" don't do it, folks. If you're almost a Christian, that ain't gonna make it. You have to go all the way.

When I was in college, I played baseball. We were playing Auburn this particular game. I think I must have been a junior. I had never hit a home run; couldn't hit it that far.

Anyway, in this game I hit the ball hard in one at bat. It went over the second baseman's head and rolled between the outfielders, all the way to the fence. Man, I started running as fast as I could. And as I rounded second and headed for third, I saw the third base coach waving me on. So, I rounded third and headed for home.

In the meantime, the outfielder picked up the ball and threw to the cutoff man, who caught the throw and turned and fired for home. The catcher had planted himself on the third base line and was waiting for the ball. The ball and I arrived at the same time. I lowered my shoulder and plowed into that catcher. He went one way and the ball went the other. I looked up at the umpire and he yelled, "Safe!"

I had hit my first home run.

But then Auburn's first baseman was calling for the catcher to throw him the ball. That dirty rat. The catcher did, and that first baseman caught the ball and stepped on first base. And the first base ump yelled, "You're out. You missed first base." And he was right.

If our lives were like a baseball field and home plate was heaven and salvation and eternal life, and first base was Jesus, and second base was all the good deeds we do, and third base was all those organizations we belong to and awards we have won, we won't make home if we don't touch first base. And we can't get to God without Jesus.

I had the greatest dad in the world. He died more than twenty-two years ago. Daddy had a stroke in 1970 when I was coaching up at West

Virginia. They operated on his brain and thought they had him fixed up. But a couple of months later, he began to do strange things. So, Momma put him back in the hospital for another operation. He never recovered from that one. He stayed in bed for about four months and we just watched his body go.

But Mother told me what Daddy did before he went into the hospital that last time. She said he went out and cut the grass, tried to fix everything around the house, and went downtown and checked on his insurance. Then he got his Bible and underlined in it how a person could be saved. And after that, he got Mother to drive him across town to my uncle Joe's house. Now, Daddy was about sixty-four years old when this happened. Uncle Joe was about seventy.

My uncle was an atheist. He had lots of money, but he didn't believe in God. I remember back when I was a kid and being raised in the church, I always wondered about him. I used to think, "I wonder what's wrong with Uncle Joe? Why don't he believe in God?"

Mother said that Daddy took his Bible with him. He wanted to try one more time to give Uncle Joe the message of salvation. And Daddy was in such bad shape that he couldn't hardly express himself.

Anyhow, Daddy died not long after that, and I went to his funeral. And you know what? It wasn't sad. I knew my daddy was saved. I knew where he went, and I know where he is today. And I know I'm gonna be with him one of these days.

Mother is dead now too. I know I'll be with her again someday. And my sister is gone too. And I know I'll see her again. Why do I know that? I know it because they were all saved and I am saved. There is no doubt in my mind that I will be with them in Paradise.

Now, let me tell you something sad. My uncle never accepted Christ. And when he died, I went to his funeral. That one was sad, very sad.

You know, as a coach I've been involved in a lot of victories. But even with all that success I know that very little in life is guaranteed.

Is your job guaranteed? Mine's not.

What I'm trying to say is there's nothing in this world that we can be positive of, except one thing. And that is, if we accept Jesus Christ we are saved. We are guaranteed the victory.

When we accept Christ—and you have to make a public profession and can't be a closet Christian—we are guaranteed the win. And that means that everything we've done that was bad in the past is forgiven. And, buddy, He's going to have to do a lot of work on my past.

It means everything in our future is taken care of, because we will live eternally in heaven with Jesus, who has gone to prepare a place for us.

Remember when Jesus was on the cross, and there was a robber on a cross on one side of Him, and another on a cross on the other side of Him? I mean, there was Jesus—who had never committed a sin—being crucified. He had those nails hammered into His hands and feet. And a sword was thrust into His side. He didn't deserve it. But He suffered it for me, and for you.

Now, those robbers up there deserved what they were getting. That's the way they punished them back in those days. And one of those guys looked at Jesus. I guess he could feel there was something special about this man. The guy said, "Master, will you remember me when you go to your kingdom?"

And do you remember what Jesus said? Gosh, those were the most exciting words I ever heard. He said, "Today, you will be with me in Paradise."

In football we deal in statistics. And there have been games where we've gained more yards, had more time of possession, and done everything better than our opponents, and yet, we've lost. So we can't count on those statistics. But there is one statistic we can all count on. One out of one of us is gonna die.

I'm reminded of some events that happened when I was coaching in West Virginia. We had some awful disasters strike the state when I was there.

I remember in 1968, I was driving through the state and heading into Ohio. I had to go to Point Pleasant, West Virginia, and cross the Ohio River on a two-lane bridge they called the "Silver Bridge" because it was painted with silver paint. It was about 5 P.M. and traffic on the bridge was bumper to bumper. There was a traffic light at one end of the bridge and only a few cars at a time could get through the light. The bridge collapsed, and about fifty-five people drowned in the Ohio River.

The next year a coal mine exploded just outside Fairmont, West Virginia, and seventy-eight coal miners were trapped in that mine. They couldn't get them out and finally had to give them all up for dead. And they sealed the entrance to the mine. Those men are still entombed there.

And the next year, the Marshall football team was returning from a game. The plane it was on came in one mountain too quick and crashed and burned. All seventy-five people on the plane were killed.

And the very next year, a dam broke. It was a dam that was holding back water and sludge from a coal mine at the head of a narrow, winding hollow between two mountains. It was a place called Buffalo Creek. The water rushed down through that hollow and 115 people were swept away. Whole families were gone.

Now, that was four terrible disasters four years in a row, disasters that killed folks who didn't expect to die on those particular days. And I know they didn't expect to die the way they died. I wonder how many of them were prepared for it? I would guess not very many. But we can't fool ourselves, folks, we may not die that way, but we're gonna die.

But we don't have to be afraid of dying because Jesus vanquished death. He defeated the grave for us. And not only did He show us that we can have life after death, He said, "I am going to prepare a place for you."

I am here because of that belief. I put my faith and trust in that. And the older I get the more I believe it. I believe that they killed Him and put Him in a tomb, and three days later He walked out of that tomb. And did you realize that is the most documented event in the history of man?

Why don't y'all believe that?

You will believe every junky thing you read. You will believe all those trashy tabloid newspapers and magazines displayed in the supermarket checkout lines, but you won't believe the death and resurrection of Jesus, an event that has withstood the test year after year after year. God told us in Luke 9:35, "This is My beloved Son. Hear Him!"

I guarantee you, when I'm gone and you're gone, and 1,000 years from now, the story of Jesus will still be told. And some will believe, and some will not. Don't be among the unbelievers.

Once there was a little boy walking one day with his momma, and the boy said, "Momma, is God up there in the sky?"

She said, "Yes."

And the boy said, "I wish He would stick his head out so I could see Him."

Well, God did come out. Two thousand years ago He came down on Earth to be with us. The Bible tells us that. It says the Word became flesh and dwelt among us. That's God. When we read the Bible we see Jesus, and therefore we see God. I believe that with all my heart.

I hope that you will too. It was so good to visit with y'all.

God bless you.

Bobby Bowden's Records

MOST VICTORIES BY ACTIVE COACHES (THROUGH 1993)

COACH	SCHOOL	NO.
1. Joe Paterno	Penn State	257
2. Bobby Bowden	Florida State	239
3. Tom Osborne	Nebraska	206
4. Hayden Fry	Iowa	200
5. LaVell Edwards	Brigham Young	197
6. Lou Holtz	Notre Dame	193
7. Jim Sweeney	Fresno State	186
8. Johnny Majors	Pittsburgh	180
9. Bill Mallory	Indiana	156
Don Nehlen	West Virginia	156

BOWDEN RECORD

SAMFORD	W	L	T	PCT.
1959	9	1	0	.900
1960	8	1	0	.889
1961	7	2	0	.778
1962	7	2	0	.778
Total (4 Years)	31	6	0	.838

WEST VIRGINIA	W	L	T	PCT.
1970	8	3	0	.727
1971	7	4	0	.636
1972 (Peach)	8	4	0	.667
1973	6	5	0	.545
1974	4	7	0	.364
1975 (Peach)	9	3	0	.750
Total (6 Years)	42	26	0	.618

FLORIDA STATE	W	L	T	PCT.
1976	5	6	0	.455
1977 (Tangerine)	10	2	0	.833
1978	8	3	0	.727
1979 (Orange)	11	1	0	.917
1980 (Orange)	10	2	0	.833
1981	6	5	0	.545
1982 (Gator)	9	3	0	.750
1983 (Peach)	8	4	0	.667
1984 (Citrus)	7	3	2	.667
1985 (Gator)	9	3	0	.727
1986 (All-American)	7	4	1	.625
1987 (Fiesta)	11	1	0	.917
1988 (Sugar)	11	1	0	.917
1989 (Fiesta)	10	2	0	.833
1990 (Blockbuster)	10	2	0	.833
1991 (Cotton)	11	2	0	.833
1992 (Orange)	11	1	0	.917
1993 (Orange)	12	1	0	.924
Total (18 Years)	166	46	3	.783
Career Totals	239	78	3	.751

WINNINGEST ACTIVE COACHES (MINIMUM 5 YEARS AS HEAD COACH)

COACH, SCHOOL	YRS.	W	L	T	PCT.
1. Tom Osborne, Nebraska	21	206	47	3	.814
2. John Robinson, Southern Cal	8	74	19	2	.789
3. Joe Paterno, Penn State	28	257	69	3	.785

	APP.	W	L	T	PCT.
4. Bobby Bowden, Fla. State	28	239	78	3	.751
5. Danny Ford, Arkansas	13	101	34	5	.739
6. Dennis Erickson, Miami, Fla.	12	103	37	1	.728

ALL-TIME BOWL WINNING PERCENTAGE (OVER 10 APPEARANCES)

COACH	APP.	W	L	T	PCT.
1. Bobby Bowden★	17	13	3	1	.812
2. Bobby Dodd	13	9	4	0	.692
3. Don James	15	10	5	0	.667
4. Joe Paterno★	24	15	8	1	.652
5. Barry Switzer	13	8	5	0	.615
6. Bill Yeoman	11	6	4	1	.591
7. Earle Bruce	12	7	5	0	.583
8. Johnny Majors★	16	9	7	0	.563
9. John Vaught	18	10	8	0	.555
10. Paul "Bear" Bryant	29	15	12	2	.552

★Active

BOWDEN IN BOWLS (13-3-1)

SEASON	TEAM COACHED	BOWL	OPPONENT	SCORE
1972	West Virginia	Peach	N.C. State	13–49
1975	West Virginia	Peach	N.C. State	13–10
1977	Florida State	Tangerine	Texas Tech	40–17
1979	Florida State	Orange	Oklahoma	7–24
1980	Florida State	Orange	Oklahoma	17–18
1982	Florida State	Gator	West Virginia	31–12
1983	Florida State	Peach	North Carolina	28–3
1984	Florida State	Citrus	Georgia	17–17
1985	Florida State	Gator	Oklahoma State	34–23
1986	Florida State	All-American	Indiana	27–13
1987	Florida State	Fiesta	Nebraska	31–28
1988	Florida State	Sugar	Auburn	13–7
1989	Florida State	Fiesta	Nebraska	41–17
1990	Florida State	Blockbuster	Penn State	24–17

1991	Florida State	Cotton	Texas A&M	10–2
1992	Florida State	Orange	Nebraska	27–14
1993	Florida State	Orange	Nebraska	18–16

NCAA ALL-TIME BOWL WINS

COACH	NO.	RECORD
1. Paul "Bear" Bryant	15	15-12-2
2. Joe Paterno★	15	15-8-1
3. Bobby Bowden★	13	13-3-1
4. John Vaught	10	10-8-0
Don James	10	10-5-0
5. Bobby Dodd	9	9-4-0
Johnny Majors★	9	9-7-0
6. Barry Switzer	8	8-5-0
Darrell Royal	8	8-7-1
Tom Osborne★	8	8-13-0
Vince Dooley	8	8-10-2

★Active

ALL-TIME COACHING VICTORIES

NO.	NAME	WINS
1.	Paul "Bear" Bryant	323
2.	Glenn "Pop" Warner	319
3.	Amos Alonzo Stagg	314
4.	Joe Paterno★	257
5.	Bobby Bowden★	239
6.	Woody Hayes	238
7.	Bo Schembechler	234
8.	Jess Neely	207
9.	Tom Osborne★	206
10.	Warren Woodson	203

★Active

BOWDEN FACTS

Born . . . .   November 8, 1929, in Birmingham, Ala.

High School . . . . . .   Woodlawn High, Birmingham, Ala.

College . . . .   Howard (now Samford University) 1953

College Football
   Experience . . . . . .   University of Alabama (QB), Freshman
                                            Howard (QB), sophomore-senior

Graduate Degree . . . .   Peabody College (Masters in Education)

Wife . . . .   The former Julia Ann Estock

Children . . . .   Robyn Hines, Steve, Tommy, Terry, Jeffrey,
                                             Ginger Madden

Head Coaching Honors   1977 Southern Independent Coach of the
                                             Year
                                             1979 National Coach of the Year (ABC-
                                             Chevrolet)
                                             1979 Southern Independent Coach of the
                                             Year
                                             1980 National Coach of the Year (Bobby
                                             Dodd)
                                             1983 Florida Sports Hall of Fame
                                             1986 Alabama Sports Hall of Fame
                                             1987 Region II Coach of the Year

Coaching
   Accomplishments   Compiled a 166-46-3 record in 18 seasons at
                                             FSU
                                             Career record of 239-78-3 in 28 years as a
                                             head coach ranks him second among active
                                             coaches in victories
                                             One of 13 coaches in college football history
                                             to record 200 or more victories
                                             FSU's all-time leader in coaching wins with
                                             166 (FSU's seven other coaches combined
                                             for 150 victories in 29 years)
                                             His teams have finished in the Top 20 four-
                                             teen times in the last 18 seasons
                                             Nation's all-time leader in bowl winning per-
                                             centage with a mark of .812 (13-3-1)

Fifteen bowl appearances in 18 seasons, including 12 straight

His teams are unbeaten in their last 12 bowl appearances (11-0-1)

Has led Florida State to seven consecutive 10-win seasons, resulting in Top Four finishes in six of those years

Eight New Year's Day bowl appearances, including Orange bowls in 1980-81-92-93, Fiesta bowls in 1988 and 1990, the Sugar Bowl in 1989, and the Cotton Bowl in 1991

His team won the national championship in 1993